Glazes
and
Glass
Coatings

Related titles published by The American Ceramic Society:

Glazes for the Craft Potter, Revised Edition
Co-Published by A&C Black, London, England
and The American Ceramic Society, Westerville, Ohio, USA
Harry Fraser
1998, ISBN 1-57498-076-9

Answers to Potters Questions II
Edited by Ruth C. Butler
1998, ISBN 1-57498-085-8

Great Ideas for Potters II
Edited by Ruth C. Butler
1998, ISBN 1-57498-068-8

Out of the Earth, Into the Fire
A Course in Ceramic Materials for the Studio Potter
Mimi Obstler
1996, ISBN (Hardcover) 1-57498-001-7,

Science of Whitewares
Edited by Victoria E. Henkes, George Y. Onoda, and William M. Carty
1996, ISBN 1-57498-011-4

Answers to Potters Questions
Edited by Barbara Tipton
1990, ISBN 0-934706-10-7

Introduction to Phase Equilibria in Ceramics
Clifton G. Bergeron and Subhash H. Risbud
1984, ISBN 0-916094-58-8

Great Ideas for Potters
Edited by Barbara Tipton
1983, ISBN 0-934706-09-3

Glaze Projects
Richard Behrens
1971, ISBN 0-934706-06-9

The Prehistory and History of Ceramic Kilns
Ceramics and Civilization Volume VII
Edited by Prudence M. Rice and W.D. Kingery
1997, ISBN 1-57498-026-2

Underglaze Decoration
Marc Bellaire
1957, ISBN 0-934706-01-8

For information on ordering titles published by The American Ceramic Society, or to request a ceramic art publications catalog, please contact our Customer Service Department at 614-794-5890 (phone), 614-794-5892 (fax),<customersrvc@acers.org> (e-mail), or write to Customer Service Department, 735 Ceramic Place, Westerville, OH 43081, USA.

Visit our on-line bookstore at <www.ceramics.org>.

Glazes
and
Glass
Coatings

by Richard A. Eppler
and Douglas R. Eppler

PUBLISHED BY

The American Ceramic Society
Westerville, Ohio

www.ceramics.org

The American Ceramic Society

The American Ceramic Society
735 Ceramic Place
Westerville, Ohio 43081

© 2000 by The American Ceramic Society.
All rights reserved. Published 2000.
Printed in Hong Kong.

08 07 06 05 04 03 02 01 00   10 9 8 7 6 5 4 3 2 1

ISBN: 1-57498-054-8

Library of Congress Cataloging-in-Publication Data

Eppler, Richard A.
    Glazes and glass coatings / by Richard A. Eppler and Douglas R. Eppler.
      p.cm.
    Includes bibliographical references and index.
    ISBN 1-57498-054-8
      1. Glazes. 2. Glass coatings. I. Eppler, Douglas R. II. Title.

    TP812 .E5 2000
    666'.427--dc21   99-087054

COVER: The pieces featured in the cover photograph: a three-handled vase (Fulper Pottery, circa 1915-1925), a small vase, and a syrup pitcher (Georgia Art Pottery, circa 1930) are from the Ross C. Purdy Museum and were photographed by Ellen Dallager Photography, Centerville, Ohio.

For more information on ordering titles published by The American Ceramic Society or to request a publications catalog, please call (614) 794-5890 or visit <www.ceramics.org>.

I first met John Marquis in 1965 when I joined Pemco Corporation, where he was in charge of glaze and pigment development. It was through his influence that I became interested in these topics and rapidly acquired the knowledge to contribute effectively to this field. John had the unique combination of a world-class knowledge of the science and technology of glazes and pigments and an equally thorough understanding of the real-world problems of making and using these products on an industrial scale.

During the period from 1965 until his untimely death in 1973, we worked together as colleagues. It was during this period that the importance of lead release from glazes was first recognized. John was a leader in the small group that worked to understand the problem, and to assist the industry to assure that the lead containing glazes then in use would be safe for use in contact with food and drink.

Even then, John had the foresight to recognize that in the future there would be need for lead-free glazes suitable for general use, and not just for the niches they occupied at that time. We began the studies that I have worked on through much of my career and that have borne fruit only in the last few years, and that are a major feature discussed in this book. It is with great pleasure that I dedicate this book to his memory.

Table of Contents

PART IV. Coating Properties

Part I

Introduction

Chapter 1
Introduction

Why are coatings applied to products? The primary reason is that in most instances all of the required bulk and surface properties do not occur in one material. By the application of a coating, the bulk and surface properties can be optimized separately.

When the substrate or body is made of a ceramic, a vitreous coating thereon is called a glaze. The term *glaze* is sometimes also applied to the prepared mixture of materials—either powder or a suspension in water—ready for application to ceramic ware by dipping or spraying. After heat treatment, this powdered mixture vitrifies, developing desirable properties for the surface of the ware.

When the substrate is a metal, a vitreous coating thereon is referred to as a porcelain enamel. Here one is trying to apply a coating material that is fundamentally very different from the substrate. Hence, one must be very concerned with the interface between the coating and the substrate.

In this book, both glazes and porcelain enamels are considered. An important reason for this is that the science and technology of the two subjects have developed differently. Therefore, each field can learn from the experience of the other. Basic glaze formulation is more highly developed than that of porcelain enamels; yet the use of mill additives has been studied more extensively in porcelain enamels. The fit of coatings to substrates has been studied with respect to glazes, while the adherence of coatings to their substrate has been studied with respect to porcelain enamels.

The origins of vitreous coating on ceramic ware are lost in antiquity. It is possible that some coated ceramic ware was produced, perhaps by chance, when the fuels or the raw materials used to make some ceramic ware gave a glassy outer skin to the fired ware.[T1] The advantages offered by such glazed ware in improved cleanability were obvious, and this led to further experimentation and eventually to general use.

Thus, the earliest glazes were made from slips composed of suspensions of clay particles in water, often with an added flux of a salt or ash.[V2] By 4000 to 3100 BC, opaque glazed beads and amphora (perfume bottles) were being produced in Egypt.[R9] Stoneware glazes containing calcium oxide and wood ash appeared in China around 1600 to 1500 BC. High-firing feldspathic glazes appeared a few centuries later, also in China. During the Han Dynasty in China (206 BC to 200 AD) glazes for pottery containing lead oxide appeared. Around 900 AD, white opaque glazes containing tin oxide opacifier were rediscovered by Islamic potters.

By 1900, then, ceramic coating was a well developed art. However, little of the science of these coatings was understood until the pioneering work of Hermann Seger in the first decade of this century.[S6] This work has continued, so that the practice of ceramic coating is well understood in many aspects. Nevertheless, progress continues. In just the last five years, the understanding of coating formulation without the use of lead oxide has been greatly expanded. Thus, much of the material in Chapter 3, for example, has not previously appeared in book form.

There are two general types of properties one must be concerned with in designing a ceramic coating.[E26] The first type derives from the fact the coating must be applied to, and must bond with the substrate. The composition must fuse to a homogeneous, viscous glass at an appropriate temperature. That temperature will either be coincident with the temperature for body maturation, or else it will be sufficiently lower that distortion of the substrate doesn't occur.

During and after fusion, the coating must react with the substrate to form an intermediate bonding layer. For porcelain enamels, components of the coating called adherence oxides may be included to produce this reaction. Just the right amount of interaction is needed. If too little, the coating will fall off. If too much, the composition of the body or coating may be degraded.

On cooling the fired ware, the whole coated substrate contracts. If the coefficients of expansion of coating and substrate are not close enough, stresses and strains lead to spalling or crazing. The thermal expansions should be close, but not identical. Ceramic coatings are much stronger in compression than in tension. Therefore, the coating is intentionally put in compression by putting it on a substrate that has a somewhat higher coefficient of expansion. During cooling, the coating shrinks less and is put in compression. In Chapter 15, the calculation of expansion mismatch will be discussed.

Finally, the coating must have a low surface tension, so it will spread uniformly over the substrate, and not crawl away from edges and holes.

The second type of important general properties are those associated with the use of the product. In a given application, a ceramic coating may render the substrate impervious, mechanically stronger, more resistant to abrasion and scratching, chemically more inert, more readily cleanable, and aesthetically pleasing to touch and eye.

Almost all vitreous coatings are expected to be homogeneous, smooth, and hard. A smooth, hard surface is required to resist abrasion and scratching. The exception is a textured coating, where an aesthetically pleasing pattern is imposed.

A smooth surface is not only visually appealing and resistant to abrasion, but also more apt to be impervious to liquids and gases, and hence more readily cleanable. Ceramic coatings are often used with food and drink, where sanitary requirements impose high standards of cleanability.

For many ceramic coatings, chemical durability in service is a prime concern and a reason for selecting ceramic coatings in preference to other materials. Vitreous coatings are formulated to be resistant to many reagents—hot water, acids, alkalies, and organic media. The only exception is hydrofluoric acid.

For some applications, the ware is to be subjected to elevated temperature in service. The coating must be able to withstand this exposure. This is a prime reason for selecting a ceramic coating, particularly in industrial and military applications.

In any surface coating material, the optical and appearance properties are of prime concern. Most ceramic products must be aesthetically pleasing as well as functional. Fortunately, the ceramic artist has many choices for designing a visually appealing product. Coatings can be transparent or opaque; high gloss, satin or matte; smooth, patterned or textured; monochrome or colored. In addition, two or more effects can often be combined in a variety of unique ways to give a plethora of visual effects.

Chapter 2
The Nature of Glass

itreous coatings are essentially glasses, bonded to a substrate. While they have additional requirements as coatings, they also have the advantages and disadvantages of glass. Therefore, it is important to understand some basic ideas about the nature of glass. This discussion will of necessity be very superficial, as a whole book could be devoted to the nature and properties of glass. Here we will only cover some elementary concepts needed for an understanding of ceramic coatings.

Glass is often defined as an inorganic product of fusion that has cooled without crystallizing.[P4] The relationship between glass, solids, and liquids is explained by the specific volume versus temperature diagram (Figure 2.1). If one slow cools a liquid of low viscosity from A to B, which is at the freezing point temperature T_f, crystallization to C will occur.

By contrast, in a liquid of high viscosity, cooling often is sufficiently rapid that crystallization does not occur at temperature T_f. Instead, supercooled liquid continues along the line BE to point E, which is at the glass temperature T_g.

At the glass temperature T_g, the material undergoes a significant change in the thermal expansion (the slope of the volume-temperature curve). Below this temperature, the expansion change resembles that of the solid. It is a glass.

The viscosity at which this transition occurs is very high—around 10^{13} poises. The variation with cooling rate reflects the nature of the transition—the material can no longer respond to the changing conditions (that is, relax). It becomes rigid. Hence, glass is a state of matter that maintains the energy, volume, and atomic arrangement of a liquid, but for which the changes in energy and volume with temperature are similar in magnitude to those of a crystalline solid.

Figure 2.1

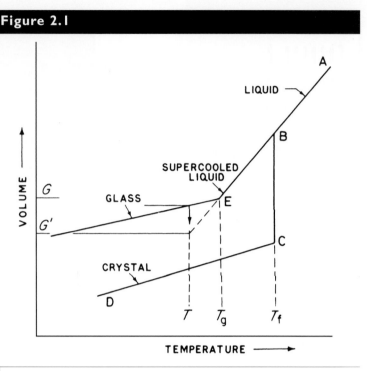

Relationship between the glassy, solid, and liquid states.

Of all the oxides, only B_2O_3, SiO_2, GeO_2, and P_2O_5 form glasses on their own. As_2O_3 and Sb_2O_3 produce glass if cooled rapidly. For coatings, we will be concerned with SiO_2 and B_2O_3. Several others; TeO_2, SeO_2, MoO_3, WO_3, Bi_2O_3, Al_2O_3, Ga_2O_3, TiO_2, ZrO_2, and V_2O_5 will not form glasses on their own, but will do so when melted with a second oxide. For example, $9TeO_2PbO$ is a glass.

A number of hypotheses have been advanced to explain glass formation. The hypothesis that has proven most helpful is Zachariasen's random network.[Z1] He noted that the mechanical properties and density of glass are similar to the corresponding crystal. Therefore, he assumed that the atoms in glass are bonded by forces similar to those in crystals, and must form extended three-dimensional networks with energy content close to that of the crystal. The diffuse X-ray patterns, however, show that this network in glass is not symmetrical and periodic, as it is in crystals. Figure 2.2 compares the symmetrical and periodic structure of a crystal with the random long-range structure Zachariasen proposed for glass.

Figure 2.2

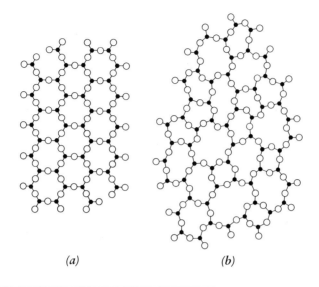

(a)   *(b)*

Schematic representation of (a) ordered form of a crystal structure, and (b) random network of a glass of the same composition.

With this concept, he proposed a set of empirical rules that an oxide must satisfy to be a glass former:

1. Oxygen atoms are bonded to no more than two cation atoms.
2. The coordination number of the cations to the oxygen is low; usually four or less.
3. Oxygen polyhedra share corners, not edges or faces.
4. At least three corners of each polyhedron must be shared. In practice they are triangles and tetrahedra.

The oxides that meet these criteria for glass formation are called network formers. Those that contribute in part to the network, but cannot form it alone, are called intermediates. The remaining ions in the glass are supposed to occupy random positions interstitially in the lattice. Their major function is to contribute additional oxygen ions, which modify the network structure. Hence, they are called network modifiers. This concept is illustrated in Figure 2.3, which portrays the concept for a sodium silicate glass.

A number of authors have tried to take the concepts of the random network hypothesis and apply structural concepts to it.[K4] One such concept is that of bond strength. The atomic rearrangements incident to crystallization usually involve the breaking of bonds.

Figure 2.3

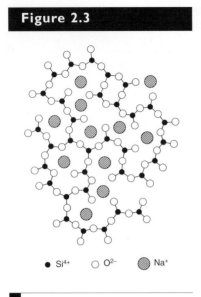

● Si⁴⁺   ○ O²⁻   ◉ Na⁺

Schematic representation of the structure of a sodium silicate glass.

Hence, there should be a correlation between bond strength and the ability to form a glass. This correlation is shown in Table 2-1, where we find bond strengths of 80 to 120 for network formers, 55 to 75 for intermediates, and 10 to 45 for modifiers.

While this simple model is very useful to our understanding of glass, and provides essential guidance for formulating vitreous coatings, it has limitations. In the first place, it suggests that the limit on the amount of modifier that can be added is the metasilicate. That is, a three dimensional network cannot be formed with less then a one-to-one modifier-to-former ratio.

For most modifiers, this is true. An exception is lead oxide. Good glasses can be formed with as much as 66 mol% PbO, many with desirable low melting characteristics suitable for coatings. Because of its large ionic size, and its polarizability, it can to some extent take part in the network formation, as shown Figure 2.4.

This characteristic of lead oxide has an important consequence when one discusses replacing a lead oxide–containing glaze with a lead-free glaze. A lead-free glaze has a totally different structure than a lead oxide–containing glaze. Hence, developing a lead-free glaze for a given application is a matter of developing a completely new glaze, not of merely making a substitution. Many thousands of research dollars have been wasted looking for a lead oxide substitute. It is definitely not a good idea!

Table 2-1. Calculated Bond Strengths of Some Oxides

Cation	Coordination Number	Single Bond Strength (kcal/mol)
Network Formers		
B	3	119
	4	89
Si	4	106
Ge	4	108
P	4	111
V	4	112
As	4	87
Sb	4	85
Zr	6	81
Intermediate		
Al	6	53–67
Zn	2	72
Pb	2	73
Modifiers		
Na	6	20
K	9	13
Ca	8	32

Figure 2.4

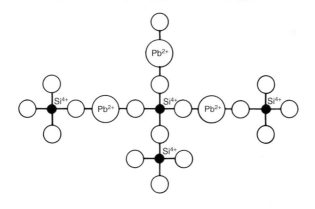

Schematic representation of a lead silicate network.

Part II
Chemistry of Glazes and Enamels

Chapter 3

Formulation of Glazes

The formulation of glazes will be discussed systematically on two planes. First, examples will be given of each of the more important types of glazes. Then, conclusions will be drawn as to the principles underlying successful glaze formulation.

3.1 Method of Presentation

As mentioned in Chapter 1, there is no simple way to classify glazes. Yet some classification must be adopted to treat such a large body of information. In section 3.3, leadless gloss glazes will be covered. In section 3.4, lead-containing glazes are discussed. After that, opaque glazes are covered in section 3.5, followed in section 3.6 by satin and matte glazes, and in section 3.7 by some glazes for special effects.

Before beginning, however, it is necessary to discuss the three ways a formula can be written. Probably the most familiar way is in terms of the weight percent of each of the oxides in the formula. We will need this way in order to convert from a formula to a batch recipe, giving the weights of the various raw materials to be used.

For understanding the behavior of a glaze and its properties, more can be learned from a formula that describes the amounts of the various oxide molecules that make up the glaze. We call such a formula a molecular formula.

Finally, there is the Seger formula.[56] Although the Seger formula is related to the molecular formula and is readily calculated from the molecular formula by a simple multiplication, its appearance is different enough to require explanation. This method of presentation is often used in glaze composition work, because it has some advantages for our understanding of the relationship of one glaze to another. In a

Seger formula, the oxides present are arranged in three categories: basic oxides, that is, monovalent and divalent oxides in one category; amphoteric or trivalent oxides in the second; and acidic oxides, or those tetravalent or pentavalent, in the third.

The basic oxides are those monovalent and divalent oxides that occupy modifier positions in the glass structure—by the Zachariasen model of glass structure.[Z1] The amphoteric oxides are trivalent oxides such as alumina and boron oxide. In some high-temperature glazes, silica will be the only acidic oxide. Other glazes will have other tetravalent and pentavalent oxides. An example of a typical earthenware glaze expressed in these three modes is given on Table 3-1. Note that in the Seger notation the oxides in the modifier column total 1, while in the mole percent and weight percent notations, the sum of all oxide percentages is 100%. Also note that the Seger notation differs from the molecular percentage only by a constant scaling factor, which for this example is 22.9.

For glazes firing at cone 5 or 6 or higher, the Seger formula is a very illuminating way of looking at glaze formulations. The melting oxides (other than boron oxide, which is not a large factor at cone 5 and above) are gathered in the modifier column, and are summed to 1. Thus, variations in the melters can be studied separately from variations in the refractory oxides.

When glazes firing at lower cones are to be considered, difficulties arise with the use of the Seger formula. First, most lower-melting

Table 3-1
Example of a Seger Formula

Oxide	Seger Formula	Corresponding Mole Percent	Corresponding Weight Percent
Basic			
Na_2O	0.16	3.7	3.1
K_2O	0.14	3.2	4.1
CaO	0.46	10.6	8.0
PbO	0.24	5.5	16.0
Amphoteric			
B_2O_3	0.32	7.3	6.9
Al_2O_3	0.34	7.8	10.8
Acidic			
SiO_2	2.70	61.9	50.5

glazes contain substantial amounts of boron oxide, which is a trivalent oxide and a melting oxide. Second, below cone 1 the alkaline earth oxides are no longer melters. Below cone 02, zinc oxide is not. Hence, at lower-firing cones, the columns in the Seger formula no longer separate the melting oxides from the refractory oxides, and the benefit of the Seger approach is lost. All that is left is the disadvantage that the total sum of oxides is variable, while in reality it is not. For these reasons, one will sometimes find it more helpful to express glaze formulations in terms of the molar ratio of each oxide in the glaze, while in other cases the Seger formula will be more illuminating. In this book the molecular formula will usually be used because this book addresses glazes at all firing conditions, including those where the Seger formula is inappropriate.

3.2 Role of the Oxides

Most of the periodic table has been used in glazes at one time or another. Among the more common oxides are:

Li_2O, Na_2O, K_2O

MgO, CaO, SrO, BaO, ZnO, PbO

B_2O_3, Al_2O_3

SiO_2, ZrO_2

Several others are used occasionally. Fluorine is sometimes used as a partial replacement for oxygen.

In a given formulation, each oxide present has a contribution to make to the glaze.[E24, R8] Silica is the most important oxide. By itself it will form a glass, given high enough temperature. Most coating formulations have more silica than all other constituents. One way of looking at vitreous coatings is to view them as a network of silica tetrahedra, to which other materials have been added as modifiers. Low-firing glazes, maturing at 1050°C or less, have one to two parts silica per part of other ingredients. Higher-firing glazes, melting at 1250°C or above, have three to five parts silica per part of others. The serious deficiency of silica as a coating constituent is its very high melting point (over 1700°C). Thus, the foremost reason for adding other oxides is to provide fluxes to reduce the firing temperature of the coating. Figure 3.1 gives the approximate effective temperature of the most commonly used fluxes. Each of these oxides has a melting point, varying from 2800°C for MgO to 886°C for PbO.

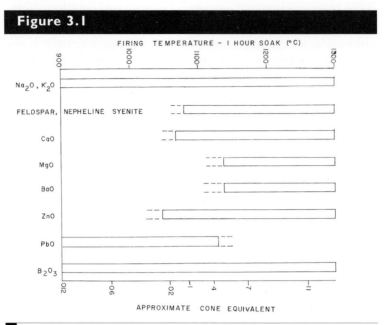

Figure 3.1

Temperatures where oxides can be used in a glaze.

However, when used with other oxides, even a material with a high melting point may function as a flux.

The chart shows that Na_2O is useful as a flux over the whole temperature range. It is very active chemically, and it functions in ceramic coatings as one of the most potent fluxes. Moreover, glazes containing soda may be brilliantly colored by the addition of appropriate coloring additives. The primary disadvantage of Na_2O is the very high coefficient of thermal expansion that soda imparts to a glaze. Glazes high in soda craze on many bodies. Also, glazes high in soda tend to be soft, easily abraded. They are also relatively soluble in acids, and they tend to weather and deteriorate. However, when used in moderate amounts and in combination with other oxides, Na_2O is very useful over a wide range of firing temperatures.

Li_2O is the most active of the alkali fluxes. Otherwise it is similar to soda. Due to its high cost, its use is normally restricted to those glazes in which its fluxing power is truly needed. Moreover, unless substantial quantities of other alkali oxides are also present, lithia promotes bubble defects in the glaze.

K_2O is very similar to Na_2O and is often used interchangeably with it when the use of naturally occurring raw material sources is specified. There are a couple of minor differences. Potash improves the gloss of a glaze, relative to soda. Second, in many formulations,

18

the high temperature viscosity of a potash system is higher than the equivalent soda system.

The alkaline earths—CaO, SrO, and BaO, as well as MgO—are active fluxes only at high temperature. Below 1100°C they may even inhibit fusion rather than promote it.

Most glazes contain CaO. It is available, inexpensive, and contributes desirable properties to glazes. Its principal function is as a flux. It acts not so much from its melting point, which is high, but from its contribution of a low viscosity in the molten glaze once formed. Thus, while it may be the principal flux in high-firing glazes, in lower-temperature glazes other fluxes, such as PbO, ZnO or Na_2O, must be used with CaO to produce the melting. If too much CaO is used in a glaze, a matte surface will result from the crystallization of anorthite.

The action of the other alkaline earths is similar to CaO. SrO is somewhat more fusible than CaO and may be substituted for it when a more active flux is desired. Conversely, BaO is more refractory than CaO, so its concentration must be limited. As a high molecular weight material, it does increase the refractive index. MgO is used primarily as a high-temperature flux, and as an additive to reduce thermal expansion. It has the steepest temperature coefficient of viscosity. Hence, while it is of little use as a flux below 1100°C, it is a powerful flux at high temperature.

ZnO is useful as a flux above 1000°C. Moreover, when used in small amounts it serves as a catalyst to promote the fusion of other oxides. In large amounts, however, it may lead to crawling, pitting, and pinholing, and to crystallization leading to a matte surface. In conjunction with other fluxes, such as alkalis and B_2O_3, it contributes to the creation of a smooth, trouble-free surface. Also, the presence of ZnO has a profound effect on the colors obtained from the various pigmenting materials. In some glazes it cannot be used.

Lead oxide is an active flux up to about 1150°C. Above this temperature, volatilization becomes excessive. While PbO has a number of advantages, its toxicity is such that it is now limited to those few applications where it is indispensable.[E38]

Boron oxide is effective at all temperatures. Moreover, because it is itself a network former rather than a modifier, it can be used with other oxides to obtain a higher level of fluxing than is possible with oxides that destroy the silica network. It also contributes to a lowering of the thermal expansion of the coating. The limitation is that, above 12 wt% in sodium borosilicate coatings, and at all levels in lead borosilicates, the coating durability deteriorates drastically.

Al_2O_3 contributes to the working properties of a glaze. The only glazes without alumina are those intended to develop crystals on cooling. Alumina in a glaze increases the melt viscosity, so it is less apt to run off vertical surfaces. In glazes containing B_2O_3 or alkaline earths, it retards phase separation or crystallization. It also increases hardness, durability, and tensile strength. In excess, it yields a matte.

ZrO_2 is primarily used in glazes as an opacifying agent. However, small amounts (less than 0.5%) improve the alkali resistance.

The fluorine ion has a size close to that of oxygen. To a limited extent, it can replace oxygen in the lattice. Being monovalent, it terminates the lattice. Hence, its effect is to drastically reduce the melting temperature and the stability of a glaze.

3.3 Leadless Gloss Glazes

When lead oxide is not used as a flux to melt a glaze, one must rely on the basic oxides such as alkalis, alkaline earths, plus magnesia and zinc oxide, along with boron oxide, to supply the fluxing power.[S12]

A number of leadless glazes have been known for many years.[E24, M7] These glazes, however, are specialties applicable to certain market niches where one or more of the limitations of lead-free systems are naturally mitigated.

The principal area of leadless glaze use has been in applications firing above 1150 to 1200°C. At these high temperatures, the need for fluxing ingredients is minimized, and thereby the defects that such ingredients often produce are also minimized.

In the first place, glazes for hard-paste porcelain, which are fired to greater than 1150°C and under reducing conditions, must be lead-less.[S12] This is because glazes containing lead break down at about 1150°C with excessive volatilization of PbO. Example A1 in Table 3-2 shows the formula of a typical glaze for these highest-firing porcelains. Essentially, these glazes are based upon studies of feldspar[R1] and the system $CaO\text{-}Al_2O_3\text{-}SiO_2$.[K1] Under the conditions used, their high silica content and low flux level produce a glaze that is transparent, very durable, and of low expansion.

For porcelains fired at lower temperature, that is, soft porcelains and hard stoneware, formulas such as A2 to A5 in Table 3-2 are satisfactory.[M7] As can be seen by studying these formulas, the overall amount of alumina and silica used is adjusted for the firing temperature required.[P1]

Table 3-2. High-Temperature Leadless Glazes

Glaze	Ref.	Cone	Composition (mole ratio)							
			Na$_2$O	K$_2$O	CaO	MgO	ZnO	B$_2$O$_3$	Al$_2$O$_3$	SiO$_2$
I. High-Silica Types										
A1	R6	15	–	0.0250	0.0583	–	–	–	0.0833	0.8333
A2	S7	11	–	0.0198	0.0693	0.0099	–	0.0198	0.0891	0.7921
A3	P4	11	–	0.0341	0.0795	–	–	–	0.0909	0.7955
A4	S10	10	–	0.0322	0.1125	0.0161	–	–	0.0900	0.7492
A5	P5	7	–	0.0408	0.1429	0.0204	–	–	0.0816	0.7143
II. High-Alkali Types										
B6	P4	11	0.0253	0.0253	0.0505	–	–	–	0.0909	0.8081
B7	G4	9	0.0256	0.0385	0.0641	–	–	0.1282	0.0769	0.6667
B8	S10	4	0.0490	0.0490	0.0980	–	–	0.0980	0.0784	0.6275
B9	S7	11	0.0220	0.0220	0.1319	–	0.0440	–	0.1209	0.6593

The usual range is the following:

- For cones 11–16, the approximate range of compositions will be RO:0.5–1.0 Al_2O_3:6.0–15 SiO_2.
- For cones 7–10, the approximate range of compositions will be RO:0.4–0.8 Al_2O_3:3.0–5.0 SiO_2.
- The ratio of the silica to the alumina is held within the narrow range from 7:1 to 10:1.

The high-alkali type of high-temperature leadless glaze, which normally has 0.4–0.5 alkali, can also be used on porcelain bodies, if the expansion is large enough. Some examples of these glazes are given in B6 through B8 in Table 3-2.

The primary use for this type of glaze is for sanitary ware. Sanitary ware glazes mature at a sufficiently high temperature that limitations imposed by fusibility do not apply.[S12] Rather, the limitation in firing is the rate at which such large ware can be heated or cooled without breakage. Typically, cycles of 15 to 20 hours are the minimum. Moreover, since tin oxide was a customary addition for opacity and it is an extremely expensive material, the composition must be considered in relation to the solubility of the opacifier in the glaze. To this end, boric oxide is normally omitted, and a substantial concentration of barium oxide or zinc oxide is added. Thus a typical fire-clay sanitary ware glaze is as given in B9 in Table 3-2.

Because of their large size and cost, defects in sanitary ware glazes are customarily ground out, and the piece reglazed.[T1] The glaze used for refire can either be the same as for the first fire (refire at the same temperature), or a variation on the first glaze where the fluxes are modestly increased so that the refire can be at lower temperature.

The Bristol glaze is a variation of the soft porcelain glaze that has been developed to produce an opaque white coating on stoneware and similar colored clay bodies.[M7] The opacity arises from the high concentrations of zinc oxide that are used. A Bristol glaze can be formulated from porcelain glazes through substitutions of large quantities of zinc oxide for the alkalies and alkaline earths. Some typical Bristol glaze formulas are given in Table 3-3. They find application on stoneware, terra cotta, and exterior building tiles.

These glazes have the advantage that their high opacity serves to mitigate the appearance of visible defects.[E44] Hence, this type of glaze has been further modified to produce glazes suitable for the glazing of wall tile at rapid firing rates.[O6] Some examples of this type of glaze are given in section IV of Table 3-3. The primary change has been to reduce the silica content in order to lower the firing temperature. In addition, boric oxide has been added in low concentrations

Table 3-3. Bristol Glazes and Wall Tile Glazes

Glaze	Ref.	Cone	Composition (mole ratio)											
			Na$_2$O	K$_2$O	CaO	MgO	SrO	BaO	ZnO	B$_2$O$_3$	Al$_2$O$_3$	SiO$_2$	ZrO$_2$	F
III. Bristol Glazes														
A10	R6	10	0.0204	0.0204	0.0816	0.0408	–	–	0.0408	–	0.0816	0.7143	–	–
A11	P4	7	0.0297	0.0396	0.0693	–	–	–	0.0594	–	0.1089	0.6931	–	–
A12	W3	7	0.0388	0.0388	0.0583	–	–	–	0.0583	–	0.1165	0.6893	–	–
IV. Wall Tile Glazes														
B13	n3	1	0.0185	0.0216	0.1481	0.0093	–	0.0154	0.0957	0.0617	0.0586	0.5802	0.0154	–
B14	n3	1	0.0520	0.0113	0.0792	0.0113	–	–	0.0724	0.0588	0.0633	0.6516	–	–
B15	n3	1	0.0682	0.0101	0.0884	0.0025	–	–	0.0808	0.0126	0.0657	0.6692	–	–
B16	n3	1	0.0388	0.0111	0.0914	–	–	0.0111	0.1247	0.0277	0.0776	0.5873	0.0166	0.0139
B17	E17	1	0.0357	0.0113	0.1071	0.0011	0.0151	–	0.0293	0.0322	0.0638	0.6416	0.0620	–
B18	E17	2	0.0330	0.0119	0.1142	0.0010	0.0175	–	0.0242	0.0270	0.0687	0.6403	0.0619	–
B19	E17	1	0.0289	0.0193	0.1343	0.0012	0.0250	–	0.0007	0.0421	0.0752	0.6693	0.0030	–

to a partially fritted formulation to further enhance the melting rate. Glazes B13 to B15 are examples of glazes suitable for firing in a kiln with a 1 to 4-hour total cycle, while glaze B16 is suitable for firing in a 10 to 30-minute cycle.

In the latest glazes,[E41] the alkali content has been reduced, while the alkaline earth concentration remains high, and zirconia and zinc oxide are used, primarily for opacification. Glazes B17 and B18 are examples of these most recent results.

Our current understanding of leadless glazes permits us to design a clear, zinc oxide–free glaze for use with strongly colored tiles. An example is glaze B19 in Table 3-3. Here the alkali content is further reduced to accommodate the higher thermal expansion of alkaline earths relative to the zinc oxide in the previous glaze. The amounts of boron oxide and silica are increased to give a clear glaze that can serve as the base for dark colors.

The changes made to formulate these glazes for tile are designed to accommodate firing on a cycle of as little as 30 minutes for glost firing of twice-fired tiles, or 45 minutes to one hour for single-fired tiles. Low alkali and boron oxide levels are needed to raise the initial melting so that gases in the body can escape, while high zinc oxide and alkaline earths are needed for rapid melting once high temperature is achieved.

The development of leadless glazes for tableware is a more difficult problem than those that have been discussed so far.[E24] Hence, some such glazes still contain lead, as we will discuss later. Among the required properties are a firing temperature of approximately cone 4, compatibility with essentially all pigment systems stable at cone 4, and a coefficient of thermal expansion no greater than $7.0 \times 10^{-6}/°C$ for semivitreous ware and $5.5 \times 10^{-6}/°C$ for vitreous hotel china.

Shortly after World War II, an extensive investigation of leadless glazes suitable for semivitreous tableware was undertaken.[M11, O4–5] Some of these formulas are tabulated in section V of Table 3-4. An important development in these formulas is the use of more than one alkaline earth. In several cases three or four such materials have been used. It was found that the properties of a glaze with several alkaline earths was superior in melting and in surface to any one of these materials alone and in larger concentrations. This work has continued, and there are several leadless glazes that find some application in the semivitreous tableware industry.[n4] Three of these glazes are listed in section VI of Table 3-4.

The study of strontium-containing leadless glazes for semivitreous earthenware having higher coefficients of thermal expansion than is customary for American practice has been carried out by Shteinberg.[G3,S10–9] Several of her more important glazes are given in section VII of Table 3-4. She finds that the most suitable glazes involve a combination of strontium oxide with magnesium oxide and calcium oxide. Both boric oxide–containing (C25) and boric oxide–free (C26) glazes have been used.

The development of leadless glazes for the lower expansion vitreous dinnerware imposes even more stringent requirements because of the lower coefficient of thermal expansion. As a result, it has rarely been attempted.[M7] Some examples of these glazes are given in section VIII of Table 3-4. It was found that suitable glazes could be prepared only within a fairly narrow range of compositions. The alkali concentrations were suitable between Seger 0.1 and 0.19 and preferably from 0.1 to 0.15. Too little alkali raises the firing temperature; too much alkali raises the coefficient of thermal expansion. The strontium concentration varies from Seger 0.3 to 0.65. Too little strontia raises the firing temperature unacceptably at these low alkali concentrations. Too much strontia results in too little calcia, which causes problems with color compatibility.

These latter glazes, however, have severe limitations. In the first place, it is very difficult to eliminate blister-type defects from these glazes. A more severe limitation, however, arises from the fact that these glazes are stiff enough that they duplicate exactly the coating that is applied. Therefore, it is very difficult to obtain acceptable surface quality in these glazes.

When the high durability requirements of a food contact surface are not required, these defects can be eliminated through the use of a more fluid glaze.[H6, K6] Some examples of glazes for use on alumina bodies for spark plugs and similar technical applications are given in section IX of Table 3-4.

One final type of leadless glaze remains to be considered, the low-expansion glazes suitable for zircon and cordierite bodies. The thermal expansion of zircon bodies is low, making for difficult glaze fit problems.[P1] The coefficient of thermal expansion is between 4 and $5 \times 10^{-6}/°C$. Glazes high in magnesium oxide have been the usual solution,[L4] as shown in Table 3-5, section X.

Cordierite bodies are even lower in expansion, from 1.5 to $4 \times 10^{-6}/°C$. It is not possible to glaze these bodies with fully vitreous glazes. However, it is possible to glaze cordierite by inducing in an appropriately formulated glaze the precipitation of a low-expansion phase.[O3] Some typical examples of these glazes are given in section XI of Table 3-5. These glazes are based on the crystallization of the low-expansion stuffed quartz phase in a vitreous matrix. Glazes B39

Table 3-4. Tableware Glazes

Glaze	Ref.	Cone	Li₂O	Na₂O	K₂O	CaO	MgO	SrO	BaO	ZnO	B₂O3	Al₂O₃	SiO₂	ZrO₂	F
V. Orlowski and Marquis's Glazes															
A20	O4	4	0.0231	0.0277	0.0092	0.1016	0.0346	0.0346	–	–	0.0531	0.0693	0.6467	–	–
A21	O4	3	–	0.0134	0.0268	0.0960	–	–	0.0580	0.0290	0.0692	0.0737	0.6384	–	–
A22	O4	5	–	0.0144	0.0287	0.0957	0.0239	0.0120	0.0239	0.0407	0.0742	0.0646	0.6920	–	–
A23	O4	5	–	0.0291	0.0304	0.0896	0.0325	0.0325	–	–	0.0497	0.0736	0.6659	–	–
A24	O4	5	0.0086	0.0289	0.0195	0.0887	0.0321	0.0321	–	–	0.0493	0.0728	0.6597	–	0.0086
VI. Semivitreous Tableware Glazes															
B25	n3	4	0.0222	0.0173	0.0132	0.0969	0.0318	0.0320	–	–	0.0504	0.0704	0.6659	–	–
B26	n3	4	–	0.0191	0.0188	0.1216	–	0.0498	–	–	0.0747	0.0710	0.6449	–	–
B27	n3	1	0.0110	0.0190	0.0270	0.1362	0.0155	0.0258	–	–	0.0402	0.0862	0.6389	–	–
VII. Russian Majolica Glazes															
C28	S8	4	–	0.1014	0.0163	0.0560	0.0139	0.0560	–	–	0.0482	0.0599	0.6481	–	–
C29	S8	4	–	0.0877	0.0219	–	0.0548	0.1096	–	–	–	0.0493	0.6767	–	–
C30	S8	1	–	0.0983	0.0223	–	0.0274	0.0547	–	–	0.0790	0.0495	0.6688	–	–

Composition (mole ratio)

Table 3-4. Tableware Glazes (continued)

Glaze	Ref.	Cone	Composition (mole ratio)												
			Li_2O	Na_2O	K_2O	CaO	MgO	SrO	BaO	ZnO	B_2O3	Al_2O_3	SiO_2	ZrO_2	F
VIII. Vitreous Tableware Glazes															
D31	M15	4	-	-	0.0313	0.0878	-	0.0899	-	-	0.0752	0.0673	0.6380	0.0104	-
D32	M15	4	-	0.0063	0.0251	0.0711	-	0.1066	-	-	0.0752	0.0673	0.6380	0.0104	-
D33	M15	4	-	0.0063	0.0251	0.0878	-	0.0899	-	-	0.0752	0.0673	0.6380	0.0104	-
D34	M15	4	0.0061	0.0607	0.0152	0.0638	0.0223	0.0911	-	-	0.0506	0.0810	0.6679	-	-
IX. Glazes for Technical Ceramics															
E35	H8	4	0.0114	0.0200	0.0200	0.0600	0.0743	0.0457	0.0400	0.0143	0.0914	0.0400	0.5829	-	-
E36	K5	4	0.0050	0.0501	0.0033	0.0284	-	0.0334	0.0584	0.0167	0.1870	0.0584	0.5876	-	-

Table 3-5. Low-Expansion Glazes

Glaze	Ref.	Cone	Li$_2$O	Na$_2$O	K$_2$O	CaO	MgO	ZnO	B$_2$O$_3$	Al$_2$O$_3$	SiO$_2$	ZrO$_2$
X. Glazes for Zircon												
A37	L3	12	–	0.0096	0.0179	0.0206	0.0893	–	–	0.0797	0.7830	–
A38	L3	10	–	0.0138	0.0215	0.0262	0.0754	0.0185	0.0277	0.0646	0.6477	0.1062
XI. Glazes for Cordierite												
B39	O6	2	0.1910	–	0.0337	–	–	–	0.0449	0.1663	0.5640	–
B40	O6	1	0.1973	–	0.0295	–	–	–	0.0204	0.1610	0.5805	0.0113
B41	O6	4	0.1722	–	0.0270	–	–	0.0083	0.0187	0.1411	0.5643	0.0685

Composition (mole ratio)

and B40 are translucent, whereas glaze B41, which contains substantial amounts of zircon as well as stuffed quartz, is opaque. The primary crystal system used is the lithia-alumina-silica system, where there are two low-expansion crystals, beta eucryptite and beta spodumene. Cordierite, in the magnesia-alumina-silica system, can also be used.

Now that leadless glazes are desired for more than a few small market niches, there is a need for a general understanding of how to formulate them. We will now discuss the conclusions that have been drawn about how to formulate a leadless glaze.[E41]

3.3.1 Let's begin with the alkalis. The alkalis, Na_2O and K_2O, are the most powerful melting oxides available. They also have other benefits, such as suppression of phase separation. However, alkalis substantially increase the thermal expansion of ceramic glazes.[E35] This property creates the limits on alkali use for almost all applications, the reasons for which are discussed in Chapter 15.

In general, as the firing temperature is increased, the thermal expansion of typical bodies decreases. To avoid crazing defects, the glaze thermal expansion must be modestly lower than the body expansion. Hence, the limits on the alkali contents of glazes are as follows.[E41]

- Glazes to be fired at cone 06 may contain up to 0.07 to 0.08 mole ratio (7 to 8 mol%)
- Glazes to be fired at cone 1 should be limited to 0.05 to 0.06 mole ratio
- Glazes to be fired at cone 4 should be limited to 0.04 to 0.05 mole ratio
- Glazes for high-firing stoneware bodies and sanitary ware bodies should be limited to 0.02 to 0.04 mole ratio

Alkalis also improve the gloss of a glaze. Thus, gloss glazes should be formulated close to the maximum levels. On the other hand, satin and matte glazes can be more easily formulated at lower alkali concentrations.

3.3.2 Boron oxide is both a glass former and a melting oxide. Using it permits the use of higher concentrations of melting oxides than is otherwise possible. However, excessive boron oxide leads to poor glaze durability.[E30] In lead-free glazes, a more serious and limiting problem is that too much boron oxide leads to gassing during the glost fire, producing pinholes in the glaze.[E41]

The amount of boron oxide that can be safely added without creating pinholes is a strong function of the heat work in firing. The greater the heat work, the less the allowable boron oxide. The limits on boron oxide addition are:

- At cone 06 the maximum boron oxide is 0.17 mole ratio
- At cone 1 the maximum boron oxide addition is 0.04 to 0.05 mole ratio
- At cone 4, it is 0.03 mole ratio, and at cone 6 it is 0.02 mole ratio
- At cone 8, little if any boron oxide should be used

3.3.3 Silica is the framework of glazes. Hence, a minimum silica level is needed to maintain the glaze structure. For gloss glazes, the level of silica should be 0.66 to 0.68 mole ratio. On the other hand, if the glaze is to melt and dissolve the refractory oxides of silica plus alumina plus zircon, the amount of refractory oxides must be limited to 0.75 mole ratio. For gloss glazes, these two limits are compatible. For satin and matte glazes, the alumina requirements of the matting crystals lead to the need for higher alumina content and lower silica content. For a satin glaze, the silica level should be 0.60 to 0.62 mole ratio. For a matte glaze the silica level should be 0.57 to 0.59 mole ratio.

These limits apply to glazes fired at cone 5 and lower, where the dissolution rate of silica is slow enough to be a limiting parameter. For higher firing heat work, both the total refractory oxides and the silica contents are increased linearly as the heat work is increased.[P1,S6] The Seger limits are:

- At cone 6 the silica content should be 0.68 to 0.70 mole ratio for a gloss glaze, and the total refractory oxides should be 0.79 to 0.80
- At cone 8 the silica content should be 0.72 to 0.74 mole ratio for a gloss glaze, and the total refractory oxides should be 0.82 to 0.83

3.3.4 Alumina is an important constituent of most glazes. It improves several properties, and serves to suppress phase separation and subsequent crystallization. On the other hand, the solubility of alumina in glazes is limited. If that solubility is exceeded, crystals of anorthite (calcium aluminum disilicate) and related phases appear.[L2] Thus, there is an optimum alumina concentration for maximum glaze clarity.[E41] That optimum alumina concentration is only slightly affected by the firing conditions. It increases slightly as the heat work increases. Hence, the limits for alumina are:

0.055 to 0.06 mole ratio at cone 06
0.07 to 0.08 at cone 1
0.075 to 0.085 at cone 4
0.08 to 0.09 at cone 6
0.09 to 0.10 at cone 8

For satin and matte glazes, where the anorthite crystals are desired, the alumina concentration can be modestly increased. However, the lower silica concentrations previously discussed have the effect of lowering the alumina solubility, so a substantial increase in alumina concentration is not required.

3.3.5 The discussion of the alkaline earths calcia, strontia, and baria has been left to this point because the melting behavior of the alkaline earth materials is complex. They have sufficiently high melting points that they must be dissolved rather than melted. Once dissolved, they lower the viscosity of the molten glaze and increase the dissolving power of the melt. Thus, at firing temperatures severe enough to dissolve the alkaline earths at an appropriate rate, they function as fluxes. However, at lower heat work they are essentially inert.

For calcia and strontia, the heat work at which the dissolving rate becomes appreciable is about cone 01. For baria it is around cone 2.

The principal alkaline earth oxide is calcium oxide. It contributes desirable properties to higher-firing glazes. Strontium oxide is similar in behavior to calcia. Barium oxide is considerably more refractory than the other alkaline earths, and it has some of the toxicity problems associated with heavy metals. Its use is not recommended.

As alkaline earths are the last of the major ingredients to be discussed, their recommended concentrations are partially determined by the requirement that the sum of all concentrations equals 1.00 mole ratio (i.e., 100%). Nevertheless, at cone O6 the goal should be to avoid the use of alkaline earths completely. For gloss glazes, at cones 1 to 6 the total alkaline earths will usually be 0.13 to 0.18 mole ratio. At cone 8 they will decline to 0.12 to 0.15 mole ratio due to the increase in silica and alumina required for that high heat work. Of this, up to 0.03 mole ratio can be strontia, the balance calcium oxide.

For satin and matte glazes, the lower silica content will permit substantially higher alkaline earth additions. Satin glazes may contain up to 0.25 mole ratio alkaline earths; matte glazes may contain up to 0.28 mole ratio alkaline earths. As before, up to 0.03 mole ratio can be strontia, the balance calcia.

3.3.6 Magnesium oxide is a powerful flux in high–heat work glazes, and it helps to control thermal expansion. However, it has a very steep viscosity-temperature curve, so it is a refractory

ingredient below cone 3. It also promotes knife marking of glazes. Its principal raw material source, talc, yields water of crystallization at 1100°C, which produces gassing. Thus, the addition of magnesia beyond that added as impurity in raw materials used for other oxides is not recommended.

3.3.7 Zinc oxide behaves in ceramic glazes in a manner similar to the alkaline earths, except that it dissolves at a reasonable rate at slightly lower heat work than the alkaline earth oxides. It acts as a flux above cone 02. When used in small quantities along with other fluxes, it is a very valuable material, producing a smooth, defect-free surface.

Zinc oxide behaves in a manner similar to boron oxide in that adding too much zinc oxide at a given heat work will lead to pitting and blistering defects.

Moreover, above 0.005 mole ratio, zinc oxide behaves as a low-grade opacifier. Finally, zinc oxide has a profound effect on the color of several ceramic pigments.[E43] Therefore, the use of more than 0.005 mole ratio zinc oxide should be a conscious, deliberate decision.

When the decision to prepare a zinc oxide–containing glaze is made, the limitations on zinc oxide are as follows:
- It should not be used in glazes fired below cone 02
- At cone 1 through 4, the zinc oxide concentration should be limited to 0.04 mole ratio, and preferably 0.03 mole ratio
- At cone 6 the zinc oxide should be limited to 0.03 mole ratio
- At cone 8 it should be limited to 0.02 mole ratio

Better results are obtained at somewhat lower zinc oxide concentrations than the limit values.

Relative to a zinc oxide–free glaze, a glaze containing zinc oxide should have no more than one-half the maximum boron oxide level previously indicated, and no more than 70% of the alkali level. Since zinc oxide is a strong flux, these limitations should not increase the heat work required to melt the glaze.

3.3.8 The best known use of zirconia is as the principal component of zircon opacifiers. For that use, the zircon should remain as a separate crystalline phase.

While the solubility of zirconia in most glazes is low, it is not zero. Up to 0.004 mole ratio zirconia may be added to a glaze without inducing crystallization. Such addition is desirable and recommended. It will tend to raise the gloss of a leadless glaze, and it will improve on the alkaline durability of a silica-based glaze.[E30]

When these various considerations are balanced in a given formulation, a suitable leadless glaze will usually result.

3.4 Lead Glazes

Today the use of lead oxide in glazes is no longer acceptable.[E38] The cost of meeting the regulatory requirements that apply to plants using lead oxide is rapidly becoming more than most producers can tolerate financially.

Traditionally, lead oxide was used in glazes for several reasons.[E14] The strong fluxing action of lead oxide allows glazes to mature at lower temperatures than their leadless counterparts. It permits maturing of the glaze over a wider firing range. Lead oxide imparts low surface tension and high index of refraction, resulting in a smooth, brilliant glaze surface. Finally, it resists crystallization of the glaze. This combination of desirable properties is difficult to duplicate without lead.

However, PbO also has disadvantages as a glaze constituent.[E26] Ware must be fired in a strongly oxidizing atmosphere, because lead is readily reduced. It volatilizes above 1200°C.

The most important problem is that PbO is poisonous. Appropriate precautions must be taken in using it, to avoid even the possibility of lead poisoning. Lead poisoning is a serious matter. It is caused by the ingestion of soluble lead compounds into the system, usually by mouth, although it can also result from breathing vapors or dust. The disease is very difficult to diagnose, since its symptoms are similar to many other ailments. Therefore, every possible precaution must be taken when preparing lead glazes to avoid poisoning.

Moreover, if glazes are not properly formulated, they are subject to attack, primarily by acidic media, which results in the release of lead into the solution. If such glazes are used in contact with food or drink, lead poisoning of the user may result. The measurement and control of lead release is discussed in detail in Chapter 16. Anyone contemplating the preparation of a lead oxide–containing glaze should study that chapter in detail before proceeding.

Some examples of lead-containing glazes for use at cone 4[E24] are given in Table 3-6. It is instructive to compare these glazes (A42–A45) with glazes A20 to B27 in Table 3-4. In general, the contents of silica, boric oxide, alumina, and calcia are similar. The use of lead oxide in glazes A42 to A45 permits the use of generally higher concentrations of alkali oxide than are found for the leadless glazes. Said another way, the concentrations of lead oxide in the lead-containing glazes are lower than the concentrations of alkaline earths (other than calcia) in the leadless glazes. The generally low thermal expansion behavior of lead oxide permits the use of the higher concentrations of alkali oxide, which results in greater fluidity, and thus improved surface.

To further reduce the maturing temperature, alumina and silica are lowered and the lead oxide content is increased.[R1] The advantage of this type of glaze is that it is compatible with a full palette of colors, including those produced by heat-sensitive pigments such as the cadmium sulfoselenide reds. The disadvantage is that they are difficult to formulate with adequate durability. Some examples of commercial clear glaze formulas suitable for cone 06 are also given in Table 3-6. These glazes are typical of those suitable for use on artware and hobbyware bodies.

At still lower maturing temperatures, glazes become simpler again, involving the use of only one basic oxide, lead oxide, and eliminating boric oxide. These glazes are based on lead bisilicate with small additions of alumina to retard phase separation. Some examples of lead bisilicate glazes are also given in Table 3-6. These glazes can be fired as low as cone 010 for special effects in artware and hobbyware glazing.

The glazes used on alumina integrated circuits to seal them represent the low temperature extreme in glazes.[F1] Because of the thermal sensitivity of the electronic chips contained in the packages, firing temperatures as low as 550°C are required. At this extreme, all other properties have to be sacrificed to low melting. The result is some very simple formulations based on lead borate shown in the last section of Table 3-6. A typical formula for a vitreous glaze is shown first, followed by a formula for a devitrifying coating. Needless to say, these coatings have very poor durability and are highly toxic.

3.5 Opaque Glazes

Opaque glazes are those sufficiently low in light transmitted that they effectively hide the body from view[E24] (see Figure 3.2). They are usually white, although light colors can also be achieved by the addition of pigments (see Chapter 8).

Opacity is introduced into ceramic coatings by adding to the coating formulation a substance that will disperse into the coating as discrete particles that scatter and reflect some of the incident light.[S12] In order to do this, the dispersed substance must have a low

Table 3-6. Lead Glazes

Glaze	Ref.	Cone	Composition (mole ratio)									
			Na$_2$O	K$_2$O	CaO	SrO	PbO	ZnO	B$_2$O$_3$	Al$_2$O$_3$	SiO$_2$	ZrO$_2$
XII. Cone 4 Tableware Glazes												
A42	M17	4	0.0356	0.0131	0.0983	–	0.0520	–	0.0625	0.0677	0.6707	–
A43	M17	4	0.0394	0.0028	0.1238	–	0.0504	–	0.0779	0.0628	0.6429	–
A44	E12	4	0.0190	0.0190	0.1223	–	0.0506	–	0.0759	0.0675	0.6459	–
A45	E12	4	0.0418	0.0165	0.0684	–	0.0760	0.0760	0.0606	0.0753	0.6281	–
XIII. Cone 06 Clear Glazes												
B46	E24	06	0.0131	–	0.0179	–	0.2170	–	0.0427	0.0675	0.6399	0.0020
B47	E24	06	0.0342	–	0.0474	–	0.1360	–	0.1103	0.0594	0.6076	0.0050
B48	E12	06	0.0125	–	0.0167	0.0467	0.1698	–	0.0585	0.0644	0.6294	0.0020
B49	E12	06	0.0337	–	0.0467	0.0141	0.1227	–	0.1141	0.0591	0.6046	0.0050
XIV. Lead Bisilicate Glazes												
C50	E12	010	–	–	–	–	0.2682	–	–	0.0719	0.6599	–
C51	E12	010	–	–	–	–	0.3125	–	–	0.0797	0.6078	–
XV. Electronic Packaging Glasses												
D52	F2	<022	–	–	–	–	0.6667	–	0.3333	–	–	–
D53	F2	<022	–	–	–	–	0.5211	0.1831	0.2958	–	–	–

Figure 3.2

Plate with an opaque glaze.

solubility in the molten glaze and a refractive index that differs appreciably from that of the clear ceramic coating.

In Chapter 8 there is a discussion of the white pigments or opacifiers used in ceramic coatings for opacification. The glazes themselves are discussed in this chapter.

The more often the path of light is broken by the dispersed crystals, the greater is the opacity of the glaze. Therefore, the finer the particle size of the crystals, the greater is the surface area and hence the greater the reflection.[R1] The particle size for optimum opacity is about 0.4 microns. Therefore, among the various zircon opacifiers available on the market, representing a range of average particle size, maximum opacity is given by that opacifier which has the finest particle size. Since this greater fineness is achieved by milling, the finer zircons are also the most expensive. On the other hand, zircon for smelting into a frit is optimum when intermediate in particle size. The effectiveness of the zircon opacifier can therefore be improved in partially or fully fritted glazes by smelting some of the zircon into the frit.[n4] Some examples of typical opacified glazes as used in the wall tile industry are given in Table 3-7. Note that in all cases a portion of the zirconia is added in the frit, whereas the rest is added as a mill additive.

3.6 Satin and Matte Glazes

Opaque glazes can be regarded as a halfway stage toward satin and matte glazes.[S12] The satin or matte appearance (see Figure 3.3) is again an effect due to the presence of small crystals dispersed in the glaze. It is the result of the devitrification produced when a completely fused glaze cools and part of the fused mass crystallizes. The crystals must be very small and evenly dispersed in order to give the glaze surface a smooth and velvety appearance. It should be possible to write on a matte or a satin glaze with ordinary pencil and then rub the mark off with the finger.[S13] Matte glazes are always more or less opaque because the crystals, as in normal opaque glazes, break up the rays of light. The crystals are of zinc silicate (willemite) as in the case of zinc mattes or calcium silicate (wollastonite) or calcium aluminum disilicate (anorthite) in the case of lime mattes. If barium oxide is added to the formulation, barium aluminum disilicate (celsian) may crystallize. Matte effects can also be obtained by undissolved material in the glaze, such as bone, feldspar, or talc. However, the quality of the matte is inferior to those produced by crystallization.[S12]

Since crystallization is required, the glaze should not be overfired, and the proper cooling cycle must be maintained.[S12] Matte glaze compositions cooled too rapidly have glossy surfaces.

Figure 3.3

Three plates: (top) plate with a gloss glaze, (left) plate with a satin glaze, (right) plate with a matte glaze.

Most glazes can be converted to a matte glaze by the addition of a matting agent. Zinc mattes (see Table 3-8, section XVII) are produced by the addition of a mixture of zinc oxide and clay in more or less equal proportions to the glaze formulation. The purpose of the clay is to introduce alumina, and thus to reduce the size of the zinc silicate crystals, which tend to be too large.[512]

Additions of whiting or wollastonite to a glaze will give lime matte glazes (see Table 3-8, section XVIII). Barium oxide, strontium oxide, and magnesium oxide can also be used, but the matting effect is more irregular and uncertain.

3.7 Glazes for Special Effects

A number of glazes exhibit unique aesthetic effects that are occasionally useful in certain applications. Some of these special effects are due to crystals dispersed in the glaze. Two examples of glazes containing crystals—opacified glazes in section 3.5 and satin and matte glazes in section 3.6—have already been discussed. These are examples of microcrystalline glazes, in which the particle size of the crystals is so small that they cannot be individually detected by the naked eye.

Figure 3.4

A macrocrystalline glaze.

By reducing the nucleation rate to lower levels, crystals can be grown in certain glazes that are large enough to be readily detectable by the naked eye.[F2] This category includes rutile break-up glazes, in which the surface may be covered with individual crystals, often clustered together, and aventurine glazes, in which the crystals are suspended in the glass matrix.

The development of macrocrystalline glazes (see Figure 3.4) is very sensitive to details of the firing process, in particular the rate of cooling through the temperature range of roughly 1000 to 400°C. Also important are the base glaze formula, which should be low in alumina, and the elements used to

Table 3-7. Opaque Glazes

Glaze	Ref.	Cone	Composition (mole ratio)									ZrO_2	
			Na_2O	K_2O	CaO	SrO	BaO	ZnO	B_2O_3	Al_2O_3	SiO_2	added in frit	added in mill
A54	n3	1	0.0379	0.0281	0.0687	-	0.0081	0.0956	0.0405	0.1145	0.5371	0.0358	0.0336
A55	n3	1	0.0291	0.0218	0.1067	-	0.0073	0.0972	0.0375	0.1064	0.5291	0.0330	0.0320
A56	n3	1	0.0462	0.0203	0.0703	-	-	0.0946	0.0405	0.1255	0.5341	0.0234	0.0453
A57	n3	1	0.0518	0.0163	0.0659	-	0.0093	0.0506	0.0682	0.0977	0.5786	0.0242	0.0374
A58	E17	1	0.0357	0.0113	0.1071	0.0151	-	0.0293	0.0322	0.0638	0.6416	0.0065	0.0555
A59	E17	2	0.0330	0.0119	0.1142	0.0175	-	0.0242	0.0270	0.0687	0.6403	0.0041	0.0578

Table 3-8. Satin and Matte Glazes

Glaze	Ref.	Cone	Composition (mole ratio)								
			Na_2O	K_2O	CaO	SrO	ZnO	B_2O_3	Al_2O_3	SiO_2	ZrO_2
XVII. Zinc Matte Glaze											
A60	n3	1	0.0445	0.0153	0.0733	-	0.2064	0.0526	0.1066	0.4382	0.0631
XVIII. Lime Matte Glazes											
B61	n3	1	0.0475	0.0016	0.2252	-	-	0.1043	0.0650	0.4941	0.0628
B62	n3	4	0.0130	0.0195	0.1615	0.0563	-	0.0571	0.0811	0.5492	0.0623
B63	E17	1	0.0229	0.0157	0.1948	0.0134	0.0087	0.0310	0.0516	0.6095	0.0502
B64	E17	1	0.0211	0.0052	0.2886	0.0084	-	0.0402	0.0689	0.5641	-

form the crystals, usually a combination of zinc, titanium, and iron oxides. Using ilmenite (iron titanate) in these glazes is very useful, as it acts as a nucleating agent for the crystals.

3.7.1 Rutile break-up glazes exhibit a crystalline effect, which develops around coarse grains of the mineral rutile.[F2,T1] While rutile dissolves easily in molten glazes, it also crystallizes easily out of the same glazes as the glaze is cooled. The break-up effect is due to the growth of titanates on titania particles in the glaze batch. The effect was initially developed in leaded glazes, where the crystal was lead titanate. In the lead-free glazes in section XIX of Table 3-9, the crystal is zinc titanate. The SiO_2 and Al_2O_3 contents of the glazes are low, in order to keep the viscosity low at crystallization temperatures. About 1% of ilmenite in the glaze batch helps to develop the crystals by acting as a nucleating agent.

As the crystals grow, they absorb iron compounds from the surrounding glaze, yielding a flecked glaze, owing to the buff-colored crystals in the brown matrix glass. The effect depends critically on the size and color of the crystals. Therefore, slow cooling is essential for the best results.

3.7.2 Aventurine glazes are transparent glazes in which crystals are suspended in the fired glassy matrix[F3,T1] (see Figure 3.5). These crystals exhibit a marked sparkling effect. Most aventurine glazes are produced by the addition of 10 to 15% of iron oxide (Fe_2O_3) to a transparent base glaze with very low molten viscosity. These glazes have also been produced with chromium, copper, and uranium. The oxide dissolves in the molten glaze, but recrystallizes on cooling. Historically, most aventurine glazes were leaded. Some current lead-free examples are given in section XX of Table 3-9. The amount of iron oxide and the rate of cooling are critical. The correct amount of iron oxide is around 11 wt%, and the glaze should be low in alumina. A well-melted glass, followed by slow cooling, is vital to developing the aventurine effect.

3.7.3 Textured tear glazes are a third crystalline effect in which the surface resembles matte islands in glossy rivers.[H11] They are called tear glazes because the glaze looks as if it had been torn. The crystals are usually zircon. An example is given in Table 3-10. The family of tear glazes is broad, but common characteristics include low SiO_2, high ZrO_2 (up to 20 wt%), and relatively high concentrations of other glass formers (B_2O_3, P_2O_5). Application and firing technique affect the final glaze appearance. Three-dimensional effects can be obtained through splatter coating.

Table 3-9. Glazes for Unique Effects

Glaze	Ref.	Cone	Composition (mole ratio)											
			Na$_2$O	K$_2$O	CaO	MgO	BaO	ZnO	Fe$_2$O$_3$	B$_2$O$_3$	Al$_2$O$_3$	SiO$_2$	TiO$_2$	SnO$_2$
XIX. Rutile Break-Up Glazes														
A65	C5	8	0.0821	0.0244	0.0493	0.0253	–	0.0394	0.0060	–	0.1164	0.5855	0.0770	–
A66	C5	8	0.0290	0.0113	0.0538	0.1121	0.0243	–	0.0050	0.0148	0.0517	0.5942	0.1082	–
A67	C5	6	0.0246	0.0106	0.1237	0.0761	–	0.1068	0.0020	–	0.0540	0.5431	0.0609	–
A68	C5	02	0.0685	–	0.1440	–	–	0.1638	0.0010	0.1347	0.0157	0.3930	0.0800	–
XX. Aventurine Glazes														
B69	C5	4	0.0934	0.0277	0.0724	0.0407	–	0.0524	0.0453	–	0.0886	0.5795	–	–
B70	C6	4	0.0891	–	–	–	0.0099	–	0.0941	0.1980	0.0149	0.5941	–	–
XXI. Crackle Glaze														
C71	n3	06	0.1426	0.0519	0.0039	–	–	0.0083	–	0.1617	0.0848	0.5461	–	–
XXII. Raku Glazes														
D72	F3	06	0.1170	0.0362	0.0034	0.0023	–	0.0056	–	0.1566	0.0723	0.5870	–	0.0192
D73	C7	06	0.1158	0.0426	0.0660	0.0113	–	0.0068	–	0.1315	0.0889	0.5115	–	0.0244

Figure 3.5

An aventurine glaze.

3.7.4 Crackle glazes are glazes that exhibit a deliberately induced crazing[F2] (see Figure 3.6). The crackle is produced by using a glaze higher in coefficient of thermal expansion than the body. Usually this means glazes high in the alkalis Na_2O and K_2O. The crazing effect is discussed in detail in Chapter 15. Section XXI of Table 3-9 gives a glaze that will craze on almost all ceramic bodies, yielding a crackle effect.

A problem with crackle glazes is controlling the extent of crazing. Too much crazing produces innumerable craze lines closely packed together.

The crackle involves multiple cracks that extend through the glaze to the interface with the body. The craze lines can afterwards be decorated by rubbing colored pigments into them. Because materials can be rubbed into the craze lines, a crackle glaze should never be used on surfaces that come in contact with food or drink. During use, organic particles can enter the cracks. They cannot be removed by washing.

3.7.5 Luster glazes pro-
duce a thin film of metal on the glaze surface as a result of the glaze being reduced[F2] (see Figure 3.7). They are usually applied to a fired glaze surface, but some in-glaze lusters are used exactly like ordinary glazes. There are two types of luster glazes: those that can be fired in oxidizing atmospheres, but which contain reducing agents; and those that must be fired in reducing conditions.

Table 3-10. Textured Tear Glaze	
Oxide	Mole Percent
Na_2O	0.1099
CaO	0.0434
ZnO	0.0680
B_2O_3	0.1332
Al_2O_3	0.0485
SiO_2	0.2553
ZrO_2	0.0703
P_2O_5	0.0086
F	0.2624
Reference H9	fired cone 1

The first type contain metal resinates produced by heating a metallic salt with resin, followed by dissolution in a suitable oil such as lavender oil. On firing the glaze to 650 to 750°C, a thin film of metal is deposited on the glaze surface.

A typical formula is:[C8]

resin	20 wt%
$Bi(NO_3)_3$	5
lavender oil	30
metal oxide	45

where the metal oxide can be any of the transition metal oxides.

The second type, which must be fired in reducing atmosphere, contains a mixture of the metallic salt with about three times its weight in clay or ochre, with a binder to hold the metallic film onto the biscuit ware. The glazes are fired oxidizing to about 750°C, followed by a strongly reduced soak for about one hour.

3.7.6 The Raku process
(see Figure 3.8) involves loading ware into a red-hot kiln.

Figure 3.6

Pitcher with a crackle glaze.

After a short soak, the ware is removed from the kiln while still at red heat. Glazes for the Raku process are those that will mature at a low temperature.[F2] Some examples of leadless Raku glazes will be found in section XXII of Table 3-9. The crackle glaze in section XXI of Table 3-9 is also suitable.

Owing to the high alkali content of the glazes, and to the fact that the Raku body is usually underfired, Raku glazes always craze. This effect is accentuated by the fact that for best results, Raku glazes are generally applied thickly. Reduction effects can be produced by quenching the glazed ware in oil or in a bed of sawdust, grass, etc.

3.7.7 Salt glazes (see Figure 3.9) are the result of throwing rock salt or common salt into a gas-fired kiln while the ware is in the hot zone.[F2] The salt volatilizes and, in the presence of steam, reacts with the ceramic body to form a very thin coat of a sodium aluminosilicate. The reactions can be written:

$$2NaCl + H_2O = 2HCl + Na_2O$$

$$Na_2O + \text{aluminosilicate body} = Na \text{ aluminosilicate}$$

Figure 3.7

A luster glaze.

Figure 3.8

Glaze subjected to the Raku process.

The salt is damp when added to create the steam, and excellent ventilation is required to remove the HCl fumes. A temperature of 1060°C, and preferably 1180°C is required, so that ware designed for cone 6 to 8 is normally used.

3.7.8 Ash glazes are glazes that contain a substantial concentration of wood ash in the formula. Ashes are so variable in composition that it is difficult to describe their formulas. The glazes in section XXIII of Table 3-11 are calculated assuming the composition of pine wood ash given by Tichane.[T2] In these glazes the wood ash acts as a flux. It contributes potassium, which disperses more effectively than potassium from feldspar. It also contributes phosphorus pentoxide, a fluxing glass former.

Figure 3.9

A salt glaze.

The textures that result from the use of wood ash are unusual, and sometimes very attractive, with subtle shade variations. Reduced firing conditions usually produce the more attractive results.[F2]

3.7.9 Celadon glazes (see Figure 3.10) at first seem to be nothing more than a simple lime/alkali glaze with about 1% of iron oxide, and fired in reduction.[C10] However, the reality is that a good celadon is very difficult to achieve.[V1] It requires the integration of glaze composition, discussed here, with firing conditions and choice of body.

Celadons have been described as the color produced in reduced feldspathic glazes by low percentages of iron.[T2] Celadons are usually soft yellow-green colors because of contamination by titania. In the absence of titania, blues can be obtained that approach "the blue of the sky as seen through rifts in the clouds after rain."

These glazes were developed during the Sung Dynasty in China (960–1279 AD). Typical is the Lung Chuan celadon (section XXIV of Table 3-11), which was produced in great quantity during the Sung period. The Lung Chuan celadon is a thick green to blue-green semi-opaque glaze with a soft satin surface resulting from barely maturing the glaze in a long firing. Producing this glaze requires much attention to detail. The impurities in the clays chosen, especially the titania content, determine the color. The higher the titania,

Figure 3.10

A celadon glaze.

Table 3-11. More Glazes for Special Effects

Glaze	Ref.	Cone	Na$_2$O	K$_2$O	CaO	MgO	BaO	Fe$_2$O$_3$	B$_2$O$_3$	Al$_2$O$_3$	SiO$_2$	TiO$_2$	P$_2$O$_5$
XXIII. Ash Glazes													
A75	C5	4	0.1874	0.0300	0.2561	0.0479	–	0.0062	0.0827	0.0673	0.3160	0.0012	0.0053
A76	C5	4	0.1681	0.0316	0.2092	0.0768	–	0.0055	–	0.1002	0.4026	0.0016	0.0044
A77	C5	6	0.1472	0.0297	0.1608	0.0859	–	0.0050	–	0.0820	0.4843	0.0011	0.0040
A78	F3	8	0.1705	0.0346	0.1740	0.0269	–	0.0058	–	0.0996	0.4826	0.0015	0.0047
A79	C5	8	0.1509	0.0309	0.1541	0.0240	0.0699	0.0053	–	0.0980	0.4611	0.0018	0.0041
XXIV. Lung Chuan Celadon Glazes													
B80	T2	6	0.0011	0.0345	0.1206	0.0065	–	0.0029	–	0.0918	0.7422	0.0002	0.0005
B81	T2	6	0.0052	0.0262	0.1412	0.0129	–	0.0033	–	0.1057	0.7055	–	–
B82	T2	6	0.0169	0.0413	0.1297	–	–	0.0060	–	0.0864	0.7197	–	–
XXV. Chun Glazes													
C83	T2	8	0.0072	0.0264	0.1000	0.0237	–	0.0064	–	0.0619	0.7718	0.0006	0.0022
C84	T2	8	0.0099	0.0217	0.0838	0.0372	–	0.0264	–	0.1376	0.6779	0.0055	–
C85	T2	6	0.0182	0.0426	0.1418	–	–	0.0071	–	0.0608	0.7295	–	–

47

the greener the color. The glaze must be applied very thickly—at least two millimeters of fired glaze is needed. It is fired in strong reduction from as low as 950°C. The firing must be very slow, in order to get a smooth surface, while barely reaching maturity.

3.7.10 The Chun ware of northern China (section XXV of Table 3-11) yield a pale to deep blue color with an occasional splash of copper red.[T2] (see Figure 3.11) While other Sung glazes, such as the Lung Chuan, are phase separated and soft in color due to bubbles and fine crystals, Chun glazes are a true opal, with a brown color in transmitted light and a blue color in reflected light.

One key to Chun glazes is titania, a common trace element in most clays. To obtain a blue color, the clay must be carefully chosen to minimize the titania content. Another key is phosphate, in low (0.5%) concentration. This was formerly achieved by using ash as an ingredient (see section 3.7.8). As with Lung Chuan celadons, the slow firing of a thick glaze in strong reduction is required.

Figure 3.11

Chun glaze.

Chapter 4
Formulation of Porcelain Enamels

Porcelain enamel is the name given to a glass coating applied to a metal substrate—usually steel.[E24] The interface between the glass coating and the metal substrate is critical to the development of bonding between these two dissimilar materials. The glass coating must not only act as a protective and aesthetically pleasing surface, but also must bond to the metal substrate.

4.1 Adherence

Before proceeding to a discussion of materials for porcelain enameling, a few words about the phenomenon of adherence is in order. A more comprehensive discussion will be found in Chapter 14.

For proper adherence, it is necessary to develop a continuous electronic structure or chemical bond across the interfacial area.[P2] As will be discussed later, this is accomplished by saturating both the enamel coating and the substrate metal with an oxide of the metal. For iron and steel substrates, this oxide is FeO. Surface roughness also generally improves adherence, although it is of little value if the chemical bond is weak.

Additions to the ceramic coating formulation of certain ions, such as cobalt oxide and nickel oxide, result in improved adherence between the glass coating and the metal. These oxides contribute substantially to the rate at which the saturation of the substrate and the coating with the critical oxide of the substrate occurs.[K4] They also play a critical role in creating and maintaining the saturation at the interface between the substrate and the coating.

In Chapter 14 the adherence process will be examined in detail and the action of these adherence oxides discussed. For now, let us merely note that their presence or absence is the fundamental difference between enamels. Ground coat enamels contain adherence oxides, while cover coat enamels do not.

4.2 Ground Coat Enamels

Table 4-1 gives some typical examples of general-purpose ground coat enamels.[n5] As the name implies, the ground coat is applied directly to the metal substrate, often as an undercoat, over which other coatings are applied. In other applications, the ground coat is used alone. Especially when used as an undercoat, the most essential property of a ground coat is adherence to the metal substrate. Certain metallic oxides are added to the enamel formulation to promote this bonding process.

Chief among these adherence oxides is cobalt oxide. Normally 0.01 to 0.02 molar ratio is considered necessary. Second in importance is nickel oxide, which may be used in molar ratio of 0.02 to 0.04. To a lesser degree, cupric oxide, manganous oxide and iron oxide may be used. The specific amounts depend upon details of the enamel's total formulation, processing, and service requirements.

Ground coats used as undercoats have comparatively simple alkali borosilicate formulations. Chemical resistance requirements are limited to minimizing surface defects that may be caused by the substrate or its preparation method. In addition, ground coats must have good workability under production conditions, which means low viscosity and low surface tension at firing temperatures.

Even this simple combination of properties is difficult to achieve in one formulation subjected to one set of processing conditions. Therefore, enamels are usually all fritted coatings. Moreover, to achieve optimum conditions, it is often necessary to use two-, three-, or four-frit combinations, with each member contributing a particular property to the combination. For example, a hard member frit may provide high resistance to sagging or hairline defects, and superior corrosion resistance. A medium-firing member may help to prevent the same defects, and it also may add resistance to burn-off or copperheading. The soft member frit fuses early in the firing process, seals off the metal, promotes bonding, and improves edge coverage. The result is a wider firing range and improved coating smoothness.

Examples A1 and A2 in Table 4-1 are typical of general-purpose ground coat enamels. Coating A1 fires for 4 minutes at 805°C, whereas coating A2 fires for 2½ minutes at 780°C. Occasionally a fourth member frit may be used to produce an appliance gray speckled effect. The end member is a titania opacified off-white frit that is

Table 4-1. Composition of Ground Coat Enamels

| | General Purpose | | | Home Laundry | Hot Water Tank | | Continuous Cleaning |
	A1	A2	A3	B4	C5	C6	D7
Ref.	n5	n5	n5	E17	E17	E17	E24
Content (mole ratio)							
Li_2O	0.0109	0.0181	0.0087	0.0173	0.0381	0.0277	0.0136
Na_2O	0.1357	0.1312	0.1254	0.1296	0.1111	0.1392	0.0927
K_2O	0.0103	0.0151	0.0155	0.0106	–	–	0.0123
CaO	0.0718	0.0681	0.0649	0.0130	0.0227	0.0226	0.0091
MgO	0.0013	–	0.0012	0.0028	–	–	–
BaO	0.0186	0.0293	0.0150	0.0030	0.0028	0.0023	–
ZnO	–	–	–	0.0020	0.0138	0.0096	–
CoO	0.0045	0.0039	0.0027	0.0030	0.0038	0.0039	0.0003
NiO	0.0101	0.0106	0.0077	0.0026	0.0012	–	0.0003
CuO	0.0019	0.0022	0.0012	–	–	–	0.1383
Cr_2O_3	–	–	–	–	–	–	0.0064
MnO_2	0.0013	0.0014	0.0027	0.0049	0.0034	0.0129	0.0003
B_2O_3	0.1299	0.1365	0.1227	0.1465	0.0644	0.0677	0.0134
Al_2O_3	0.0382	0.0385	0.0366	0.0719	0.0136	0.0123	0.3191
SiO_2	0.4987	0.4531	0.5054	0.4410	0.5759	0.5782	0.3167
ZrO_2	–	–	0.0073	0.0329	0.0557	0.0586	0.0462
TiO_2	–	–	0.0184	0.0203	0.0176	–	0.0003
Sb_2O_3	0.0003	–	0.0002	–	–	–	0.0008
P_2O_5	0.0016	0.0031	0.0027	0.0020	–	–	–
F	0.0650	0.0882	0.0620	0.0774	0.0706	0.0715	0.0300

compatible with the other member frits. Coating A3 is an example of a coating made with a four-frit combination, one of which is a titania-opacified off-white frit. This coating fires for 4 minutes at 780°C.

Ground coat frits can also be designed to meet a variety of end use purposes. For example, coating B4 in Table 4-1 has been formulated for alkali resistance through the addition of substantial quantities of zirconium oxide. It is typical of coatings used in the home-laundry industry. The amount of zirconium oxide added is a compromise between the need for alkaline durability, served by adding more zirconium oxide, and the need for workability, which zirconium oxide hinders. For an application such as strong alkali resistance in a chemical reactor, the amount of zirconium oxide would be increased at the expense of workability.

Enamels can also be formulated for acid resistance. Silica is highly acid resistant, so acid-resistant enamels tend to be high in SiO_2. Titania, below the level at which crystallization occurs, around 5% by weight, also improves acid resistance. That is why the laundry enamel has some titania in its formula.

Enamels can also be formulated for thermal resistance in service. This is normally accomplished by raising the refractoriness, or firing temperature, of the enamel. Coatings C5 and C6 in Table 4-1 are examples of the formulations used when the outstanding thermal and corrosion resistance required of hot water tank systems are needed.[E17] The higher concentration of silica and lower concentration of boron oxide in these coatings reflects the substantially higher firing temperature of 7 minutes at 860°C. The composition of these enamels bears a similarity to that of the home laundry enamels because the action of water on these enamels is similar to that of alkali attack.

It is instructive to compare these formulations with formulations B6 through B8 in Table 3-2. It can be seen that the two important differences are the addition of adherence oxides to facilitate bonding to a metal substrate and the use of greatly increased concentrations of boric oxide and reduced concentrations of alumina and silica to permit the very much lower firing temperature.[E24]

A substantially different type of ground coat formulation is given in D7 in Table 4-1. This coating has been developed to provide a way to oxidize and hence remove food soils from the surfaces of ovens at normal operating temperatures. In these materials, various active ingredients chosen from a wide variety of metal oxides such as copper, vanadium, niobium, bismuth, chromium, molybdenum, tungsten, manganese, rhenium, iron, cobalt, nickel, cerium, rhodium, palladium, and platinum are incorporated into the formulation.[W3] In addition, to make the coating only partially vitreous and substantially porous, approximately one-half of the silica is replaced with alumina.

4.3 Cover Coat Enamels

Porcelain enamel cover coats are designed to provide specific color and appearance characteristics combined with resistance to atmospheric and liquid corrosion, surface hardness, abrasion resistance, and resistance to heat and thermal shock, as required.[n5] Cover coat formulations are available to provide a wide variety of appearance properties. They range from opaque whites through pastels and medium-strength colors to strong, dark colors. A wide selection of glosses is also available, ranging from the high-gloss sanitary ware finishes to the full-matte architectural enamels.

Porcelain enamel cover coats are classified as opaque, semi-opaque, and clear. Opaque enamels are used for white and pastel cover coats, semi-opaque enamels are used for most of the medium-strength colors, and clear enamels are necessary to produce bright, strong colors.

Although zirconia and antimony oxides were used for opacification in the past, current opaque enamels are opacified with titanium dioxide. In most cases, all the titanium dioxide is smelted into a clear frit that crystallizes to anatase and rutile during the firing process to provide the required opacification.[E9,E2,P3,S8] Therefore, the properties of the product depend on the concentration of crystals present in the vitreous matrix, which in turn responds to the firing parameters of time and temperature.

Some fully opaque titania-opacified porcelain enamels are given in section A of Table 4-2. These materials have been formulated to show excellent acid resistance and in most cases fairly good alkaline resistance. Titania-opacified enamels are produced with reflectances ranging from 78%, as with enamels A8 or A9, up to 88%, as with enamel A10. The firing temperatures range from 770°C to 830°C. The five examples shown here are all suitable for application directly to decarburized steel. However, not all titania-opacified porcelain enamels are suitable for application direct-on, because they do not produce a satisfactory surface.

As with the other porcelain enamels, these systems are basically alkali borosilicates. To the basic formulations have been added large concentrations of titanium dioxide, in the range where it will be soluble at the melting temperature of 1400°C but only partially soluble at the firing temperature of 800°C. In addition, large concentrations

53

Table 4-2. Composition of Opacified Cover Coat Enamels

	Opaque Cover Coat Enamels					Semi-opaque Cover Coat Enamels	
	A8	A9	A10	A11	A12	B13	B14
Ref.	n5	n5	E3	n5	n5	n5	n5
Content (mole ratio)							
Li_2O	0.0087	0.0160	0.0186	0.0054	0.0200	0.0218	–
Na_2O	0.0927	0.0828	0.0949	0.0659	0.0845	0.0822	0.0737
K_2O	0.0511	0.0438	0.0333	0.0657	0.0411	0.0577	0.0479
MgO	–	0.0019	–	–	–	–	–
ZnO	0.0070	–	–	0.0091	0.0027	0.0076	0.0357
B_2O_3	0.1208	0.1205	0.1448	0.1405	0.1386	0.1408	0.1437
Al_2O_3	0.0116	0.0114	0.0079	0.0096	0.0099	0.0078	0.0085
SiO_2	0.3891	0.3905	0.4261	0.4524	0.4110	0.4615	0.5361
ZrO_2	0.0148	0.0100	–	0.0079	0.0040	–	0.0189
TiO_2	0.1341	0.1410	0.1640	0.1477	0.1357	–	–
P_2O_5	0.0054	0.0055	0.0057	0.0056	0.0056	–	–
Nb_2O_5	–	0.0001	0.0001	0.0001	0.0001	–	–
WO_3	–	–	0.0001	–	0.0001	–	–
F	0.1750	0.1763	0.1043	0.0901	0.1465	0.1224	0.0745
Firing conditions	780°C, 3 min.	770°C, 3 min.	780°C, 3 min.	830°C, 3 min.	770°C, 3 min.	770°C, 3 min.	815°C, 3 min.

of fluoride are added to reduce the stability of the vitreous matrix. Finally, small additions are often made of materials that affect the color of the enamel by altering the crystallization properties. These materials include phosphorus pentoxide,[E4] niobium pentoxide, and tungsten oxide.[E11]

Two examples of semi-opaque cover coat enamels are also given in Table 4-2. These materials do not differ in essential constituents from the fully opaque enamels. Instead, the concentration of titanium dioxide is reduced to the point where the system is compatible with the use of pigments for the production of medium-strength colors.

Clear cover coat porcelain enamels are used in conjunction with appropriate pigments for the production of strong and medium-strength colors. Some typical examples are given in section A of Table 4-3. There is a rather wide variation in formulation between these products compared with the opaque and semi-opaque enamels. Although some titanium dioxide is present in order to improve acid resistance, the concentrations are low enough that substantial crystallization does not occur. Therefore, the inclusion of pigment in the mill formulation will permit the development of strong colors.

Particularly in the architectural industry there is need for cover coat enamels with lower gloss but with no reduction in weatherability and durability. Traditionally, this need was met by adding from 5 to 25% of silica or 2 to 10% titania to a high-gloss enamel. There are several deficiencies in this technique, however, and recently coatings have been developed specifically for matte finishes. Table 4-3 includes examples of these coatings. Example B19 illustrates a fully opaque matte coating, whereas example B20 is typical of a semi-opaque coating suitable for use with darker colors.

Table 4-3. Composition of Cover Coat Enamels

	Clear Cover Coat Enamels				Matte Cover Coat Enamels	
	A15	A16	A17	A18	B19	B20
Ref.	n5	A1	A1	A1	n5	n5
Content (mole ratio)						
Li_2O	0.0357	–	–	–	–	–
Na_2O	0.1200	0.1770	0.1993	0.1586	0.0494	0.0600
K_2O	0.0947	0.0070	0.0036	0.0089	0.1366	0.1320
CaO	–	0.0446	0.0574	0.0488	0.0016	0.0016
ZnO	–	–	–	–	0.0371	0.0416
B_2O_3	0.0621	0.1733	0.1741	0.1918	0.0903	0.0876
Al_2O_3	0.0162	0.0355	0.0251	0.0382	0.0099	0.0092
SiO_2	0.5979	0.4145	0.3797	0.4673	0.4553	0.4766
ZrO_2	0.0388	–	–	–	0.0157	0.0177
TiO_2	0.0273	–	–	–	0.1813	0.1739
P_2O_5	–	–	–	–	0.0025	0.0033
Sb_2O_3	–	–	–	–	0.0018	0.0019
MoO_3	0.0020	–	–	–	–	–
F	0.0753	0.1481	0.1609	0.0863	0.0184	0.0122
Firing conditions	815°C, 3 min.	790°C, 3 min.	790°C, 3 min.	790°C, 3 min.	805°C, 3 min.	805°C, 3 min.

Chapter 5
Raw Materials For Ceramic Coatings

For a number of reasons, one of which is cost, ceramic coatings are not prepared by mixing the separate oxides.[E24] Instead, as far as possible, naturally occurring minerals are used in order to achieve the most rapid melting, and the lowest possible batch cost, consistent with processing requirements.

Many of these minerals contain more than one of the constituent oxides. Hence, the choice of raw materials is limited by the presence of all the oxides in a given material. Table 5-1 shows most of the raw materials commonly used in the formulation of ceramic coatings.

As will be discussed in Chapter 7, most ceramic coatings are applied as an aqueous slip. For this reason, materials that are highly soluble in water are not included in Table 5-1. Such materials can only be used after fritting, a process to be discussed in Section 5.3.

While no water-soluble materials are included in Table 5-1, a few of these materials are toxic, and are more or less soluble in mild acids. Great care is required when handling such materials to prevent the ingestion or breathing of dusts. One should always read the Material Safety Data Sheets supplied with materials to determine appropriate handling procedures.

A number of factors must be considered in selecting a raw material for use in a ceramic coating.[T1] These factors include:

- The chemical composition of the material, including the impurities to be expected
- The uniformity of the composition over extended periods of time
- The particle size distribution of the material
- The availability of the material and the location(s) of its source

- Its behavior in transit and in storage
- Its behavior in water suspension
- Its behavior in processing
- Its effect on the environment
- Cost

Chemical composition involves not only the desired elements, but also the impurities. Among impurities, ferric oxide (hematite), titania (rutile), iron chromite, and zircon are particularly undesirable. Also undesirable is any element that is not called for in the formulation. On the other hand, some impurities may be desirable. As a general rule, less pure materials, especially those containing volatiles that decompose below 500°C, are more reactive than materials of high purity.

Consistency of composition over time is very important. Most mined materials can vary slowly over time. To combat this problem, some producers, especially in the clay mining business, blend material from various parts of their mines, in order to produce a uniform product over time.

The particle size and its uniformity over time are major concerns.[M13] Finer particles will melt and homogenize more rapidly, and with less energy. On the other hand, the increased surface-energy-to-bulk-energy ratio of a fine particle will lead to agglomeration. Agglomerates melt very slowly and must be avoided. Thus, a balance is required.

The location of a raw material source affects shipping costs and delivery times. For some of the less expensive raw materials, shipping cost can be an appreciable part of the delivered cost. On the other hand, some unique materials are worth the added cost and inconvenience.

Behavior in transit and storage can seriously affect the ability to use a material. Hygroscopic materials, for example, must be protected from water. Excessive humidity can cause cementing reactions to take place.[R5] Fine particles can cause dust clouds, with consequent loss of material.

As will be discussed in detail in Chapter 7, the water solubility of a material affects its behavior in an aqueous suspension. Even materials considered to be relatively insoluble, such as feldspars, can leach alkalis when left for a long time in aqueous suspension.[T1]

The behavior of a material during processing can have a significant effect on the results obtained. This will be discussed in detail in Section 5.4. In particular, it is important to realize that reactivity is generally inversely related to purity. High-purity materials are often relatively inert and difficult to use. Moreover, the melting rate and

Table 5-1 Commonly Used Raw Materials

To Add	Possible Raw Materials	Other Oxides Introduced
Li_2O	Spodumene	Al_2O_3, SiO_2
Na_2O	Feldspars	K_2O, Al_2O_3, SiO_2
	Nepheline syenite	K_2O, Al_2O_3, SiO_2
K_2O	Feldspars	Na_2O, Al_2O_3, SiO_2
	Muscovite mica	Al_2O_3, SiO_2
CaO	Wollastonite	SiO_2
	Calcium carbonate (whiting)	-
	Dolomite	MgO
MgO	Heavy magnesium oxide	-
	Magnesium Carbonate	-
	Dolomite	CaO
	Talc	CaO, SiO_2
SrO	Strontium carbonate	-
BaO	Barium carbonate	-
ZnO	Zinc oxide	-
PbO	Lead bisilicate	SiO_2
Al_2O_3	Corundum (heavy alumina)	-
	Alumina hydrate	-
	Feldspars	Na_2O, K_2O, SiO_2
	Nepheline syenite	Na_2O, K_2O, SiO_2
	Kaolin clay	SiO_2
	Ball clay	SiO_2
	Muscovite mica	K_2O, SiO_2
	Pyrophyllite	SiO_2
SiO_2	Quartz sand, Flint	-
	Feldspars	Na_2O, K_2O, Al_2O_3
	Nepheline syenite	Na_2O, K_2O, Al_2O_3
	Wollastonite	CaO
	Kaolin clay	Al_2O_3
	Ball clay	Al_2O_3
	Muscovite mica	K_2O, Al_2O_3
	Pyrophyllite	Al_2O_3
	Talc	CaO, MgO
	Zircon	ZrO_2
ZrO_2	Zircon	SiO_2
TiO_2	Anatase	-

homogenization of the coating materials are enhanced by choosing raw materials that are chemically most similar to the final coating composition, and to appropriate eutectics.[E45]

Increasingly, environmental concerns enter into the selection of raw materials. Fluorine is a volatile element that is of value in reducing the viscosity of glass melts, but its use is restricted by air pollution regulations. Lead oxide is an oxide with many useful properties. However, its use entails the handling of a toxic substance of acute concern to regulatory authorities. Among the most intractable environmental problems are the disposal of the bags that many powdered materials are shipped in, and the used refractories obtained when kilns are periodically relined.

5.1 Sources of Each of the Oxides

The principal raw materials used in formulating ceramic glazes are listed in Table 5-1. In this section, each of these materials will be briefly discussed, with emphasis on their place in glaze formulation. Note that only materials that are essentially insoluble in water are considered here.

5.1.1 Spodumene, and the related mineral petalite, are the only acceptable sources of lithium oxide other than frits. Both are lithium aluminosilicates that can be refined to low iron oxide impurity content.[M10]

While these minerals are more refractory than the soda or potash feldspars, they form powerful eutectics with them.[O2] Hence, the major use of these minerals is in combination with the other feldspars, to both lower thermal expansion and increase melting rate.

The sources of these minerals are Gwalia Consolidated (Western Australia) and Tantalum Mining Corporation (Manitoba) for spodumene, and Bikita Minerals (Zimbabwe) for petalite. They are supplied through F. & S. International, Inc. (Pittsburgh, PA).

5.1.2 Feldspars are alkali aluminosilicate minerals, with varying amounts of sodium, potassium, and calcium.[P7] While very abundant (60% of the earth's crust), only selected deposits are suitable. The principal requirement is that the concentrations of colored ions, principally iron, must be low.

The various commercial feldspar products vary primarily in the ratio of their alkalis. So-called potash feldspars generally contain 2 to 3% Na_2O and 10 to 11% K_2O by weight. So-called soda feldspars generally contain 6 1/2 to 7% Na_2O and 4 to 4 1/2% K_2O. The variation is sufficiently large that one should always use the stated composition of the particular product used.

The major suppliers of potash feldspars are Pacer Corporation (Custer, SD) and Zemex Industrial Minerals, Inc. (Atlanta, GA). Soda feldspars are supplied by Zemex Industrial Minerals, Inc. and Unimin Corporation (New Canaan, CT).

Feldspars are major fluxing components of most glazes that are fired at cone 02 or above. They are the only suitable sources of soda and potash other than nepheline syenite (see section 5.1.3) and frits. Their use in most glazes is limited by their alkali content. The choice between potash feldspar and soda feldspar is partially a matter of the firing temperature. In glazes firing at cone 6 and above, better properties, especially gloss and resistance to runoff from vertical surfaces, are achieved with potash feldspar. For glaze firing between cone 02 and cone 6, the faster melting rate of soda feldspar becomes more important and generally yields better-quality coatings.

5.1.3 Nepheline syenite is a holocrystalline, granular, igneous rock composed of nepheline ($K_2O \cdot 3Na_2O \cdot 4Al_2O_3 \cdot 8SiO_2$), potash feldspar, soda feldspar, and minor amounts of other minerals. It is found only in a few places in the world. The principal location is Blue Mountain, near Sudbury, Ontario. Because it is essentially a eutectic of nepheline and feldspar, it is a somewhat more powerful flux than feldspar. Its relatively low silica, high alumina composition makes it particularly appropriate for satin and matte glazes.[O2] Otherwise, its behavior in coatings is similar in most respects to feldspar. The limit to its use in glazes—its alkali content—is more restrictive than that of the feldspars, as the alkali content of nepheline is higher.

The supplier of nepheline syenite is Unimin Corporation (New Canaan, CT).

5.1.4 Muscovite mica is a phyllosilicate mineral that exhibits a platy structure.[H4] In ceramic coatings, the interest is in low iron ground grades, where it acts as a powerful flux material, yet adds to the coating only 5 wt% of potassium oxide as a non–lattice forming material. These grades are produced as a coproduct or byproduct of feldspar, kaolin, and lithium beneficiation; from mica schist; and from scrap muscovite sheet.

Some principal suppliers include Zemex Industrial Minerals, Inc. (Atlanta, GA), KMG Minerals (Kings Mountain, NC), Pacer Corporation (Custer, SD), and Spartan Minerals Corporation (Pacolet, SC).

5.1.5 Wollastonite is a natural calcium silicate. Because of its superior performance, its use is probably the fastest-growing among raw materials used in ceramic coatings.[R6] Commercial products are 98 to 99% pure. The specific impurities and the performance of the product vary somewhat from location to location.

The Essex County, New York material (NYCO Minerals, Willsboro, NY) is separated from garnet and other impurities by high-intensity magnetic separation to produce a 99% pure product that is somewhat more reactive than other wollastonites used in glazes. The Governeur, New York material (R.T. Vanderbilt Company, Norwalk, CT) is sufficiently pure an ore that a 98% pure product is produced without beneficiation. Its impurities include calcite and prennite. Starting up in 1997 was a large mine near Hermosillo, Sonora, Mexico (also NYCO Minerals, Willsboro, NY), which will serve the United States market. This plant will use froth flotation to separate calcite impurity, a process that is also used by a producer in Finland (Partek).

Wollastonite is the preferred raw material source for calcium oxide in glazes. Compared to calcium carbonate plus flint, it dissolves much more readily, permitting the glaze to smooth out more rapidly and completely. It substantially reduces the tendency for bubble defects to occur (see Chapter 13), both by eliminating carbonate volatilization and by removing silica particles that can act as pins preventing gas from escaping.

5.1.6 Calcium carbonate (whiting) in the United States is usually processed from marble or calcite ores, primarily by wet grinding. It is widely available, and low in cost, so that proximity of the supplier to the customer is a major consideration. Commercial products are 98 to 99% pure, with most of the impurity hydroxide.

Some major suppliers of calcium carbonate include ECC International (Roswell, GA), Franklin Industrial Minerals (Nashville, TN), Genstar Stone Products Company (Hunt Valley, MD), and J. M. Huber Corporation (St. Louis, MO).

The major limitation on the use of calcium carbonate in ceramic coatings is the 44% carbon dioxide that escapes during the firing process. If great care is not taken, bubble defects in the coating will result from the use of calcium carbonate.[O2]

5.1.7 Dolomite is a double carbonate mineral of calcium and magnesium.[H7] High-purity dolomite sources are fairly common. Such sources have at least 20% magnesium carbonate and less than 2% impurities.

Companies that produce high-purity dolomite in North America include Baker Refractories (York, PA), Martin Marietta Magnesia Specialties (Baltimore, MD), and National Refractories and Minerals (Livermore, CA)

5.1.8 Magnesium oxide is the most important product of the magnesium compounds industry.[C9] It is usually produced by the thermal decomposition of magnesite (magnesium carbonate—see section 5.1.9) or magnesium hydroxide obtained from seawater or magnesium-rich brines. The physical properties of the magnesia are governed by the precursor, the time, the temperature of the calcination, and the impurities. Dead-burned magnesia is produced at temperatures greater than 1400°C and is characterized by low chemical reactivity. For this reason, its use is limited to small quantities in glazes firing at cone 6 and higher.

Suppliers include Aluchem (Reading, OH), American Minerals, Inc. (King of Prussia, PA), Martin Marietta Magnesia Specialties (Baltimore, MD), and National Magnesia Chemicals (Moss Landing, CA).

5.1.9 Magnesium carbonate (Magnesite) occurs in several parts of the world and is usually mined selectively, followed by beneficiation.[C9] The beneficiation methods include crushing, screening, and froth flotation. The latter processing results in a very low density product. This very low density limits the use of this material in coating applications to 1 wt% or less. Otherwise, the coating application will be too low in density, leading to bubble and crawling defects in the coating (see Chapter 13).

Suppliers include J.M. Huber Corporation (St. Louis, MO), Morton International (Danvers, MA), and Premier Services Corporation (Middleburg Heights, OH).

5.1.10 Talc is a soft, hydrous magnesium silicate mineral.[J3] Commercial talcs range from products approaching the theoretical mineral to mineral products that have properties common to pure talcs but contain little of the actual mineral. Talc mined in Montana is close to the pure mineral. In Texas, associated minerals include quartz, magnetite, chlorite, tremolite, and anthrophyllite. Tremolite (nonasbestiform) and serpentine are found in New York talc.

The principal talc producers are Dal-Tile Corporation (Dallas, TX), R.T. Vanderbilt Company (Norwalk, CT), and Luzenac America (Englewood, CO). Their products, respectively, come from Texas, New York, and Montana.

Talc is often used as the residual source of magnesium oxide in ceramic coatings. The major problem with this strategy is that talc yields its water of hydration at about 1100°C, which is very close to the top temperatures in a cone 1 firing. Above cone 6, this is not a problem.

5.1.11 Strontium carbonate is obtained from two minerals, celestite (strontium sulfate) and strontianite (strontium carbonate).[O1] Of these two, celestite is the more common. The black ash and soda ash processes are used to convert the celestite to chemical-grade strontium carbonate. Purity of 97 to 98% is normally obtained. The preferred method is the black ash method, which involves reacting the celestite with coal to produce strontium sulfide, which is then aerated in water solution with carbon dioxide to produce the strontium carbonate.

United States celestite requirements are supplied from Mexico. Strontium carbonate is supplied by Cometals, Inc. (New York, NY), and Chemical Products Corporation (Cartersville, GA).

Strontium oxide is a very valuable constituent of glazes fired at cone 1 and higher. However, because of the high decomposition temperature of the carbonate, obtaining strontium values from a frit usually gives better results.

5.1.12 Barium carbonate is produced primarily from the mineral barite (barium sulfate), which is reacted with coal to produce barium sulfide, a water-soluble product that can be further reacted with soda ash or carbon dioxide to yield barium carbonate.[G6]

Substantial amounts of this material are imported, primarily from China, which has the world's largest reserves. The major domestic suppliers are Basstech International (Englewood, NJ), Chemical Products Corporation (Cartersville, GA), Cometals, Inc. (New York, NY), and Kraft Chemical Company (Melrose Park, IL).

This material has limited use in glazes. It is used primarily in the formulation of barium mattes. However, because of the high decomposition temperature of the carbonate, obtaining barium values from a frit usually gives better results.

5.1.13 Zinc oxide is a fluffy white powder produced by one of two processes.[P6] In the French process, zinc metal is vaporized and then burned off to zinc oxide powder. In the American process, oxidized ores of zinc sulfide are reacted with coal, and then smelted, vaporizing zinc metal, which is then burned to zinc oxide as it escapes the smelter.

The only remaining American process plant (Eagle Zinc Company, Hillsboro, IL) produces a grade of zinc oxide specifically designed for ceramic glaze application (trade name Denzox), which is coarser than other zinc oxides. Suppliers of French process zinc oxide include Kraft Chemical Company (Melrose Park, IL) and Zinc Corporation of America (Monaca, PA).

Zinc oxide is used extensively in glazes for ceramic tile, where it offers fluxing power, control of thermal expansion, and enhanced gloss. It also acts as a low-grade opacifier.

5.1.14 Lead bisilicate is the only source of lead oxide that is sufficiently acid insoluble that it can be considered for use in ceramic coatings. It is actually a fritted product, made by smelting together 65% lead oxide, 34% silica, and 1% alumina, by weight.[N1] The principal supplier is Hammond Lead Products (Hammond, IN).

Lead bisilicate is one of the most powerful flux materials that can be used in ceramic coatings. It provides a number of important advantages, one of which is that it combines great fluxing power with only a modest increase in thermal expansion. However, lead oxide is a toxic material that requires extensive precautions to be used successfully (see section 3.4 in Chapter 3). Today, this has become a political as well as a technical problem, so that lead oxide is being phased out in most applications.

5.1.15 Kaolin is a relatively pure form of the phyllosilicate mineral kaolinite.[Y1] It is found along the fall line in a continuous belt from central Georgia to the Savannah River area of South Carolina. The kaolin used by the ceramic industry is called airfloated kaolin, and it is produced by flash drying, roller milling, air classification, and packaging. The air classification process removes the major contaminants, primarily muscovite mica, quartz, pyrite, siderite, and hematite.

Some major producers include Kentucky-Tennessee Clay Company (Sandersville, GA), Zemex Industrial Minerals, Inc. (Edgar, FL), R. T. Vanderbilt (Bath, SC), Albion Kaolin (Hepzibah, GA), and Dry Branch Kaolin Company (Dry Branch, GA). In addition, a limited amount of kaolin is imported from England, primarily by ECC International, Inc. (Roswell, GA). The English kaolin has a different geological origin from the United States material, has somewhat different impurities, and thus can behave differently in a glaze.

In addition to serving as a source of alumina and silica in the glaze formulation, kaolin clay acts as a suspending agent in ceramic coating slips (see Chapter 7). Its use, however, must be limited by its effect on the shrinkage of the glaze slip on drying. Too much kaolin in the formulation will result in too much shrinkage, leading to crawling defects (see Chapter 13).

When the requirements for alumina and silica cannot be supplied by other ingredients, and the use of airfloated kaolin is limited by the shrinkage effects, calcined kaolin can be considered. Calcining kaolin removes the water of hydration, which is the cause of the shrinkage that leads to crawling defects. It also converts any residual FeOOH to hematite, which can be removed magnetically. However, it also increases the particle size to the point where it is not very effective as a suspending agent.

A supplier of calcined kaolin is Burgess Pigment Company (Sandersville, GA).

5.1.16 Ball clay is a sedimentary clay, primarily kaolinic, but also containing amounts of illite, smectite, and other interstratified clay minerals.[M14] They are characterized by fine particle size (5 to 0.2 microns) and exhibit high plasticity. These materials contain in varying amounts carbon, iron, and titanium. Thus, only the highest purity ball clays are sufficiently white-firing to be useful in coating applications. Table 5-2 shows the composition and properties of two ball clays that are used in glazes.

Most ball clays come from the northeast corner of the Mississippi embayment region in southwest Kentucky and northwest Tennessee. The principal suppliers are Kentucky-Tennessee Clay Company (Mayfield, KY), Old Hickory Clay Company (Hickory, KY), H. C. Spinks Clay Company (Paris, TN), and United Clays, Inc. (Brentwood,TN).

Table 5-2 Ball Clays Suitable for Coating Applications

Property (wt %)	Old Mine #4[a]	#1 Glaze Clay[b]
SiO_2	57.5	58.6
Al_2O_3	27.3	28.9
Fe_2O_3	1.3	0.9
TiO_2	1.6	1.0
Alkali	1.5	0.7
LOI	10.6	9.2
Surface area (m^2/g)	24.9	18.0
Particle size (% $< 1\mu$)	60	55

[a] Kentucky-Tennessee Clay Company, Mayfield, KY
[b] Old Hickory Clay Company, Hickory, KY

The use of ball clays in glazes is determined primarily by their behavior in the glaze slip, where they are used to provide slip suspension (see Chapter 7). Their use, however, must be limited by their effect on the shrinkage of the glaze slip on drying. Too much ball clay in the formulation will result in too much shrinkage, leading to crawling defects (see Chapter 13).

5.1.17 Alumina (corundum) is produced commercially by the calcination of alumina hydrate (see section 5.1.18), a coproduct of the Bayer process for aluminum refining.[M1] A number of grades are available, based on particle size, shape, and soda content. For glaze application, the low-soda grades are not required; neither are the grades with unique particle shape. Hence, the basic A1 grade is usually acceptable. The usual particle size is -325 mesh. The chemical purity is mostly a matter of excluding colored impurities, and should be 99 wt% alumina.

The principal suppliers are Alcoa Industrial Chemicals (Bauxite, AR), Alcan Chemicals (Cleveland, OH), Aluchem, Inc. (Reading, OH), and Reynolds Metals Company Chemical Division (Bauxite, AR).

A major concern in using alumina in glazes is its very slow dissolution rate. For satin and matte glazes, this may be desirable, but for gloss glazes it is a major limitation. For them, it can only be used in limited quantity, in glazes fired at cone 4 or higher.

5.1.18 Alumina hydrate is the commercial name given to aluminum hydroxide. It is a poorly crystalline material that is 65 wt% alumina, 35 wt% water. Its particle size is low, often submicron. On heating, the water disassociates and evaporates at about 300°C, which is low enough that it usually does not cause bubble defects in glazes.

It is one of the products produced in the Bayer process for aluminum refining.[M1] Hence, the major producers are the same as for alumina.

Its use in glazes is as a final source of alumina. It is more reactive than calcined alumina, but less so than some other alumina sources such as the feldspars, nepheline syenite, pyrophyllite, and the various clays. Hence, the allowable quantities are limited to a few percent except at the highest firing temperatures.

5.1.19 Glass sand (Flint) is the highest grade of commercially mined quartz.[B5] It must meet rigid specifications with respect to purity and silica content, which should be at least 99.5 wt%. Of particular concern are elements that induce color. Only a small amount of iron oxide and chromium compounds can be tolerated, and aluminum, calcium, and magnesium oxides should be minimized.

The most commonly used grades of glass sand are -200 mesh material and -325 mesh material. The former is limited to the highest firing glazes (cones 8–10).

Unimin Corporation (New Canaan, CT), and U.S. Silica Company (Berkeley Springs, WV) are the largest producers. Other producers include Nicks Silica Company (Jackson, TN) and Oglebay Norton Industrial Sands (Zanesville, OH).

The use of glass sand in glaze formulation is limited by its well-known slowness of dissolution in most molten glazes. Hence, while glass sand (flint) finds extensive use in sanitary ware glazes fired at cones 8 to 10, its use in cone 4 glazes must be limited, and its use in cone 1 glazes (and those fired lower) is not recommended.

5.1.20 Pyrophyllite is a nonplastic aluminosilicate mineral, which provides a source of those elements that melt more readily than alumina or flint. It has a higher SiO_2 content than kaolin or ball clays.

The largest producers are Resco Products, Inc., North State Pyrophyllite Division (Greensboro, NC), and R.T. Vanderbilt (Norwalk, CT).

5.1.21 Zircon (zirconium silicate) is the principal opacifier used in coatings fired above 1000°C. It is also the source of zirconia for all ceramic coatings. It is mined from alluvial beach sands by a process of dredging, wet concentration, and dry separation, and is usually associated with rutile, ilmenite, monazite, and other heavy-mineral sands.[W2]

About half of the world's production comes from Australia, some of which is imported into the United States. About one-sixth of the world's production is in Florida. For ceramic coating applications, the ore must be purified and milled to controlled particle size. Several grades are offered. As the particle size is reduced, the opacifying power increases, but so does the cost. Suppliers include Johnson Matthey Ceramics (Niagara Falls, NY) and Elf Atochem North America (Philadelphia, PA).

5.1.22 Anatase is one of the phases of titanium dioxide. It is the only phase of titanium dioxide with significant application in ceramic coatings. It is produced by the sulfate process from ilmenite ore.

Anatase grades of titanium dioxide are white pigments used in the ceramic industry in the manufacture of opacified porcelain enamels. Titanium dioxide is used for the opacifier because it has a high refractive index. Anatase grades are used in this application because their absorption edge is further away from the visible than is rutile, and, unlike rutile, the crystals do not grow to sizes where the absorption edge overlaps the visible.[58] Anatase is limited to firing temperatures of 850°C or less, due to the inversion of the crystal to rutile.

The principal suppliers of anatase grades of titanium dioxide are Kemira, Inc. (Bridgewater, NJ), NL Chemicals (Hightstown, NJ), and SCM Chemicals, (Baltimore, MD).

5.2 Raw Materials to Avoid

There are a number of raw materials on the market which, from time to time, have been used in glazes, yet are best avoided.

First, the alkali carbonates soda ash (Na_2CO_3), potash (K_2CO_3), and lithium carbonate (Li_2CO_3) are all highly soluble in water. Once dissolved in a slip, they will alter its rheology (see deflocculation in Chapter 7). Thus, aside from small amounts of mill added as deflocculants, they should not be used.

While calcium carbonate and dolomite can be used in glazes with a sufficiently high seal-over temperature (see sections 5.1.7 and 5.1.8, respectively), strontium carbonate and barium carbonate should be avoided. The reason is that the decomposition temperatures of these materials (see Table 13-1) are so high that gaseous carbon dioxide will be trapped in the glaze, producing bubble defects (see Chapter 13).

A different problem arises with the use of the borate minerals Gerstley Borate and colemanite.[22] These minerals are produced in such small volume that it is not economical to maintain uniformity of composition. Substantial variation can and does occur (sometimes from bag to bag), which can be the cause of several glaze defects. Thus, with these materials it is not possible to produce a uniform product over any length of time.

Moreover, these minerals are hydrates. In a water-based slip, they will gradually dissolve and alter the slip rheology. Thus, a glaze containing Gerstley Borate may have proper rheology initially, but after slip storage it may produce pinholes and blisters.

Hence, even for a limited production run or a one-of-a-kind piece, extra precautions are required.[22] Enough material for the entire run must be purchased, all from one lot. The glaze for each day's work must be mixed/milled and used at once.

As discussed in sections 3.4 and 16.6, lead oxide and cadmium oxide are toxic materials. The regulatory requirements for safe handling in the plant or studio and for the disposal of wastes contaminated with lead oxide are now very extensive and costly to implement. Thus, the use of lead bisilicate or other lead oxide–containing raw materials is to be avoided.

5.3 Frits

Frits are glasses prepared by melting suitable raw materials in a gas- or oil-fired furnace, or in an electric melting unit.[G1] The primary reason for the use of frits is that some of the ingredients required for glazes are soluble in water. If such materials were used directly, the normal methods of preparation by wet grinding and application in an aqueous suspension would not be possible. These water-soluble ingredients must first be made insoluble. This is done by mixing them dry with all or some of the other glaze ingredients and premelting them to a glasslike substance called a frit.

The solubility problem is particularly important with respect to boron, as there are no insoluble sources of that element. Other difficulties are encountered with the alkalis, where the alumina content of felspathic minerals limits the amount that can be used.

A second important reason for using frits is melting rate. When raw glaze materials have been fritted, the reactions between them have already been largely completed. Therefore, there is less heat work required to fire the glaze coating. As a result, the surface of a high-frit glaze can be superior to that of a raw glaze of the same composition. Alternatively, the firing time can be reduced for a fritted glaze.

There are several other reasons for using a frit. One is the poisonous nature of lead oxide. When lead oxide is fritted with sufficient quantities of appropriate oxides, it becomes insoluble and much less dangerous to handle. Second, some raw materials are substantially different in density from the others. Hence, during slip preparation, these materials may settle out, and layered sedimentation may occur. Finally, certain raw materials, such as magnesium carbonate, would cause difficulty because of their fine particle size and low bulk density.

The raw materials for frit manufacture are similar to those that have already been discussed. In addition, borax, boric oxide, and sodium and potassium carbonates are used. Although high purity is generally not required, consistency of product over time is, because frit making is a high-volume, continuous process. The other limita-

Figure 5.1

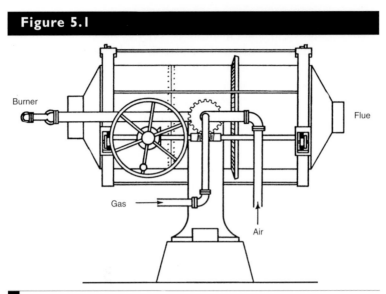

Burner

Flue

Gas

Air

Rotary smelter for frit manufacture.

tion is the need, in most cases, to exclude chromophores.[H2] The one exception is ground coat porcelain enamels, where the deliberately added adherence oxides are colored. Primarily, this limitation is a matter of limiting iron oxide and titania.

Frit manufacture begins with weighing out the batch, usually by feeding the major raw materials from silos into a weighing hopper by a conveyor system.[A1] Smaller ingredients are weighed out directly from bags. Allowance must be made for any moisture associated with the material.

The next step is blending. The goal of mixing is for every grain to be adjacent to grains of other ingredients, but the end result of random tumbling will be a random mixture. In most cases this is adequate. Raw materials differing widely in physical properties are not easy to mix homogeneously. Differences in specific gravity, particle shape, or grain size will result in natural segregation during mixing. Heavier and smaller particles tend to sink through lighter, larger, or ragged grains.

After blending, the batch is fed to the melting furnace, several types of which are commonly used. In the laboratory, frits can be made by melting the ingredients in a crucible. The crucible selected must be able to withstand the corrosive nature of molten glass. Commercial frits are melted in furnaces fired by gas, oil, or electricity. They are either box-like or rotary type, and they have refractory linings.

The rotary melter shown in Figure 5.1 is used when a number of frits are required in small quantities—1000 pounds or so.[A1] In this process, a charge of material is placed in the preheated melter, brought up to temperature, and held for the time necessary to achieve reasonably complete solution of the batch, typically 15 minutes to two hours. In the rotary melter, the furnace is slowly rotated during melting to enhance mixing and heat distribution. After melting, the burners are shut off and the molten frit discharged and quenched.

The rotary melter is cylindrical and is mounted so that it can be rotated and also tilted. The ends are made conical to retain the batch while rotating. An opening at one end serves for the burner, and an opening in the opposite end serves as a flue. Rotary melter capacities range from 10 pounds to one ton.

The rotary is charged by a screw feeder that can reach to the back end of the furnace and deposit the batch as it is withdrawn. The burner is then swung into place and lighted. The melter is rotated only fast enough to bring the batch up on one side, so that the material, as it melts, can roll down to the bottom of the melter. This subjects the new batch constantly to the flame, giving maximum speed in melting. When melting is complete, the burner is shut off, and the furnace is tilted so the batch can flow out.

The continuous frit smelter is illustrated in Figure 5.2.[n6] It is of a simple incline design. Raw material is continuously added to a pile at one end of the preheated box-like melter by a screw feeder. Burners are directed at the raw material pile, and molten material flows by gravity to the other end of the melter and is continuously discharged and quenched.

These melters are longer than they are wide, and they are built so that the floor slopes from the charging end to the opposite end of the melter, where the material is fined and drawn off continuously and quenched or fritted. The heat is supplied by a main burner firing from the front of the furnace, and the products of combustion thus pass countercurrent to the flow of the molten frit. Situated at the higher end of the furnace are two secondary burners, which assist in the melting process.

Because frit making is a high-volume, continuous process, this work is normally done by firms specializing in this process.[E24] It is inefficient for a glaze or enamel user to make small batches of frit. More important, it is difficult to maintain quality control when small batches are prepared. Quality frit must be made in large batches, preferably using continuous melters operating under stable conditions.

Figure 5.2

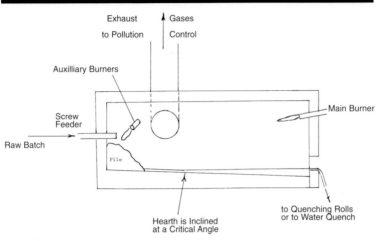

Continuous smelter for frit manufacture.

The physical and chemical changes taking place during the melting process are complicated and imperfectly understood.[K2, K3] Even at early stages, pronounced changes take place. For example, sodium nitrate melts at 307°C, forming a liquid that dissolves and reacts with other constituents. Borax begins to give up some of its water of crystallization as steam, and it melts at a red heat. This evolution of steam and melting causes considerable agitation in the batch. The molten borate readily dissolves metal oxides and initiates chemical reactions with other constituents. Probably, the presence of steam greatly accelerates the reaction rate in the furnace.

If alkali or alkaline earth carbonates are present, they decompose to carbon dioxide and oxides. At 900°C soda ash and lead oxide melt. Above 900°C, the molten alkalis are active fluxes, attacking the other ingredients. Any fluorides present soon are in solution, and they add to the reaction rate. Finally, the silica and other refractories are dissolved, not melted.

5.4 Kinetic Effects in Glazing

There are two steps in formulating a glaze, especially a lead-free glaze, for defect-free production. As discussed in Chapters 3 and 4, the first step is deciding on the oxide formula of the glaze. The several oxides that can be used each have limitations that must be allowed for.[E41] The second step is selecting appropriate raw materials that, when combined and then fired onto the ware, will yield a defect-free glaze.

5.4.1 Raw material selection is not a trivial consideration for a number of reasons.[E45] The first reason is melting and/or dissolution rate. During the time when the glaze is at the high temperature during the firing process, all of the various raw materials must either melt or dissolve. That time may be as short as 2 to 10 minutes in a fast-fire operation. Even for slow-fire, the time is only 1 to 6 hours. Moreover, as kinetic processes, melting and dissolution are strongly temperature dependent. Thus, while these processes may be of little concern in a sanitary operation firing at cones 7 to 10, they are major concerns for tile operations with a cone 1 fast-fire.

The most rapid melting and/or dissolution rate is achieved when the raw materials selected are chemically most similar to the fired glaze composition.[E45] Thus, for example, feldspar melts more rapidly in a gloss glaze (which requires higher silica content), while nepheline syenite melts more rapidly in a satin or matte glaze (which requires lower silica content). The rate is further maximized at the eutectic composition for the relevant oxides. The closer a raw material is to the eutectic for the relevant oxides, the faster it will melt or dissolve. Thus, for example, wollastonite dissolves more rapidly than whiting plus silica.

Second, the glaze melting process releases large quantities of gas, which must be eliminated during the firing process.[E32] The space between the particles in the dried-but-not-fired glaze alone amounts to over 40% of the total volume, and it is but one of several sources of gas. This imposes several limitations. One limitation arises because, while gas escapes readily during the initial stages of firing, once the glaze seals over, the only way to eliminate gas is by diffusing it to the glaze surface, where a bubble of gas may burst and the surface heal over. This diffusion process is too slow for current manufacturing processes. Hence, there is a need to maximize the temperature at which seal-over occurs.[L3]

Another limitation is that some raw materials release substantial amounts of gas on heating. If the temperature of decomposition is not several hundred degrees below the firing temperature, substantial gas may be trapped, producing bubble defects.[E32]

Moreover, it has been shown[D7,D8] that unmelted particles of silica and other refractory materials can serve as anchors for gas, promoting its retention in the glaze. This can leave bubble defects in the glaze even when the particle does finally dissolve before the end of the firing process. Thus, it is important to maximize the use of complex natural minerals, in order to minimize the use of flint and other refractory oxides.[E45]

A third important factor is particle size distribution. The particle size of raw materials has an important influence on the behavior of the material in making a glaze.[E28] Dissolution or melting occurs from the outer particle surface inward toward the center of the particle. Hence, it will take longer for a large particle to react than a small one.

There is a limitation, however, due to agglomeration. As particle size decreases, the tendency to agglomerate increases. Agglomerates do not melt efficiently. Thus, optimum particle size in most cases turns out to be −325 mesh material free of submicron particles.

5.4.2 Behavior of Raw Materials During Glaze Maturation.

In discussing the behavior of the various raw materials during glaze maturation, it is useful to group them, discussing together those with similar properties.[E45] First we have the refractories, those materials with high melting points and inertness, with great resistance to degradation either thermally or chemically. Hence, the temperature must be high enough for an adequate melting rate. These raw materials come in two categories, the plastic and the nonplastic.

Plastic raw materials are those that can be mixed with a little water to form a mass that can be easily worked into a desired shape. They work because their molecules can attract and loosely bond to water molecules. Hence, they have value in glazes as suspending agents.

The most common such materials are the clays. There are three important classes of clay; kaolin, ball clay, and montmorillonite. Kaolin is the name of a group of clays, produced mostly in Georgia, that are very pure and white burning. They are often used in concentrations up to 10% in glazes to provide slip suspension. During the firing process, they first lose their water of hydration at temperatures of 500 to 650°C.[E32] Afterward, the remaining material is an aluminosilicate of moderate refractoriness. In firings at cone 4 or above, they can be used without risk. At lower firing conditions, the amount that can be used depends on the soak time available. Glazes that are soaked for one hour or more can contain 6 to 8 wt% at cone 1, and 3 to 4 wt% at cone 02. For fast-fire operations, kaolin is not recommended at cone 1 or less for gloss glazes. Limited amounts (3–4 wt%) can be used in satins and mattes, where residual unmelted material may not be noticeable.

Ball clays are a less pure family of clays produced mainly in Kentucky and Tennessee. They are darker burning but offer superior suspending power. Because of the color problem, only the most white-burning grades should be considered. Their behavior on firing is similar to the kaolins.

Finally, montmorillonite clays, often called bentonite or hectorite, are hydrous clays produced largely in Wyoming. Their great virtue is that they are about five times as effective in suspending glaze slips as other clays. Hence, even when used alone, no more than 2 wt% is sufficient to provide adequate slip suspension.

The nonplastic refractories are materials such as alumina and silica that are very high melting and very resistant to dissolution. In glazes fired at high temperatures, such as sanitary ware, substantial amounts of these materials can be dissolved in the molten glaze. At lower firing temperatures, their use must be severely limited.

Quartz (flint) is dissolved readily in glazes fired to cone 5 (1210°C) or higher. Sanitary ware glazes fired at cones 8 to 10 may contain 20 to 30 wt% flint without difficulty. On the other hand, in firings at lower temperatures, it is difficult or impossible to eliminate residual unmelted silica. This is a particularly serious problem, because unmelted silica is very effective at preventing the escape of gas.[D7-D8] Thus, at cone 4 (1180°C), the amount of flint in the glaze batch should be limited to 8 to 10 wt%, and at lower temperatures it should not be used.

Calcined alumina is even slower melting than flint. Hence, it is not recommended for use in glazes. Alumina hydrate (aluminum oxyhydroxide) yields up its water of hydration at around 300°C, and is much finer in particle size than calcined alumina. Hence, it can be used in limited quantity (2–3 wt%) in glazes fired at cones 2 to 4 (1140–1180°C) or higher. A better source of alumina, beyond that added by feldspars and other materials that also contribute alkali oxides, is calcined kaolin. Calcining kaolin eliminates the rheological properties of uncalcined clay. Also, calcining clay converts iron oxide impurities to hematite, which can be removed by magnets. It melts readily enough that up to 10 wt% can be used at as low a temperature as cone 1 fast-fire (1130°C), and in addition to the clays added for suspending the slip.

Zircon has a solubility in glazes of about 5 wt% at high temperature, and 2 to 3 wt% at room temperature. Thus, it has an important use as an opacifier.[E29] Moreover, it is a very inert refractory material that dissolves in a molten glaze with difficulty. However, a low quantity of zircon can be a useful glaze component,[E41] imparting alkaline durability. For that purpose, the amount added should be limited to 1 wt% at cone 2 (1140°C) and to 0.75 wt% for cone 1 fast-fire (1130°C).

Titania behaves similarly in that it has a high-temperature solubility of about 10 wt%, and a low-temperature solubility of about 5 wt%. It is also a difficult material to dissolve, but less so than either zircon, alumina, or flint. Quantities of 2 to 3 wt% can be added to ceramic coatings without difficulty.

The second important group of materials are the fluxes. These materials are used to provide the glue that fuses the various raw materials into a single solid mass. In ceramic coatings, they are a large and essential portion of the formulation. They must form a molten glass that is powerful enough to dissolve the refractory ingredients in the short time that the glaze is molten. Like the refractories, there are two important types of fluxes. First, there are the melters—those materials that will melt, or soften in the case of frits, and provide the initial liquid phase at the firing temperature.

One such material is feldspar, which is an alkali aluminosilicate mineral produced in North Carolina and in South Dakota. Most partially fritted glazes contain substantial quantities of this material. The melting properties of the feldspars, and the viscosity of the resulting melt, depend somewhat on the soda-to-potash ratio. The soda feldspars melt effectively at about 1100°C, although their formal melting point is lower. The reason is that the viscosity of the material at somewhat lower temperature is so high that melting is not apparent. Thus, they are usable as primary melters in glazes firing at cone 1 or higher, and they can be used as secondary melters as low as cone 02 (1050°C). The potash feldspars do not melt effectively until a temperature around 1150°C is reached, and the viscosity of the resulting melt is very high, making homogenization of the melt difficult.

Thus, at cone 1, where tile is fired, soda feldspar is preferred to potash feldspar. On the other hand, at cones 8 to 10, where sanitary ware is fired, potash feldspar is preferred, because the very high viscosity serves to prevent runoff from vertical surfaces.

A related material is nepheline syenite. This alkali aluminosilicate rock is a eutectic mixture of nepheline and feldspar. It is a more powerful melter than the feldspars and yields a lower melt viscosity. However, it has a higher alkali content than feldspar, so less can be used in achieving a given alkali content.

Another related material is muscovite mica. Although its alkali is potash, and it has a higher alumina-to-silica ratio than feldspar, it is at least as powerful a melter as soda feldspar. Also, it has a higher alumina-to-silica ratio. Thus, combinations of feldspar and mica can be used to adjust the alumina-to-silica ratio.

The lithium minerals, spodumene and petalite, are also powerful melters. They are effective at temperatures as low as 1000°C. They can be considered whenever lithium oxide in the glaze formula is appropriate.

The other important class of melters are the frits, which are pre-melted and shattered glass of various compositions. They are used primarily to provide elements such as boron oxide that do not have any water-insoluble raw materials. As they are glasses, they begin to soften at temperatures of 500°C to 700°C. Thus, if care is not taken in the choice of frit, the glaze may seal the body before it has given up all of its contained air. The result will be blisters and similar gaseous defects.

The softness of a frit can be judged by its glass temperature, which is a property reported by the frit manufacturers for their products. For a glaze firing at cone 06 (1000°C), the glass temperature of the frit(s) used should be about 530°C or higher. For a glaze firing at cone 1, it should be about 600°C or higher. For a glaze firing at cone 3 or 4 or more, it should be about 665°C or higher.

About the lowest melting flux is lead bisilicate. It is used as a melter even in glass colors at temperatures as low as 600°C. Thus, it is almost always necessary to use it in a glaze applied to a previously fired body, as the seal-over temperature of a glaze containing lead bisilicate will be very low. It must never be used in a glaze fired above cone 2 (1140°C) due to excessive volatilization. Finally, it is highly toxic, requiring extensive precautions for safe use.[M20]

The other category of fluxes are those materials that do not have low melting points, but are readily attacked by molten oxides at firing temperatures, and once dissolved, contribute to the reactions forming the final product.

The most effective material in this category is wollastonite. At temperatures above 1050 to 1100°C, wollastonite is readily attacked by molten oxides. Once dissolved, it is autocatalytic. It lowers the viscosity of the molten oxides, making them more aggressive in dissolving other ingredients. At cone 1 and higher, substantial quantities can be used. Gloss glazes can contain up to 10 wt%. Satin and matte glazes, where residual unmelted material may even be desired to lower the gloss, may contain up to 30 wt%. Lower-firing gloss glazes require limitations on the wollastonite content. At cone 03 (1080°C), the wollastonite should be limited to 8 wt%, and at cone 06 (1000°C), it should not be used.

The principal alternative material to wollastonite is whiting or calcium carbonate. It has similar behavior and limitations, although at one to two cones higher firing temperatures. One reason is the additional flint required to balance the silica content of wollastonite. In addition, calcium carbonate yields 44 % of its weight as gaseous carbon dioxide at approximately 900°C.[E32] The overall glaze must therefore be formulated to assure that the seal-over temperature is above 900°C. Thus, the use of substantial quantities is limited to glazes firing above cone 3 (1160°C), and limited quantities (3–4 wt%) to glazes firing at cone 1 (1130°C) or above.

Dolomite is similar in behavior to calcium carbonate, and is often substituted for it in glazes in which MgO can be tolerated.

Another alternative material is talc. It is the principal residual source of MgO in glazes. The major limitation to its use is that it yields its water of hydration at approximately 1100°C. Hence, it is very difficult to use talc in tile glazes fast-fired at cone 1 (1130°C) without producing bubble defects. At least cone 3 (1160°C) is required to use talc safely in a glaze.

The other two MgO sources, magnesium oxide and magnesium carbonate, also have limitations. Magnesium oxide is almost as slow as the refractories in its dissolution rate, although it contributes substantially to viscosity reduction once dissolved. Magnesium carbonate, in addition to yielding up its carbon dioxide as a gas, has an extremely low bulk density, increasing the interparticle air that must be eliminated in firing a glaze. Hence, these two raw materials are seldom used.

Zinc oxide is attacked and dissolved in molten oxides at reasonable rates at temperatures above approximately 1050°C. Once dissolved, it helps to lower viscosity and increase the dissolving power of the melt. Hence, it can be used in glazes to be fired at cone 04 (1050°C) or higher.

5.4.3 The successful formulation of a glaze is not just a matter of achieving the proper oxide formula, important as that is. Raw materials must be chosen that will melt or dissolve in a time frame coincident with the time the glaze is in the hot zone of the firing kiln. The melting must not begin before the gas produced by the maturing of both the glaze and the body can escape. When appropriate allowance is made, a defect-free glaze will be the result.

Chapter 6
Batch Calculations

In the discussion of coating formulations in Chapters 3 and 4, mole ratios and the Seger formula (a modified mole ratio) were used. While these types of formulas are the most useful way to understand glazes and enamels, they are not suitable for compounding the coating in the laboratory or plant. For that purpose, one needs a batch recipe, that lists what materials to mix together, and in what amounts.

Many readers will be aware that there are computer programs available to assist in the batch calculation process. This will be discussed in section 6.4. However, even when one plans to use a software program, it is important to understand the calculation process by going through it step-by-step. It is especially important to understand where judgment is required.

To get to the batch recipe, you must first convert the mole ratio or Seger formula to an oxide weight percent. Then you must select the ingredients, at least one for each oxide to be used. Then, from the chemical analyses of the raw materials, which are usually available from the manufacturers, the weight percent formula can be converted to a batch recipe.

The reverse process also has uses. You may have found a recipe somewhere and wish to know its molecular formula, in order to compare it with other formulas. Since this reverse process is straightforward, while the forward process requires judgment in selecting raw materials and frits, it will be considered first.

6.1 Batch to Oxide

One of the easiest ways to understand a calculation process is to go through some examples. Let's consider the following batch formula for a Bristol glaze:

potash feldspar	56.2 wt%
whiting	9.4
zinc oxide	6.6
china clay	10.5
kaolin	2.8
flint	14.5
	100.0

It contains potash feldspar, whiting, zinc oxide, china clay, kaolin, and flint or silica.

Appendix IV is a tabulation of raw material formulas. We will use this table to determine the oxide contents of each material. From that information, we can derive the weight ratios, and thence the weight percent for each oxide.

Let's look up potash feldspar. Note that this material contributes five oxides: soda, potash, calcia, alumina, and silica. The amount of each oxide contributed by the potash feldspar is calculated by multiplying the weight percent of the feldspar in the batch by the weight fraction of the appropriate oxide:

$$
\begin{array}{lll}
Na_2O & 56.2 \times 0.035 = & 1.967 \\
K_2O & 56.2 \times 0.095 = & 5.339 \\
CaO & 56.2 \times 0.013 = & 0.731 \\
Al_2O_3 & 56.2 \times 0.195 = & 0.959 \\
SiO_2 & 56.2 \times 0.659 = & 37.036
\end{array}
$$

Similarly, whiting contributes calcia:

$$CaO \quad 9.4 \times 0.56 \ = 5.264$$

Zinc oxide contributes zinc oxide:

$$ZnO \quad 6.6 \times 1.0 \ = 6.600$$

China clay contributes alumina and silica:

$$
\begin{array}{ll}
Al_2O_3 & 10.5 \times 0.395 = 4.148 \\
SiO_2 & 10.5 \times 0.465 = 4.883
\end{array}
$$

Kaolin also contributes alumina and silica:

$$
\begin{array}{ll}
Al_2O_3 & 2.8 \times 0.396 = 1.109 \\
SiO_2 & 2.8 \times 0.47 \ = 1.316
\end{array}
$$

Flint contributes silica.

$$SiO_2 \quad 14.5 \times 1.0 \ = 14.500$$

Table 6-1. Weight Ratios

Material	Na₂O	K₂O	CaO	ZnO	Al₂O₃	SiO₂
potash feldspar	1.967	5.339	0.731		10.959	37.036
whiting			5.264			
zinc oxide				6.600		
china clay					4.148	4.883
kaolin					1.109	1.316
flint						14.500
Totals	1.967	5.339	5.995	6.600	16.216	57.735
Grand Total	**93.852**					

Note that more decimal places have been carried than is appropriate in the final answer. In these calculations it is important to avoid rounding off before reaching the final result.

The next step is to summarize the weight ratios for each of the oxides, as shown in Table 6-1.

The weight percents can now be calculated by scaling the total to 100 percent. This is done by multiplying each weight ratio by 100 and dividing the result by the grand total. Thus, the weight percents in the example are:

$$Na_2O \quad 1.967 \times 100/93.852 = 2.096$$
$$K_2O \quad 5.339 \times 100/93.852 = 5.689$$
$$CaO \quad 5.995 \times 100/93.852 = 6.388$$
$$ZnO \quad 6.600 \times 100/93.852 = 7.032$$
$$Al_2O_3 \quad 16.216 \times 100/93.852 = 17.278$$
$$SiO_2 \quad 57.735 \times 100/93.852 = 61.517$$

To convert the weight percents to the Seger formula, or to mole ratios, the weight percents must be divided by the molecular weights of each oxide, which are also to be found in Appendix IV.

$$Na_2O \quad 2.096/62 = 0.03381$$
$$K_2O \quad 5.689/94 = 0.06052$$
$$CaO \quad 6.388/56 = 0.11407$$
$$ZnO \quad 7.032/81 = 0.08681$$
$$Al_2O_3 \quad 17.278/102 = 0.16939$$
$$SiO_2 \quad 61.517/60 = 1.02528$$

To obtain a Seger formula, the factors for the modifiers, that is, the monovalent and divalent cations, are summed, and the answer divided into each factor:

$$\text{sum of modifiers} = 0.03814 + 0.06052 + 0.11407 + 0.08681$$
$$= 0.29501$$

OXIDE	SEGER FORMULA
Na_2O	$0.03381/0.29501 = 0.114$
K_2O	$0.06052/0.29501 = 0.205$
CaO	$0.11407/0.29501 = 0.387$
ZnO	$0.08681/0.29501 = 0.294$
Al_2O_3	$0.16939/0.29501 = 0.574$
SiO_2	$1.02528/0.29501 = 3.475$

To obtain a mole ratio, all the factors are summed, and the answer divided into each factor:

$$\text{sum of factors} = 0.03814 + 0.06052 + 0.11407 + 0.08681$$
$$+ 0.16939 + 1.02528$$
$$= 1.48968$$

OXIDE	MOLE RATIO
Na_2O	$0.03381/1.48968 = 0.0226$
K_2O	$0.06052/1.48968 = 0.0406$
CaO	$0.11407/1.48968 = 0.0766$
ZnO	$0.08681/1.48968 = 0.0582$
Al_2O_3	$0.16939/1.48968 = 0.1137$
SiO_2	$1.02528/1.48968 = 0.6883$

Thus we have calculated a Seger formula and a mole ratio from a given batch formula.

Now, let's complicate matters a bit, and consider a glaze containing a frit as one of its components. Consider the following recipe for a cone 1 tile glaze:

Frit F13	20.3 wt%
flint	16.9
soda feldspar	29.5
kaolin	9.3
whiting	12.9
barium carbonate	1.1
zinc oxide	10.0
	100.0

Again we begin by calculating the oxide contents of each of the raw materials. In Table 6.2 is a compilation of frit formulas available from one of the commercial suppliers. The other suppliers have similar products. Let's look up the formula of frit F13.

From the composition given, one can calculate the oxides contributed by the frit:

amount in formula × fraction of frit = amount contributed

OXIDE	AMOUNT CONTRIBUTED
Na_2O	20.3 × 0.085 = 1.7255
K_2O	20.3 × 0.0015= 0.0305
CaO	20.3 × 0.18 = 3.6540
B_2O_3	20.3 × 0.185 = 3.7555
Al_2O_3	20.3 × 0.045 = 0.9135
SiO_2	20.3 × 0.5035= 10.2211

Next, a similar calculation is performed for the other ingredients, in the same manner as the previous example. For the flint:

SiO_2 16.9 × 1.0   = 16.9000

For the soda feldspar:
Na_2O	29.5 × 0.067 =	1.9265
K_2O	29.5 × 0.045 =	1.3275
CaO	29.5 × 0.016 =	0.4720
Al_2O_3	29.5 × 0.189 =	5.5755
SiO_2	29.5 × 0.682 =	20.1190

For the kaolin:
Al_2O_3	9.3 × 0.396 =	3.6828
SiO_2	9.3 × 0.47 =	4.3710

For the whiting:
CaO   12.9 × 0.56   = 7.2240

For the barium carbonate:
BaO   1.1 × 0.777 = 0.8547

For the zinc oxide:
ZnO   10.0 × 1.0   = 10.0000

This is summarized in Table 6-3.

Table 6-2. Commercially Available Frits

Frit	Use	Composition (wt%)												Expansion ×10⁻⁶	Melting point (°C)
		Li_2O	Na_2O	K_2O	CaO	MgO	SrO	BaO	ZnO	B_2O_3	Al_2O_3	SiO_2	ZrO_2		
I. Alkali-Boron Frits															
F15	Low Expn.	–	2.60	3.60	–	–	–	–	–	23.00	3.81	67.00	–	4.42	915
F43	Cone10 Flux	–	11.20	0.50	8.00	–	–	–	–	22.50	9.50	48.30	–	8.22	790
F79	AluminaFlux	0.50	4.00	1.20	4.80	–	1.00	–	–	26.50	9.00	53.00	–	5.72	820
F105	Alkali Flux	–	19.20	1.50	–	–	–	–	–	21.00	6.80	51.50	–	9.53	790
F245	Bond Frit	–	7.31	–	2.96	–	–	–	–	36.35	0.94	52.44	–	4.61	845
F496	Clear Frit	–	5.80	1.60	–	–	–	–	–	16.00	1.60	75.00	–	4.66	900
II. Opaque Frits															
F49	Tile	–	7.50	–	12.50	–	–	–	–	16.50	2.50	51.00	10.00	6.76	870
F125	Wall Tile	–	10.90	2.00	7.00	–	–	–	–	21.50	–	43.60	15.00	7.01	815
FZ376A	Fast Fire	–	4.60	2.80	6.00	–	–	–	1.10	13.20	7.60	56.20	8.50	6.54	925
F403	Ba Matte	–	0.50	–	4.80	1.00	–	35.00	–	1.50	6.20	49.00	3.00	6.92	1000
F541	Fast Fire	–	3.00	3.00	8.50	–	4.20	–	–	5.60	11.00	52.70	11.00	7.23	1000
III. Strontium Frits															
F18	Dinnerware	–	2.60	2.40	11.80	–	8.00	–	–	8.90	6.80	59.50	–	7.13	955
F38	Sr Flux	–	5.50	–	4.20	–	16.80	–	–	15.00	4.20	53.10	–	6.18	845
F300	Sanitary	–	2.70	1.80	9.96	–	8.17	–	–	4.95	10.08	62.36	–	7.29	985
F506	Dinnerware	–	–	4.00	13.50	–	4.50	–	–	7.00	10.50	60.50	–	6.45	1010

Table 6-2. Commercially Available Frits (continued)

Frit	Use	Li$_2$O	Na$_2$O	K$_2$O	CaO	MgO	SrO	BaO	ZnO	B$_2$O$_3$	Al$_2$O$_3$	SiO$_2$	ZrO$_2$	Expansion ×10^{-6}	Melting point (°C)
IV. Zinc Frits															
FZ16	Soft ZnFlux	–	8.60	1.20	4.00	–	–	–	15.00	31.00	–	40.50	–	6.20	730
FZ25	Tile Flux	–	15.50	4.80	–	–	–	–	0.70	17.00	12.50	49.50	–	10.07	780
FZ390	Soft ZnFlux	–	8.20	2.00	2.00	–	–	–	0.85	18.50	5.50	65.00	–	5.84	790
FZ430	Ca Zn Frit	–	4.00	2.00	10.00	–	2.00	–	1.50	11.50	10.50	58.50	–	7.45	815
FZ557	Fast Fire	–	0.30	4.70	11.00	2.50	–	0.80	11.00	4.50	5.50	59.70	–	6.63	980
V. Calcium Frits															
F12	ArtwareFlux	–	10.40	–	20.00	–	–	–	–	23.80	0.80	45.00	–	8.18	790
F13	Fast Fire	–	8.50	0.15	18.00	–	–	–	–	18.50	4.50	50.35	–	8.03	830
F19	Dinnerware	–	7.00	–	14.20	–	–	–	–	14.60	9.70	54.50	–	7.90	845
F495	Dinnerware	–	4.50	1.00	13.50	–	–	–	–	14.50	9.00	57.50	–	7.01	980
F520B	Dinnerware	–	1.40	6.50	7.00	–	–	–	–	11.60	7.50	66.00	–	6.55	925
VI. High Lithium Frit															
F493	High Li	11.00	11.70	6.00	–	–	–	–	–	13.20	6.30	51.80	–	14.13	705

Composition (wt%)

(from ref. n5)

Table 6-3. Weight Ratios

	Na_2O	K_2O	CaO	BaO	ZnO	B_2O_3	Al_2O_3	SiO_2
Frit F13	1.7255	0.0305	3.6540	-	-	3.7555	0.9135	10.2211
flint	-	-	-	-	-	-	-	16.9000
soda								
feldspar	1.9765	1.3275	0.4720	-	-	-	5.5755	20.1190
kaolin	-	-	-	-	-	-	3.6028	4.3710
whiting	-	-	7.2240	-	-	-	-	-
barium								
carbonate	-	-	0.8547	-	-	-	-	-
zinc oxide	-	-	-	-	10.0000	-	-	-
Totals	3.7020	1.3580	11.3500	0.8547	10.0000	3.7555	10.0918	51.6111
GRAND TOTAL		92.7231						

The weight percents can now be calculated by scaling the total to 100 percent. This is done by multiplying each weight ratio by 100 and dividing the result by the grand total. Thus, the weight percents in the example are:

Na_2O	3.7020 $\times$	100/92.7231 =	3.9925
K_2O	1.3904 $\times$	100/92.7231 =	1.4995
CaO	11.1490 $\times$	100/92.7231 =	12.0240
BaO	0.8547 $\times$	100/92.7231 =	0.9218
ZnO	10.0000 $\times$	100/92.7231 =	10.7848
B_2O_3	3.7941 $\times$	100/92.7231 =	4.0919
Al_2O_3	10.1933 $\times$	100/92.7231 =	10.9933
SiO_2	51.6395 $\times$	100/92.7231 =	55.6922

To convert the weight percents to the Seger formula, or to mole ratios, the weight percents must be divided by the molecular weights of each oxide, which are found in Appendix IV.

Na_2O	3.9925/62	=	0.06440
K_2O	1.4995/94	=	0.01595
CaO	12.024/56	=	0.21471
BaO	0.9218/153	=	0.00602
ZnO	10.7848/81	=	0.13315
B_2O_3	4.0919/70	=	0.05846
Al_2O_3	10.9933/102	=	0.10778
SiO_2	55.6922/60	=	0.92820

To obtain a Seger formula, the factors for the modifiers, that is, the monovalent and divalent cations, are summed, and the answer divided into each factor:

sum of modifiers = 0.06440 + 0.01595 + 0.21471 + 0.00602
+ 0.13315
= 0.43423

OXIDE	SEGER FORMULA
Na_2O	0.06440/0.43423 = 0.148
K_2O	0.01595/0.43423 = 0.037
CaO	0.21471/0.43423 = 0.494
BaO	0.00602/0.43423 = 0.014
ZnO	0.13315/0.43423 = 0.307
B_2O_3	0.05846/0.43423 = 0.135
Al_2O_3	0.10778/0.43423 = 0.248
SiO_2	0.92820/0.43423 = 2.138

To obtain a mole ratio, all the factors are summed, and the answer divided into each factor:

sum of factors = 0.06440 + 0.01595 + 0.21471 + 0.00602
+ 0.13315 + 0.05846 + 0.10778 + 0.92820
= 1.52867

OXIDE	MOLE RATIO
Na_2O	0.06440/1.52867 = 0.0421
K_2O	0.01595/1.52867 = 0.0104
CaO	0.21471/1.52867 = 0.1405
BaO	0.00602/1.52867 = 0.0039
ZnO	0.13315/1.52867 = 0.0871
B_2O_3	0.05846/1.52867 = 0.0382
Al_2O_3	0.10778/1.52867 = 0.0705
SiO_2	0.92820/1.52867 = 0.6072

Thus we have again calculated a Seger formula and a mole ratio from a given batch formula.

6.2 The Role of Judgment

Unlike the calculation of a mole ratio from a batch recipe, the calculation of a recipe from a mole ratio or a Seger formula involves judgment in the selection of what raw materials to use.

In the first place, neither boron oxide nor strontium oxide has a convenient, water-insoluble raw material source. If either of these oxides is in the desired glaze formula, an appropriate frit must be used for at least a portion of the recipe to provide a source for these oxides.

Kinetics also has a role in the decision whether or not to use a frit or frits, and, if so, how much frit to use. Frits soften at lower temperatures than most raw materials melt. As they are already premelted, they become fluid rapidly, as soon as adequate temperature is achieved. On the other hand, as frits are themselves made from raw materials, they are usually more expensive than those materials.

Secondly, as was discussed in section 5.4, kinetic effects play an important role in the selection of raw materials. The material chosen must melt or dissolve in the molten glaze at a temperature and time compatible with the desired firing conditions. There must be adequate time and temperature to eliminate the gases produced during the firing process. These factors are affected by the choice of materials, as well as by the particle sizes of the chosen materials.

Finally, as will be discussed in detail in Chapter 7, if the glaze batch is to be suspended in water to make a slip that can be used for application to a substrate, the recipe must contain an ingredient or ingredients with platelike structures, such as clays. These platelike materials serve to keep the heavier-than-water oxide materials in suspension. Typical solutions for this requirement are 8 to 10 wt% kaolin, or 1 to 2 wt% bentonite, or a combination thereof (such as 4 wt% kaolin plus 1/2 wt% bentonite).

In glaze slips, moreover, the amount of platelike material must be neither too low nor too high. Too little will result in inadequate suspension and settling out of the oxide materials. Excessive additions of these materials will induce crawling defects caused by drying cracks.

These factors should be kept in mind as the batch calculation process is demonstrated by example in the next section.

6.3 Oxide to Batch

Keeping in mind the choices discussed in section 6.2, one can undertake the process of compounding a glaze from its Seger formula or its mole ratio. The process will be illustrated by an example. Consider the development of a batch recipe for a cone 4 dinnerware glaze having the following Seger formula:

Oxide	Amount	Oxide	Amount	Oxide	Amount
Na_2O	0.146	B_2O_3	0.209	SiO_2	3.389
K_2O	0.077	Al_2O_3	0.368		
CaO	0.490				
MgO	0.148				
SrO	0.139				

The first step is to convert the Seger (or mole ratio) formula to a weight percent oxide formula. This is accomplished by first multiplying the Seger (or mole ratio) factors by the appropriate molecular weights to obtain a set of weight ratios:

Seger amount × molecular weight = weight ratio

Oxide	Weight Ratio
Na_2O	0.146 × 62 = 9.052
K_2O	0.077 × 94 = 7.238
CaO	0.490 × 56 = 27.440
MgO	0.148 × 40 = 5.920
SrO	0.139 × 104 = 14.456
B_2O_3	0.230 × 70 = 16.100
Al_2O_3	0.368 × 102 = 37.536
SiO_2	3.389 × 60 = 203.340
Total	321.082

The weight percents are then obtained by multiplying each weight ratio by 100 and dividing the result by the total of the weight ratios:

weight ratio × 100/321.082 = weight percent

Oxide	Weight Percent
Na_2O	9.052 × 100/321.082 = 2.819
K_2O	7.238 × 100/321.082 = 2.254
CaO	27.440 × 100/321.082 = 8.546
MgO	5.920 × 100/321.082 = 1.844
SrO	14.456 × 100/321.082 = 4.502
B_2O_3	16.100 × 100/321.082 = 5.014
Al_2O_3	37.536 × 100/321.082 = 11.690
SiO_2	203.340 × 100/321.082 = 63.330

The next step is the first place where some judgment is needed. A decision must be made as to what raw materials and/or frits are to be used. The first step is to note that the formula contains boron oxide and strontia, neither of which has a convenient, insoluble raw material. Therefore, we must select a frit to supply them. The table of frits (Table 6.2) is consulted, looking for a frit with these two ingredients in about the correct proportion. One finds that frit F18 has about the correct ratio of strontia to boron oxide, and it has no ingredients that are not wanted. If such a frit could not be found, one would have to use two frits, or alter the Seger formula.

From the boron oxide requirement, one can calculate the amount of frit to be added:

$$\text{amount of frit} = B_2O_3 \text{ needed}/B_2O_3 \text{ in frit}$$
$$= 5.014/8.900$$
$$= 56.337\ \%$$

Now one must calculate the amounts of all the ingredient oxides that this amount of frit F18 supplies.

frit amount $\times$ amount in frit = amount of oxide

OXIDE	AMOUNT OF OXIDE			
Na_2O	56.337	$\times$	0.026 =	1.465
K_2O	56.337	$\times$	0.024 =	1.352
CaO	56.337	$\times$	0.118 =	6.648
SrO	56.337	$\times$	0.080 =	4.502
B_2O_3	56.337	$\times$	0.089 =	5.014
Al_2O_3	56.337	$\times$	0.068 =	3.831
SiO_2	56.337	$\times$	0.595 =	33.521

With this information, one can then calculate what oxides remain to be supplied by other raw materials:

amount needed $-$ amount in frit = amount remaining

OXIDE	AMOUNT REMAINING			
Na_2O	2.819	$-$	1.465 =	1.354
K_2O	2.254	$-$	1.352 =	0.902
CaO	8.546	$-$	6.648 =	1.898
MgO	1.844	$-$	0 =	1.844
SrO	4.502	$-$	4.502 =	0.000
B_2O_3	5.014	$-$	5.014 =	0.000
Al_2O_3	11.690	$-$	3.831 =	7.859
SiO_2	63.330	$-$	33.521 =	29.809

Note that all of the strontia and boron oxide have been provided, leaving the oxides shown.

Now observe that there is still some alkali to be provided. The most economic way to add alkali is with feldspar. As there is more soda than potassium, let's try soda feldspar. From the soda content, we calculate the need for 20.209% soda feldspar:

$$\text{amount. of soda feldspar} = Na_2O \text{ needed}/Na_2O \text{ in feldspar}$$
$$= 1.354/0.067$$
$$= 20.209\%$$

Then, we calculate the amounts of all oxides provided by the feldspar:

amount soda feldspar $\times$ amount of oxide in feldspar = amount provided

OXIDE	AMOUNT PROVIDED
Na2O	$20.209 \times 0.067 = 1.354$
K_2O	$20.209 \times 0.045 = 0.902$
CaO	$20.209 \times 0.016 = 0.323$
Al_2O_3	$20.209 \times 0.189 = 3.820$
SiO_2	$20.209 \times 0.682 = 13.783$

Subtracting these from the amounts of oxides to be supplied, one gets a new list of oxides remaining to be supplied:

amount needed $-$ amount from feldspar = amount remaining

OXIDE	AMOUNT REMAINING
Na_2O	$1.354 - 1.354 = 0.000$
K_2O	$0.902 - 0.902 = 0.000$
CaO	$1.898 - 0.323 = 1.575$
MgO	$1.844 - 0 = 1.844$
Al_2O_3	$7.859 - 3.820 = 4.039$
SiO_2	$29.809 - 13.783 = 16.026$

Next, the magnesia requirement can be conveniently supplied by a talc addition, for which we calculate a 6.046% requirement:

$$\text{amount. of talc} = MgO \text{ needed}/MgO \text{ in talc}$$
$$= 1.844/0.306$$
$$= 6.046\%$$

Calcia and silica are also supplied by talc:

amount of talc × amount of oxide in talc = amount provided

OXIDE	AMOUNT PROVIDED
CaO	6.046 × 0.078 = 0.472
MgO	6.046 × 0.306 = 1.844
SiO_2	6.046 × 0.547 = 3.307

leaving the following oxides yet to be provided:

amount needed − amount from talc = amount remaining

OXIDE	AMOUNT REMAINING
CaO	1.575 − 0.472 = 1.103
MgO	1.844 − 1.844 = 0.00
Al_2O_3	4.039 − 0 = 4.039
SiO_2	16.026 − 3.307 = 12.719

In section 5.3 it was pointed out that wollastonite is the preferred source of residual calcia:

amount. of wollastonite = CaO needed/CaO in wollastonite
= 1.103/0.421
= 2.620%

Silica is also supplied by wollastonite:

amount wollastonite × amount of oxide in wollastonite = amount provided

OXIDE	AMOUNT PROVIDED
CaO	2.620 × 0.421 = 1.103
SiO_2	2.620 × 0.519 = 1.360

leaving the following oxides to be provided:

amount needed − amount from wollastonite = amount remaining

OXIDE	AMOUNT REMAINING
CaO	1.103 − 1.103 = 0.000
Al_2O_3	4.039 − 0 = 4.039
SiO_2	12.719 − 1.360 = 11.359

At this point, the next complication in formulating a glaze must be considered. As was discussed in section 6.2, to suspend the glaze in water to make a slip one can use to apply the glaze to a substrate, the formula needs an ingredient with platelike structure, such as about 8 to 10% kaolin, or 1 to 2% bentonite. Since we have about 4% alumina left, let's use kaolin. From the alumina, we calculate that we can add 10.199% kaolin:

$$\text{amount of kaolin} = Al_2O_3 \text{ needed}/Al_2O_3 \text{ in kaolin}$$
$$= 4.039/0.396$$
$$= 10.199\%$$

Although it is at the top of the recommended range, this is not excessive.

Note, that had the calculation indicated more than about 12% kaolin, one would have had to add some of the alumina another way, in order to avoid crawling defects, as was discussed in section 6.2. This will be discussed in detail in Chapter 13, section 13.3.

The kaolin clay also supplies silica:

amount of kaolin × amount of oxide in kaolin = amount provided

OXIDE	AMOUNT PROVIDED
Al_2O_3	10.199 × 0.396 = 4.039
SiO_2	10.199 × 0.470 = 4.794

After adding the kaolin, we see that the only oxide remaining is silica:

amount needed − amount from kaolin = amount remaining

OXIDE	AMOUNT REMAINING
Al_2O_3	4.039 − 4.039 = 0.000
SiO_2	11.359 − 4.794 = 6.565

As this is a cone 4 glaze, the use of modest amounts of flint, such as needed here, is acceptable (see section 5.3). The amount needed is 6.565%, as flint is pure SiO_2.

Summarizing the results of the calculation:

WEIGHT RATIO

frit F18	56.337
soda feldspar	20.209
talc	6.046
wollastonite	2.620
kaolin	10.199
flint	6.565
Total	101.976

Because these raw materials contain some material that doesn't end up in the glaze, such as the H_2O in the talc and the kaolin, the numbers we have calculated add up to a bit more than 100%. Therefore, the final step is to scale to 100%. This is done by multiplying each weight ratio by 100 and dividing the result by the total of the weight ratios. The result is:

weight ratio × 100/total = weight percent

MATERIAL	WEIGHT PERCENT		
frit F18	56.337 ×	100/101.976 =	55.24
soda feldspar	20.209 ×	100/101.976 =	19.82
talc	6.046 ×	100/101.976 =	5.93
wollastonite	2.620 ×	100/101.976 =	2.57
kaolin	10.199 ×	100/101.976 =	10.00
flint	6.565 ×	100/101.976 =	6.44

For those who would like some additional practice, here is an additional problem for you to work on. Find a suitable batch for the following cone 6 stoneware glaze:

OXIDE	MOLE RATIO
Na_2O	0.0323
K_2O	0.0081
CaO	0.1515
MgO	0.0101
B_2O_3	0.0253
Al_2O_3	0.0657
SiO_2	0.7070

One solution is in the appendix at the back of the book, but it is not the only possible one. Try to work it out yourself before you look at that solution.

6.4 Computer Programs

While it is important to understand batch calculation procedures and the judgments that must be made, today much of the drudgery of making these calculations can be transferred to a computer.

6.4.1 For anyone familiar with spreadsheet programs such as Lotus 1-2-3 or Excel, it is possible to develop one's own worksheets to perform these calculations. The batch-to-molecular calculation is handled in a straightforward manner. Each material in the batch formula is multiplied by the fraction of each oxide to obtain the amount of that oxide. The amounts of each oxide are summed and then scaled to a weight percent. Finally, the molecular percent or Seger formula is calculated. The procedure is identical to that described in sections 6.1 and 6.2.

For the molecular-to-batch calculation, a teardown procedure is recommended. The first step is to calculate the weight percent. Then, a material is selected, and the amount calculated from a selected oxide or oxides. Next, the amount of each oxide contributed by that material is calculated and subtracted from the weight percent to obtain the amount remaining. The procedure is repeated until all the materials have been selected, and all the oxides accounted for. Finally, the amounts are scaled to the batch size desired.

There are also some excellent software programs available for purchase.[M2-4] Two of the best, and best established, are Insight and Hyperglaze.

6.4.2 Insight PC, for both MS-DOS and Macintosh computers, is an enormously powerful tool for glaze calculations.[M2,4] For MS-DOS computers, it is available in both Windows and DOS versions. It has a well-done manual and an excellent tutorial, but it takes several hours before one begins to feel competent in using it.

Classic glaze calculation is the heart of the program. The opening screen has a recipe window and a molecular formula window. The recipe window gives an adjustable recipe total and a batch cost. The calculation window is set up for the Seger formula but can be exchanged for a molecular percent.

Speed is one of the most attractive features of Insight. Because all of the materials data are loaded into memory when the program is first run, calculations are almost instantaneous.

A glaze calculation program is only as good as its database of raw material formulas. A great deal of effort has gone into selecting the best analyses to be included. In earlier versions, the only difficulty with the database was that it was not easy to edit it. The latest Windows version has alleviated this problem.

Insight is particularly good in its ability to rapidly examine dozens of minor adjustments to a recipe and determine instantly how they will affect the molecular formula. By combining this with Insight's reference column feature, a desired formula can be matched quickly.

Insight is written by Tony Hansen, Medicine Hat, AB, Canada, and is available in the United States from Axner Company, Inc., P. O. Box 621484, Oviedo, FL 32762, tel. 800-843-7057.

6.4.3 Hyperglaze, for Macintosh computers, is a collection of programs, including glaze calculation, materials database, and glaze recipe database storage, in one easy-to-learn package. It runs under the program HyperCard, which is usually shipped with Macintosh computers.

In addition to the calculation of the Seger formula, it calculates the molecular percentage, cost per batch, coefficient of expansion, silica-to-alumina ratio, and adjustable batch sizes.

The molecular-to-batch calculation runs smoothly, with a great deal of assistance, in the form of recommendations for raw material selection. The program stresses the need to select the complex raw materials first, leaving those with only one or two oxides for later. HyperGlaze also serves as a recipe database, with the ability to search it for particular characteristics.

Hyperglaze comes with a clear, well-written manual, and an elaborate on-screen help system. A major feature is the ability to edit information almost anywhere on its user interface.

The only limitation of this program is its speed of calculation, which is much slower than that of Insight. This can be a limitation when running "what if" calculations on a series of possibilities.

HyperGlaze is available from the author, Richard Burkett, 3027 Olive Street, San Diego, CA 92104.

6.4.4 There are also some newer programs that deserve consideration.[M4] One highly recommended shareware program is GlazeChem 1.2. It is an excellent blend of glaze calculation and glaze recipe database. A particularly useful feature of this program is the ability to compare several related recipes against preselected formula limits. Exporting and importing recipes from Insight or Hyperglaze are done easily. GlazeChem 1.2 is available from Robert J. Wilt, 92 Bay State Avenue, #2, Somerville, MA 02144.

Glaze Calculator for Windows is a unique approach to this topic. It is useful in the evaluation of changes to a recipe. However, it has a British materials database, and it lacks some functions, such as adjusting batch size. Glaze Calculator comes from Christopher Green, Seegreen Software, P. O. Box 115, Westbury-on-Trym, Bristol BS9 3ND, United Kingdom.

Glaze Simulator for Windows attempts to predict glaze properties from the formula. As with all such efforts, it suffers from the fact that the accuracy of property predictions is quite limited. In Chapter 15 there is a discussion of the most commonly attempted property prediction, that of coefficient of thermal expansion. The practical conclusion from many years' experience in designing this prediction is that property predictions are useful in a relative sense but are next-to-useless on an absolute basis. That is, for example, if you calculate the thermal expansion coefficient of two glazes, and one is higher than the other by a given amount, that difference will be accurate in direction, and usually in amount. BUT, the absolute values of the two will often differ from measured values by 10 to 20 percent.

Chapter 7
Mill Additives and Slip Rheology

I

t is rare for a mixture of ground frit and raw materials suspended in water to be usable as is, particularly with any degree of reproducibility.[T1] The rheological properties of the slurry mixture are influenced by the particle sizes and shapes of the various components, and these flow properties change with time. Control is needed over the thickness of coating application, and the evenness of deposition. Hence, additions of rheology modifiers are required to control slip sedimentation, improve wetting properties on and bonding to the substrate, control drying time, prevent drying cracks, and improve unfired or green strength. Control over these properties is the means to controlling the application process.

The increasing use of leadless glazes and porcelain enamels makes this subject even more important than before, as leadless systems are very sensitive to rheologically derived defects. Unfortunately, most additives often influence more than one of the rheological properties. These properties are also somewhat dependent on details of the process equipment used in preparing and applying the coating material. Thus, several trials are usually required to find a suitable combination of additives for a given application. However, once a suitable combination of additives has been developed for a given coating preparation and application process, that combination of additives will usually be applicable to all coatings prepared and applied at that facility.

In this chapter the types of additives will be reviewed, and the most-often-used materials in each category discussed. This information is summarized in Table 7-1, which lists some of the more important mill additives and their uses.

Table 7-1. Mill Additives

Material	Function	Amount Used
Water-soluble cellulose	Binder. Hardens bisque. Reduces handling damage.	0–1%
Gum tragacanth	Binder. Hardens bisque. Reduces handling damage.	0–1/4%
Polyvinyl alcohols	Strong binder. Greatly hardens bisque. Prevents handling damage.	0–1/4%
Tetrasodium pyrophosphate	Rapidly decreases set. Must be used with care.	0–1/4%
Sodium tripolyphosphate	Decreases set.	0–1/4%
Sodium metaphosphate	Decreases set.	0–1/4%
Sodium nitrite	Widely used deflocculant. Increases set.	0–1/2%
Borax	Slurry stabilizer. Increases set.	0–1/2%
Sodium aluminate	Strongly increases set.	0–1/2%
Ammonium hydroxide	Weak deflocculant. For alkali-free systems.	0–1%
Sodium or potassium carbonate	Increases set. Aids other deflocculants.	0–1/2%
Potassium chloride	Increases set. Brightens whites. Difficult to avoid defects.	0–1/2%
Urea	Reduces tearing. Add just before use.	0–1/2%
Calcium chloride	Long time flocculant	0–1/4%
Magnesium sulfate	Long time flocculant	0–1/4%
Calcium sulfate	Longest time flocculant.	0–1/4%
Alum	Short time flocculant.	0–1/4%
Ammonium chloride	Short time flocculant. Suitable for alkali-free systems.	0–1/4%
Kaolin	Suspender. Increases bisque strength.	0–10%
Ball clay	Strong suspender. Increases bisque strength.	0–10%
Bentonite, hectorite	Strong suspender. Five times stronger than other clays. Causes thixotropy.	0–2%
Colloidal silica	Aids suspension. Improves gloss and acid resistance.	0–2%
Pigments	Produce color. Reduce acid resistance.	0–10%

7.1 Binders

While some glaze compositions high in clay content can be easily handled in the green state (after drying, but before firing), most dry coating layers are friable and can easily be damaged in the process of preparing the ware for firing. The addition of binders or hardeners is, therefore, necessary. The binder acts as a temporary cement, holding the glaze particles on the surface until firing.

The amount of binder added can range up to 3%, but 0.5% is typical.[T1] Excessive amounts embrittle the coating and introduce shrinkage on firing.

Several types of organic binders are used. The ideal binder burns away freely below 400°C without ash and doesn't cause shrinkage or disruption of the coating. Both natural gums and synthetic polymers are used, sometimes mixed.

The most commonly used binders are cellulose ethers. They are chosen as coating hardeners because their properties are more consistent than those of natural gums and starches. In a coating with a stable degree of flocculation, there is an improvement in the stability of the viscosity. Hence, coating layers of consistent and controllable thickness can be applied by various techniques. Drying shrinkage is also predictable.

Cellulose is a partly amorphous, partly crystalline solid, insoluble in water. By etherification, derivatives are prepared that are water soluble. In these materials the properties of the basic cellulose molecule are modified by the positioning of carboxy groups on the molecule. Hence, products are available with a range of viscosities, depending on the degree of polymerization. In water, polymerized cellulose swells to give clear solutions with viscosity dependent on the concentration and molecular weight of the polymer.

In a coating application, the binder must be strong enough to permit handling of the ware in the dried-but-not-fired state, but soft enough to accommodate the drying shrinkage while bonded to the substrate. Hence, lower-viscosity grades are preferred for glaze hardening. It is almost never possible to use the same grade of carboxymethyl cellulose as is used for binding a ceramic body.

The polymer properties are affected by temperature, pH, and the presence of electrolytes and preservatives. Vigorous stirring permits solution in cold water. Usually a 10% solution is made up, from which additions up to 1% are made to the coating slip. In commercial-scale operations, these additions should not be made in the mill, because mechanical stress and heat can degrade the polymers. Rather, they should be added after milling.

Choice can be made from a range of cellulose products, including sodium carboxymethyl cellulose (CMC) and methyl cellulose (Methocel).

There are side effects that cannot be ignored. Carboxymethyl cellulose, although a preferred binder, acts as a deflocculant in most glazes. Methocel is not. Cellulose solutions require protection against biological and mold attack.

Natural gums are carbohydrate polymers of high molecular weight. Gum tragacanth is a natural hydrophilic gum found on a bush in much of Asia. It is only partially soluble in water, in which it swells to form first a gel and then a sol. These sols have low surface tension and are useful as coating stabilizers.

Starch has wide application in industry as a thickener, extender and adhesive. It is only occasionally used in ceramics. The amount of ash remaining after firing is a major limitation on starch use. Two types of starch are available. Normal starch requires dissolution in hot water. Pretreated grades can be dispersed in cold water. Usually a 10% solution is made first and used to make additions to a glaze to give 0.1 to 0.5% by weight of starch.

There is a range of polyvinyl alcohol compounds (PVA), which are efficient binders.[57] Low molecular weight versions disperse more readily and are necessary for coating applications. Additions of up to 1% to the slip produce tough, coherent layers. Wetting agents improve the use of polyvinyl alcohol.

Other possibilities include alginates, water-soluble acrylics, and resin emulsions.

7.2 Deflocculants

In a slip, the solid particles can either be individually dispersed or agglomerated into flocs. Stokes' law shows that larger particles or agglomerates settle out much faster than small particles. Hence, control of the dispersion of the particles is critical.

This control is achieved by adding deflocculants. Their action in the suspension may be compared to magnets, having a north and south pole, or a positive and negative charge.[M8] For example, when ionized in water, sodium nitrite has a positive charge on the sodium and a negative charge on the nitrite. Clay in suspension carries a negative charge. Hence, the positively charged sodium will adhere to the clay particle surface. This charged clay, with sodium ion, will in turn attract water, forming a three-part sphere known as a clay micelle. Instead of a small clay particle moving about freely in water, there is now a much more bulky shape that cannot move with the same freedom as the original clay particle. Hence, the slurry becomes able to suspend larger quantities of the frit and other solid particles.

While all deflocculants work the same way, they vary in effectiveness, and in their balance between improving suspension and altering viscosity, or set (the ability of a suspension to adhere to a vertical surface and not run off). Thus, some of the milder agents may increase set, while the overall effect of some strong agents is to produce a free-flowing suspension of lower viscosity.

Materials that have this effect are called deflocculating electrolytes, or deflocculants. They come in two types: the polyanion and the alkali cation deflocculants.

The polyanion deflocculants are complex salts of sodium and phosphoric acid—sodium tripolyphosphate, tetrasodium pyrophosphate, and sodium metaphosphate.[T1] Tetrasodium pyrophosphate is a particularly powerful deflocculant. Very small amounts will reduce the viscosity of pastes to fluid suspensions. These phosphates can be added to the mill during the grinding stage to aid in the milling.

Alkali ion deflocculants include monovalent salts such as the following:[M8,T1]

- Sodium nitrite is used particularly with enamels, where it is also an antirust agent. It increases set.
- Borax increases set and stabilizes the slurry. It is only usable in slips that do not leach boron from the frit.
- Sodium aluminate strongly increases set, with only modest suspension improvement.
- Ammonium hydroxide is a weak deflocculant used when alkalis are undesirable.
- Sodium carbonate or potassium carbonate are rarely used alone, but they improve the effectiveness of other deflocculants.
- Sodium silicate, usually N brand, is often used with Na_2CO_3. It also has binding characteristics.
- Potassium chloride is sometimes used with colored coatings. Chloride ion is often undesirable.

7.3 Flocculants

Flocculants are less often used, but they have certain uses. Figure 7.1 shows that flocs settle to less dense coatings.[T1] Hence, flocculants can be used to control coating density. Second, ions can be leached from most coating materials, given sufficient time. These ions tend to be alkalis, which thin the slip to a viscosity below that needed for application. This often occurs during slip storage. Flocculants can counteract this trend.

Flocculants are generally divalent or higher cation salts. They are very powerful, so they are used in very small quantities, from 0.005 to 0.1%. They include the following:
- Calcium chloride provides stable suspension over a long time.
- Magnesium sulfate also is a long time agent.
- Calcium sulfate is sometimes added. It is the longest acting of the flocculants.
- Calcium hydroxide can even be used in clay-free suspensions.
- Alum and ammonium chloride are short time flocculants.

7.4 Suspending Agents

For application from an aqueous slurry, coating formulations require a proportion of colloidal material, which provides the means to support in suspension the inert pseudospherical components.[M8] The most common such suspending agent is clay.

Clays come in two general classes—kaolins and ball clays. Kaolins are white burning, and are comparatively pure kaolinite. They are moderately powerful suspending agents. They find use primarily in white and light-colored coatings, where the impurities in ball clays cannot be tolerated. Ball clays are less pure, often containing substantial free silica and/or micas, in addition to kaolinite. Many contain substantial concentrations of iron oxide and titania, and are thus darker burning. Thus, they can alter the color of the coating. But 70 to 80 percent of their total particles are less than 1 micron in diameter, so they are more powerful suspending agents. Clay additions (either kaolin or ball clay, or some combination) up to 12% by weight are often used.

Bentonite and hectorite are the names given to a class of montmorillonite clays that have higher-than-normal water contents and very fine particle size.[T1] They are somewhat diffi-

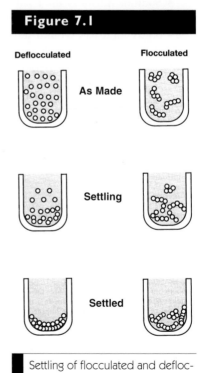

Figure 7.1

Deflocculated   Flocculated

As Made

Settling

Settled

Settling of flocculated and deflocculated suspensions.

Figure 7.2

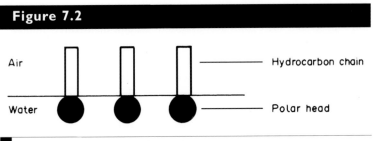

Air — Hydrocarbon chain

Water — Polar head

Schematic representation of a wetting agent.

cult to disperse in water, but once dispersed they attach a very high water concentration, forming strong gels that are up to five times more effective in suspension power than normal clay. Hence, they are effective at concentrations of 0.5 to 2%, well below the 10% or more used with more conventional clays. Bentonite is particularly useful with a fully fritted coating, which can be formulated in many cases with 99% frit, 1% bentonite. Unlike organic agents, bentonite does not cause loss of viscosity if coating slip is heated. It does not degrade due to bacterial action.

A final suspending agent is fine particle silica. There are several suppliers. It is a relatively pure silica made by chemical processing, and is a powerful suspending agent.

Most of the materials that have been previously discussed as binders also have some suspending power and can be considered suspending agents. Similarly, the several clays have some binding capability, particularly when present in large quantities.

7.5 Other Additives

Certain substances, such as soaps, can lower the surface energy of liquids.[T1] They act by orientation at the interface, as shown in Figure 7.2. They are of particular interest when underglaze decoration is practiced. The pastes used for such decoration are organic based.[59] Without wetting agents, those organics must be carefully burned off before coating application. It is less expensive to add a wetting agent to the coating, which permits coating over the organic media used for underglaze printing.

A major consideration in the choice of a wetting agent is the need for low-foaming or nonfoaming characteristics.[T1] Otherwise, bubble defects will be introduced into the coating. The wetting agent additions are small, usually less than 1%.

Whatever the source, foam is deleterious. Hence, small quantities of an antifoam agent may be helpful. Phosphate ion is an effective foam control agent, particularly if it can be added as discussed in section 7.2, so that the cation acts as a deflocculant deliberately added.

All glazes, even those with coloring pigments added, appear white in the green state. This can cause confusion in a plant where several coatings are being processed. The solution is to add a small amount of an organic dye, so as to color-code each coating used. Of course, dyes must be selected that will completely burn off in firing.

Many of the organic additives that have been discussed will undergo degradation in storage due to bacterial action. Bacteriocides are needed to prevent this. One example is a material called Tris nitro. It is added in very small quantity, about 0.01%.

There is one additional large class of additives: the pigments and opacifiers. These will be discussed in Chapter 8.

7.6 Slip Rheology

The additives discussed in sections 7.1 to 7.5 are added largely for the purpose of controlling the rheology of aqueous slips. The property of most immediate concern is the viscosity of the slurry. The viscosity of simple liquids, such as water, used in making ceramic slips is said to be Newtonian.[R1] If we push a fluid down a pipe or a channel, a stress develops between the moving fluid and the stationary container through which it is flowing. For liquids which are Newtonian, the stress is proportional to the velocity gradient across the fluid:

$$\tau = -\mu \frac{dv}{dr}$$

The constant of proportionality μ is the viscosity. It indicates the resistance to flow due to friction between the molecules and between

Figure 7.3

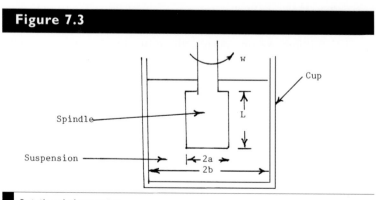

Rotational viscometer.

Figure 7.4

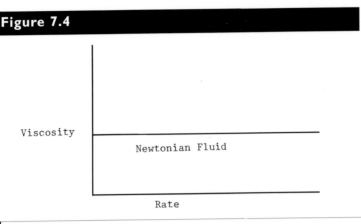

Viscosity of a Newtonian fluid.

the fluid and its stationary container. With stress expressed in dynes/cm^2, and rate in s^{-1}, the units of viscosity will be dynes, s/cm^2 or poises.

7.6.1 Viscosity measurement of ceramic slips can be done several ways. The most widely used viscometer for ceramic suspensions is the variable speed, rotating cylinder viscometer, illustrated in Figure 7.3. The inner cylinder of this device, of length L, rotates at an angular frequency w, and the torque produced by the viscous medium is measured. In the most commonly used version of this device[1], the measurement is made by the force on a spring in the head that drives the spindle. For this design, the viscosity is:

$$\mu = \frac{[T][1 - (a^2/b^2)]}{[w][a^2\ 4\pi L]}$$

Various spindle designs are used to increase the viscosity range of the instrument. The larger the spindle, the lower the viscosity it measures.

For suspensions, it is assumed that the spacing between the spindle and the housing $(b - a)$ is much greater than the particle size of the solid particles; the viscous material makes continuous contact with the spindle surfaces; no slippage occurs; and laminar flow is fully developed.

This instrument is widely used in ceramic laboratories because it is straightforward to use and simple to interpret the results. However, strictly speaking, it is only correct for Newtonian fluids. For other systems, it provides an apparent viscosity, by measurements at more than one rotational speed.

---

[1] Brookfield Engineering Laboratories, Inc., Stoughton, MA.

7.6.2 For Newtonian fluids, viscosity is a true constant, independent of velocity gradient, and a plot of viscosity versus velocity gradient is a straight line (Figure 7.4).

Unfortunately, ceramic slurries are rarely Newtonian. Consider the effects of adding a binder to the slip. Binder molecules have a large sphere of influence relative to their molecular size. Dissolved in the slip, they may significantly increase the apparent viscosity. As shown in Figure 7.5, as the binder molecular weight is increased, the increase in viscosity with a given amount of binder also increases. At low concentrations the increase is proportional to the concentration of binder, and to the size of the binder molecule.

In addition, as the flow rate of a binder containing fluid increases, the binder particles tend to align with the direction of flow, in such a way as to present a smaller cross section to the direction of flow. Hence, they gradually reduce the resistance of the fluid to flow, lowering viscosity. This behavior, where apparent viscosity decreases monotonically with increase in velocity gradient, is called pseudoplastic flow. Figure 7.6 shows the pseudoplastic behavior of some binder-water solutions. Note that the reduction in viscosity due to alignment is greatest for the highest molecular weight binders. The low molecular weight binder-water solutions used with coatings have less deviation from Newtonian flow.

Ceramic slurries also contain solid particles suspended in the fluid. Initially, at low concentrations of solid particles, the effect is merely to gradually increase the viscosity, as the liquid medium has to flow around the solid particles:

$$\frac{\mu_S}{\mu_L} = 1+kf_P$$

Here μ_S is the viscosity of the suspension, μ_L the viscosity of the pure liquid portion, and f_P the volume fraction of solid particles. The constant K is 2.5 for spherical particles, more for those with an aspect ratio greater than 1.

At a concentration above 5 to 10 volume percent, the solid particles begin to interact. They become entangled with each other as the velocity gradient is increased. Thus the viscosity

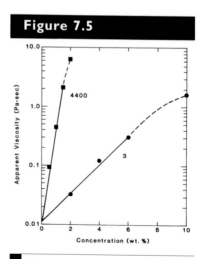

Figure 7.5

Viscosity of a slurry as a function of binder concentration.

Figure 7.6

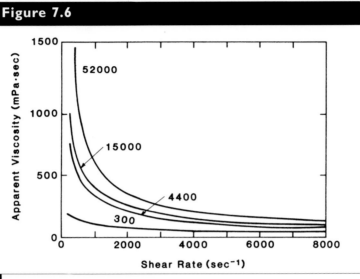

Viscosity of a pseudoplastic fluid.

also increases as the velocity gradient increases. This is called dilatant flow, which is shown in Figure 7.7. Dilatant flow is characteristic of large particles. Either polymer additives or agglomerates of ceramic particles, especially clays, can produce dilatant flow.

As the concentration of solids is increased much further, eventually a concentration is reached at which no flow occurs. This breakdown concentration due to flow stoppage is an important parameter in all thick coatings and slurries. It is, for example, one of the basic parameters in the compounding of paints, where it is called the critical volume content.[K7] It refers to the minimum amount of medium necessary to fill in the gaps between the solid particles. It is measured for paints by a technique called oil absorption. One determines the amount of linseed oil necessary to barely hold together a 1 g ball of solid, and then calculates the volume of oil/volume of solid. Then:

$$CPVC = 1/[1 + OA]$$

Values of the critical pigment volume content vary from about 55% for pseudospherical particles to less than 25% for platelike particles, such as clays. The latter is due to the house-of-cards effect.

An additional complication to viscosity behavior is time dependence. For example, consider a pseudoplastic slip in which the anisotropic particles are increasingly aligned as the flow rate is increased. If the flow rate is reversed, the particles do not immedi-

Figure 7.7

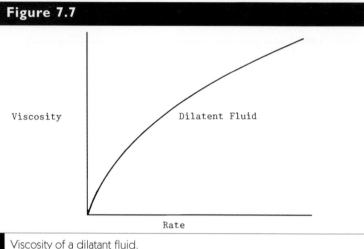

Viscosity   Dilatent Fluid

Rate

Viscosity of a dilatant fluid.

ately randomize, but continue for a while to flow in an aligned manner. This time dependence is called thixotropy, as shown in Figure 7.8.

Many high-solids coating slips exhibit thixotropy. It is a property that can both help and hurt an application process. On the one hand, a mill charge may have to be energized to get it out of the mill. On the other hand, thixotropy can assist in application, permitting the coating to flow over the ware and smooth out, then set and remain in place during drying.

Figure 7.8

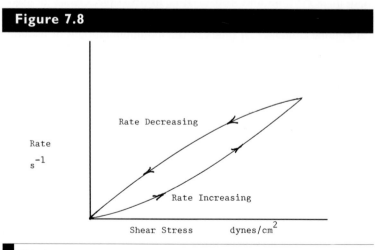

Rate Decreasing

Rate
s^{-1}

Rate Increasing

Shear Stress   dynes/cm^2

Thixotropy.

Chapter 8
Color in Glazes and Enamels

One of the most important reasons for applying a ceramic coating is to improve the appearance of the product. While it is not the only aspect of appearance, the color of a product is a major component of it. Thus, most ceramic coatings contain components added to give a desired color.

8.1 What Is Color?

Color is a sensation that most of us are familiar with, as an aspect of what we see with our eyes. A method of describing color must therefore relate to our human perception of this property.

From this viewpoint, the production of color requires three components:[B3] a source of light, the object that it illuminates, and a way to detect the color of the object. Therefore, in describing the color of a ceramic coating, a known standard source and a standard method of detection will be required.

For the source, the International Commission on Illumination has selected several standard light sources for use in describing color. One of these, CIE Source A, is a tungsten-filament lamp operating at a color temperature of 2854 K. CIE Source C is derived from Source A by passing its light through liquid filters. It is an approximation of average daylight. As sources, these are real physical lights that can be used in color experiments. CIE has also defined CIE Illuminant D_{65}, which is a closer approximation to the power distribution of average natural daylight. However, so far it has not been possible to make a source representing it. Thus, when a color measuring instrument reports Illuminant D_{65} data, it is reporting data mathematically converted to what a D_{65} would yield if such a source could be made.

When the light from one of these sources strikes a solid object such as a ceramic coating, there are only a limited number of

Figure 8.1

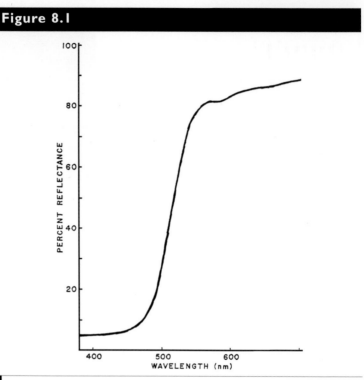

Spectral reflectance of a yellow glaze.

possibilities for what happens. The first of these is transmission—the light passes through the coating. With ceramic coatings this is a rare response.

Reflection occurs whenever there is a boundary with a change in the refractive index. For many ceramic coatings, with refractive indices near 1.5, the amount reflected is about 4% at each boundary with air. Higher-index coatings reflect more.

Light may also be absorbed, or converted into energy outside the visible spectrum, primarily as heat. If the material absorbs part of the light, it appears colored. If all the light is absorbed, the material is black and opaque.

Finally, light may be scattered. Some light is absorbed and re-emitted at the same wavelength, but now part of the light travels in one direction, part in another. When there is enough scattering, the light is diffusely reflected from the material, and the material is said to be opaque. If there is no absorption, and the amount of scattering at each wavelength is the same, the sample will appear white; otherwise it will be colored.

Scattering is caused by light falling on small particles with refractive indices different from that of the surrounding material, as, for example, small particles of a pigment dispersed in a glaze. The amount of scattering is strongly dependent on the difference in refractive index between the two materials. Scattering is also a function of the particle size of the scatterer, being most effective when the particle diameter resembles the wavelength of the light.

The most efficient pigments for glazes are thus materials with refractive indices very different from that of the glass matrix, and particle size approaching that of the wavelength of light.

With respect to color, the effect of a ceramic coating on light can be described by its spectral reflectance curve. This curve shows the fraction of light reflected at each wavelength from the material. Figure 8.1 gives the spectral reflectance curve of a yellow tile. It absorbs wavelengths in the blue below 500 nm, while reflecting those in the yellow. Figure 8.2 shows the spectral reflectance curve of a light red tile. The wavelengths of absorption are centered in the blue-green. Figure 8.3 shows the spectral reflectance curve of a deep red tile. Here the absorption is extended almost to 600 nm and is

Figure 8.2

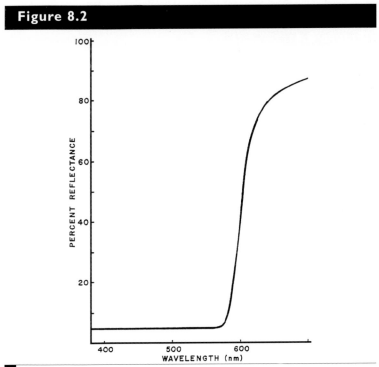

Spectral reflectance of a light red glaze.

Figure 8.3

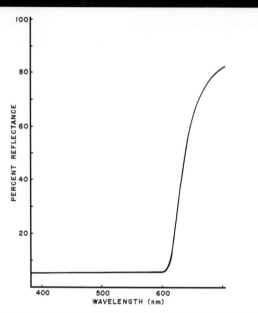

Spectral reflectance of a very deep red glaze.

Figure 8.4

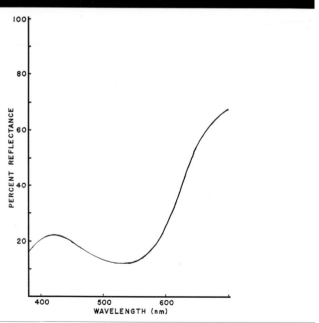

Spectral reflectance of a magenta glaze.

Figure 8.5

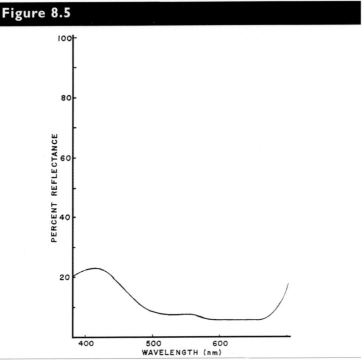

Spectral reflectance of a dark blue glaze.

centered in the green. Figure 8.4 shows the spectral reflectance curve of a magenta tile. Its absorption is centered in the yellow green near 520 nm. Figure 8.5 shows the spectral reflectance curve of a dark cyan-blue tile. It absorbs the longer wavelengths from 520 to 670 nm and reflects at the edges of the visible. Figure 8.6 shows the spectral reflectance curve of a turquoise blue tile, which absorbs red light of wavelength 600 to 700 nm. Figure 8.7 shows the spectral reflectance curve of a green tile. This tile absorbs both ends of the spectrum and reflects the middle.

As detectors, the only important alternatives to the human eye-brain system are photomultiplier tubes and silicon photodiodes. Their response curves are very different from each other, and from the human eye. Hence, their response must be mathematically related to the response of a typical human eye.

8.2 Color Spaces

Now let us turn to the question "How can we describe colors?" Specifically, let's ask how a person of normal color vision might

Figure 8.6

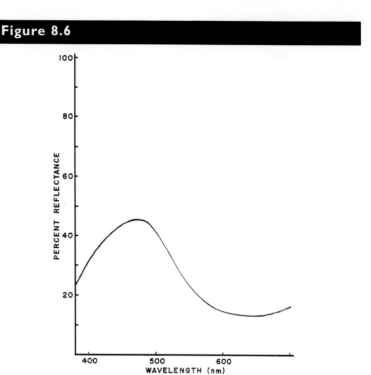

Spectral reflectance of a turquoise blue glaze.

describe the colors he or she has seen in daylight. The answer is that color can be described in any one of several three-coordinate systems, which are called color spaces.[B3]

The first of the three coordinates describes fully those colors without hue—the blacks, grays, and whites—and separates them from those with a recognizable hue. This coordinate is variously called lightness or value.

The chromatic colors provide a more complicated situation, because they differ from one another in several ways, not just by differences in lightness. In addition to lightness, they can be separated by hue—that is, into red, orange, yellow, green, blue, etc. This is the second coordinate. But, this is still not the whole story. For example, one might have a brick red pebble and a bright tomato red pebble with the same hue—red, and the same lightness. But they don't look alike. These colors differ in the third parameter—their departure from grayness, which is called chroma, or saturation.

With these three parameters—hue, lightness or value, and saturation or chroma—one can describe color. Note that these three parameters describe color, not appearance. Appearance is a more complex concept, involving qualities such as size, gloss, surface texture, etc.

Earlier, we stated that the color of a ceramic coating depends on its spectral reflectance curve. Can that curve be related to these three quantities of hue, value, and chroma? The answer is yes, one can calculate from the spectral reflectance curve sets of three numbers that describe color. However, the spectral reflectance curve contains more information than do color coordinates, so the reverse is not true—one cannot define a spectral reflectance curve from a set of color coordinates. This is the effect called metamerism, which is two different spectral reflectance curves that give the same color coordinates in a given illumination. Under a different illuminant, they will not have the same color coordinates.

While there are any number of color spaces possible, some are more relevant to color in ceramic coatings. Color spaces are of two kinds, those based on collections of physical samples, and those based on theoretical considerations. We will first consider a color space based on a collection of physical samples.

The Munsell system[M22] is a collection of samples painted to represent equal intervals of visual perception between adjacent samples. It describes colors in terms of its three coordinates: Munsell

Figure 8.7

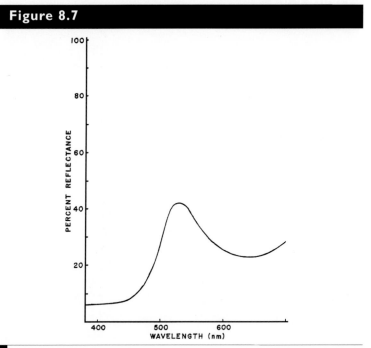

Spectral reflectance of a green glaze.

hue, Munsell value, and Munsell chroma.

Figure 8.8 is a photograph of a color tree made out of the Munsell samples. The scale of grays (Munsell value) is the trunk of the Munsell color tree. Hue is around the circumference of the tree, and chroma is the radius. The outstanding feature of the Munsell system is its conformance to equal visual perception. There is very little evidence for deviation from equal steps of perception in any of the Munsell coordinates. Hence, it is the standard against which all other systems are compared.

We now come to the description of color spaces that are only incidentally associated with collections of samples. The basis for all these systems is the CIE system,[C3] produced by the Commission Internationale de l'Eclairage, or International Commission on Illumination. The CIE has developed a standardization of sources and of observer, and a methodology for deriving numbers that provide a measure of color, as seen by the standard observer in a standard illuminant.

CIE has recommended several illuminants. The most important of these is Illuminant D_{65}, having a correlated color temperature of 6500 K. This illuminant is a proxy for natural sunlight. The only

Figure 8.8

Munsell color wheel.

other important illuminant is Illuminant A, which is an incandescent light bulb.

CIE has also recommended a standard observer, a representation of the average of the vision of the human population having normal color vision. It consists of the response at each wavelength to a set of three primary colors. If the colors of the three primary colors are quite different, a wide range of colors can be matched in this way, but not all. The problem is the violets, which are split between the two ends of the spectrum. This problem is overcome by, in effect, subtracting the response to one primary from the response to the other two.

CIE could have selected any of a number of sets of imaginary primaries to define the standard observer. The set they did select, X, Y, and Z, has a number of advantages. One of them is that Y was selected to be exactly the same as the eye's response curve to the total amount of light power. As a result, the tristimulus value Y provides information on a color's lightness.

Now we can calculate the CIE tristimulus values from information on the reflectance of the object in question, the power distribution curve of the CIE standard illuminant, and the color-matching function of the CIE standard observer:[B3]

$$X = \sum_{380}^{700} P_i \, R_i \, x_i$$

$$Y = \sum_{380}^{700} P_i \, R_i \, y_i$$

$$Z = \sum_{380}^{700} P_i \, R_i \, z_i$$

The values of the power distribution function P and the color-matching function x, y, or z are tabulated in various texts.[W5, C4, H9, J4] They are multiplied by each other and thence by the reflectance value R at each of many equally spaced wavelengths across the spectrum. These are then summed up to give the tristimulus values.

By convention, when dealing with reflecting objects such as ceramic coatings, one assigns the value $Y = 100$ to an ideal nonfluorescent white reflecting 100% at all frequencies. This scaling is done by adjusting the products Px, Py, and Pz so that $Py = 1$.

For convenience in preparing a two-dimensional map of colors, it is conventional to calculate the relative tristimulus values, which

Figure 8.9

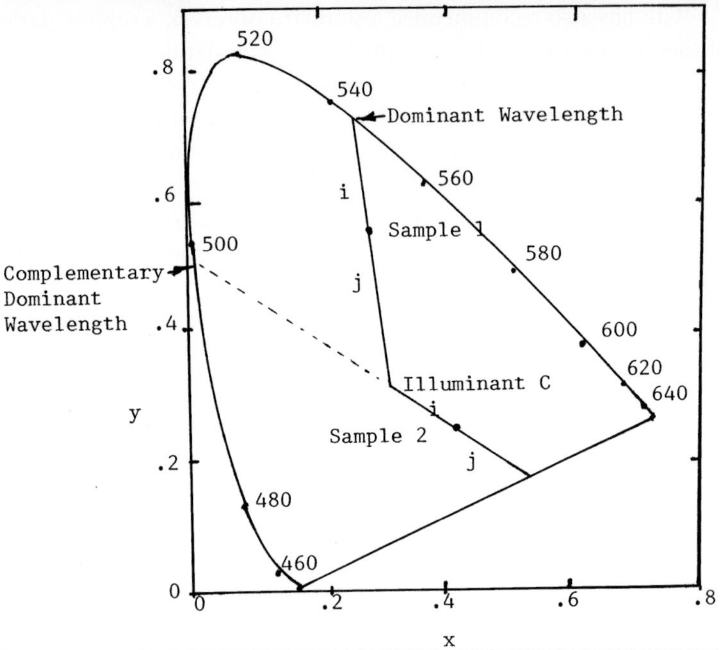

CIE chromaticity diagram.

are called chromaticity coordinates:[B3]

$$x = \frac{X}{X + Y + Z}$$

$$y = \frac{Y}{X + Y + Z}$$

$$z = \frac{Z}{X + Y + Z}$$

They describe the qualities of a color in addition to its lightness. One of the tristimulus values, usually Y, must also be specified.

Color as described in the CIE system can be plotted on a chromaticity diagram, usually a plot of the chromaticity coordinates x and y (Figure 8.9). The most familiar feature of this plot is the horseshoe-shaped spectrum locus, the line connecting the points representing the spectrum colors. Also shown are dominant wavelength and purity. The dominant wavelength is the wavelength of the

Figure 8.10

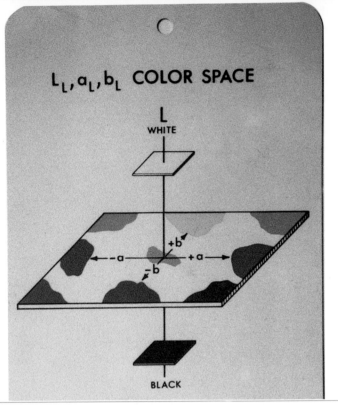

Opponent-color system diagram.

spectrum color whose chromaticity is on the straight line between the sample and the illuminant point. Purity is the fractional distance of the sample from the illuminant point to the spectrum locus.

This plot illustrates an important weakness of the CIE system. Where is black? White is clearly in the center of the diagram, but black can be anywhere, for it corresponds to all three tristimulus values being equal to zero.

This weakness of the CIE system has led to a search for an alternate description of color. The system most commonly used in the ceramic industry today is based on the concept of opponent-color coordinates, which is illustrated in Figure 8.10. In opponent-color coordinates, the argument is that a color cannot be red and green at the same time, or yellow and blue at the same time, although it can be both red and yellow as in oranges and browns, or red and blue, as in purples, etc. Hence, redness or greenness can be expressed as a single value a, which is positive if the color is pink or red, and negative if it is green. Similarly, yellowness or blueness is expressed by the coordinate b, which is positive for yellows and negative for blues. The third coordinate describes the lightness of the color, and is called L.

Probably the most widely used of all color spaces except the CIE system is the Hunter L, a, b system introduced in 1942.[H6] This system has introduced the opponent-color concept to industrial practice in many industries, including ceramics. Today this type of system is often known as an L-a-b system, regardless of whether Hunter's coordinates are used. A major factor in the popularity of the Hunter system is the availability of low-cost colorimeters that read directly in L-a-b.

The equations relating the Hunter to the CIE tristimulus values are:

$$L = 100\left(\frac{Y}{Y_n}\right)^{1/2}$$

$$a = 175\left(\frac{0.0102X_n}{Y/Y_n}\right)^{1/2}\left[\left(\frac{X}{X_n}\right)-\left(\frac{Y}{Y_n}\right)\right]$$

$$b = 70\left(\frac{0.00847Z_n}{Y/Y_n}\right)^{1/2}\left[\left(\frac{Y}{Y_n}\right)-\left(\frac{Z}{Z_n}\right)\right]$$

The lightness equation is based on an early observation that lightness is roughly proportional to the square root of luminance factor. While the Hunter system is an important improvement in color uniformity over the CIE system, it is not perfect.

Hence, a number of refinements have been made, which have been combined into the L^*-a^*-b^* system recommended by CIE in 1976 with the official abbreviation CIELAB.[C5] The equations for this system are:

$$L^* = 116(Y/Y_n)^{1/3} - 16$$

$$a^* = 500[(X/X_n)^{1/3} - (Y/Y_n)^{1/3}]$$

$$b^* = 200[(Y/Y_n)^{1/3} - (Z/Z_n)^{1/3}]$$

These three equations apply for L^* values greater than 1%—the usual case. There is a modified value for L^* of low value:

$$L^* = 116[f(Y/Y_n) - (16/116)]$$

$$a^* = 500[f(X/X_n) - f(Y/Y_n)]$$

$$b^* = 200[f(Y/Y_n) - f(Z/Z_n)]$$

where

$$f(Y/Y_n) = (Y/Y_n)^{1/3} \text{ for } Y/Y_n > 0.008856$$

$$f(Y/Y_n) = 7.787(Y/Y_n) + 16/116 \text{ for } Y/Y_n < 0.008856$$

and $f(X/X_n)$ and $f(Z/Z_n)$ are similarly defined.

With this system there is a unique coordinate for the perfect black—0,0,0 for $L,a,b,$ respectively.

It is important to stress that the CIELAB official system is a refinement of the Hunter system. The designations L, a, and b are often used interchangeably for both. While the two sets of equations for them are quite different, the values calculated are usually quite similar. Hence, for most industrial practice, one L-a-b system is as good as another, as long as the same system is used throughout any given study. This type of color space is the one normally used in describing colors of ceramic coatings.

8.3 Color Measurement

In order of ascending accuracy, the available techniques to measure color are unaltered white light, colorimeters, and spectrophotometers.

Lets begin with spectrophotometers.[B3] For the measurement of color, it is necessary only to consider spectrophotometry in the visible portion of the spectrum—380 to 750 nm—carried out on instruments designed specifically for color measurement.

The principal parts of a spectrophotometer are a source of light, a means of isolating monochromatic light, and a detection system. In most spectrophotometers, white light from a tungsten filament lamp is spread out into a spectrum by means of a prism or a grating. Then, a slit is used to select a small portion of the spectrum to illuminate the sample. The wavelength of light passing the slit is varied by automatic scanning to cover the entire visible spectrum. Finally, the light reflected from the sample is collected and detected.

Other instruments reverse the procedure, using polychromatic illumination. The reflected light is passed through the monochromator before being detected.

Abridged spectrophotometry, the method used in most commercially available instruments today, is a term referring to the measurement of a few—usually 16 or 32—preselected regions of the spectrum usually at even 20- or 10-nanometer intervals. Abridged spectrophotometers are less expensive than full spectrophotometers, and are as accurate as full spectrophotometers for color measurement work.

A recent innovation offered by the makers of abridged spectrophotometers is the portable measuring head. This is a hand-held device that can be taken out in the shop and placed against any flat surface to make a measurement. The device gives immediate readout, but also stores up to about 40 measurements, which can be taken back to the main unit and the color data read in for analysis.

In section 8.2, the calculation of tristimulus coordinates or L,a,b values from spectral data was discussed. All spectrophotometers produced today for color measurement are provided with built-in computational power or are connected to a user's computer system to make those calculations. They also normally have software to permit color difference to be obtained between a sample and a standard.

Modern color measuring spectrophotometers are capable of very high precision. In most cases, the uncertainty in sample preparation is much larger than the uncertainty in the instruments' precision. Their accuracy is a function of accurate calibration of the instrument, using standards furnished by the instrument manufacturer.

Colorimeters are instruments for color measurement using three or four colored lights. This is usually done with glass filters placed in the light beam of the instrument. The filters thus provide an optical analogue of the numerical data used to obtain tristimulus values from spectrophotometric data. The degree to which the instrument readings approximate the true CIE tristimulus values of samples depends on how well these glass filters duplicate the CIE data. Because this duplication is less than perfect, colorimeter readings should never be considered absolute, and they should never be used for standardization, purchase specification, or the like.

The great virtue of colorimeters, aside from their lower cost than spectrophotometers, is their sensitivity in detecting and measuring small differences between two samples that are nearly alike in color. The differential measurement is highly reproducible from one properly calibrated colorimeter to another, and this is the correct way to use these instruments.

A decision about which color-measuring instrument to use requires careful consideration. Too little or too much instrumentation for the task can lead to dissatisfaction or excess cost. Some of the questions to be asked include:

- How many samples are to be run? Many instruments require only a few seconds to make a measurement.
- Are absolute tristimulus values needed? Or just color differences? In short, is a spectrophotometer needed, or just a colorimeter?
- Are suitable standards and data on them available?
- Are there any reproducibility problems? If so, consider that problems in sample preparation are usually much larger than reproducibility problems with the instrument.

Some principal manufacturers of color measuring equipment are listed in Appendix 2.

8.4 Sources of Color in Vitreous Coatings

There are three ways to obtain color in a vitreous matrix.[E27, E29] In the first method, certain transition metal ions can be added directly to the coating formulation. On firing, they dissolve and become part of the glassy coating, imparting their color to the coating. This method is difficult to use in coatings, because adequate tinting strength and purity of color can rarely be obtained in the very small thickness of a coating. In addition, unless care is taken in the selection of the raw material, coating defects will occur.

A second way to obtain color is to induce the precipitation of a crystal. Certain oxides such as titania and zirconia dissolve to the extent of several weight percent in a vitreous material at high temperature. If the temperature is reduced, the solubility is also reduced, and precipitation occurs. This method is widely used for opacification, which is the production of an opaque white color. That is, an opacifier is a white pigment. Normally, at least a significant portion of the opacifier added to the coating slip dissolves during the firing process and recrystallizes upon cooling. For colors other than white, however, this method lacks the necessary control for reproducible results and is, therefore, seldom used.

The third way to obtain color in a vitreous matrix is to disperse in that matrix an insoluble crystal or crystals that are colored. The color of the crystal is then imparted to the transparent matrix. This method is the one most commonly used to introduce color to vitreous coatings.

Most of the crystals used for ceramic colors are oxides. The reason is the greater stability of oxides in molten silicate glass. The one major exception is the family of cadmium sulfoselenide red pigments. This family is tolerated because it yields colors not found in oxide

Figure 8.11

COLORED CRYSTALS	COLORLESS CRYSTALS
True Colored Crystals	Doped Crystals
$CoAl_2O_4$	$ZrSiO_4{:}V$
$3CaO{\cdot}Cr_2O_3{\cdot}3SiO_2$	$ZrSiO_4{:}Pr$
(Victoria Green)	$ZrSiO_4{:}Fe$
$Pb_2Sb_2O_7$ (Naples Yellow)	$Al_2O_3{:}Cr$
Solid Solutions	Mordant Pigments
$Co(Al_xCr_{2-x})O_4$	$ZrO_2{:}V$
$(Zn,Fe)(Fe,Cr)_2O_4$	$SnO_2{:}V$

Classification of oxide pigments.

systems, so that it is necessary to put up with the difficulties of a toxic non-oxide system.

Oxide pigments can be classified as shown in Figure 8.11. In some cases, pigments can be made from crystals that are themselves colored. Examples include the cobalt aluminate blue, Victoria green, and zinc-iron-chromite brown. By judicious use of the principles of solid state chemistry (see section 8.6), it is possible to prepare a wide variety of pigments that are solid combinations of several elements within a selected crystal structure. Some examples are the cobalt chromate-aluminate bluegreens and the zinc-iron-chromite browns.

The use of colored crystals is severely limited by the simultaneous requirements of intense color and acceptable values of the other properties required of a ceramic pigment. These requirements can be optimized separately by the use of a colorless host crystal, to which a chromophore is added in small amounts during manufacture. In most cases, the dopant is trapped in the lattice of the host. Examples of this type of ceramic pigment include the various zircon pigments, and some chrome alumina pinks.

In other cases, it has not been determined whether the chromophore is dispersed in the lattice of the matrix, or if it is absorbed on the surface of the host. These colors, which include the tin-vanadium and zirconia-vanadium yellows, are called mordant pigments.

Doped pigments can be further classified on the basis of the nature of the chromophore. The most common technique is to add as the chromophore one of the transition metals titanium, vanadium, manganese, iron, cobalt, nickel, or copper, or one of the rare earths. These oxides are themselves colored, due to the presence of the partially filled 3d or 4f shells in the atomic structure of the cation.

Several other effects are also used. In some cases, the host crystal permits the stabilization of an unusual valence state of the dopant ion. The effect is particularly important in the case of the zircon pigments, where the tetravalent state is imposed.[E16] Thus, the addition of vanadium produces the blue color of tetravalent vanadium.

When the host crystal cation can have more than one valence, charge compensation effects can occur. For example, in the tin-vanadium yellow, the ability of tin ions to be reduced to the +2 state permits the stabilization of pentavalent vanadium in the tetravalent tin oxide structure.

In some cases, the geometry of the host crystal distorts the dopant ion so that unique colors result. Probably the best known example of this effect is the ruby, where the alumina lattice distorts the chromium ion from a green to a red color. The same effect occurs with some of the chrome-alumina pink pigments.

To be suitable as a ceramic color, a material must have a number of properties.[E29] These properties fall into two categories: strength of pigmentation and stability.

The first requirement is high tinting strength or intensity of color. It is also desirable that the color be pure and free of grayness or muddiness. Related to the intensity of color is the diversity of colors obtainable with similar and compatible materials, as for example different pigments obtainable with the same host crystal. The latter is important, because many users will blend two or more pigments to obtain the shade they want.

The other important property of a ceramic color is stability under the high temperatures and corrosive environments encountered in the firing of glazes. The rates of solution must be very low in spite of the very fine particle sizes—near 10 microns. Neither should gases be given off as a result of the contact of the ceramic color with the molten vitreous material. These requirements limit ceramic colors to those materials that are fully reacted and relatively inert.

For these reasons, colors useful at one temperature of firing may not be useful at a higher temperature.[E28] For example, at firing temperatures near 1000°C, cadmium sulfoselenide reds and oranges are stable. At the higher temperatures used in the white-wares industry, these materials will decompose and react with the molten glaze. In these cases, the requirements for resistance to attack lead to the adoption of the more stable pigments based on zirconia or zircon.

Another desirable property of a ceramic color is a high refractive index. For example, valuable pigments are based upon spinels, which have a refractive index of 1.8, and upon zircon, which has a refractive index of 1.9, but no valuable pigments are based up on apatite, which has a refractive index of 1.6, even though the lattice of apatite is as versatile for making ionic substitutions as is that of spinel.

8.5 Pigment Manufacture

Although there are a number of different pigment systems, most of them are prepared by similar manufacturing techniques.[E27, S9] The first step in pigment manufacture is close control over the selection of raw materials. Most of these raw materials are metallic oxides or salts of the desired metals. Considerable differences in the required chemical purity are encountered. Some raw materials must be of industrial chemical purity. Even impurity levels in the low parts-per-million range may be critical. On the other hand, conventional ceramic raw materials such as clays, silica, and alumina also find use in pigment formulations. Moreover, it is a fact of pigment manufacture that purity does not equal quality. The reason is that the reaction mechanisms in solid state reactions are often intricate and not well understood. Often less pure raw materials prove superior for producing a given pigment.

The raw materials are weighed, then thoroughly blended. This is usually done in the dry state, although a wet ball milling operation may be used to achieve more thorough mixing, together with some size reduction.

The reaction that forms the pigment crystal occurs during a high-temperature calcining operation. The temperature may range from 500°C to 1400°C, depending on the system. Although controlled atmospheres can be used, normally air is the atmosphere of choice. The reason is that the pigments must ultimately be stable to a high-temperature molten coating, so materials sensitive to oxygen have limited use. During the calcination process, any volatiles are driven off, and the pigment crystal is developed in a sintering reaction. Some of these reactions occur in the solid state, but many involve a fluid phase mineralizing pathway.[E6, E10] Although a few large-volume pigments may be made in continuous rotary kilns, most pigments are placed in 50- to 100-pound-capacity saggers for the calcining operation.

Following calcination, the product may require milling to reduce the particle size to that necessary for use. This size reduction may be carried out wet or dry. If there are soluble by-products, a washing operation may also be required. Finally, it is almost always necessary to break up agglomerates by a process such as micronizing.

8.6 Crystal Chemistry of Pigments

The structures of ionic, inorganic solid state materials are governed by several principles of crystal chemistry.[E25] These principles are a set of general rules or guidelines that bring some order to rather extensive sets of empirical data. They permit the development of a rational correlation of the crystal structures of materials, and they lead to a knowledge of which chemical elements may appear in a given structure.

In the first place, the principal component of the free energy of a ceramic material at room temperature is its lattice energy, which, in turn, is determined almost totally by the nearest-neighbor cation-anion distances:

$$U = \frac{NAe^2 Z_a Z_b}{r_a + r_b} \left(1 - \frac{1}{n} \right)$$

Here the Z's are the charges on the various ions, N is the number of ions, A the effective cross-sectional area, e the charge on the electron, and the r's the ionic radii of the various ions. Hence, the stability of an ionic ceramic pigment is directly dependent on the charge on the ions, and the interionic separation, as represented by the ionic radii.

Secondly, the coordination polyhedra of the anions about each cation are determined almost unequivocally by the ratio of the ionic size of the cation to that of the anion, which is called the radius ratio. If too many anions are grouped around one cation, the anion-anion

Table 8-1. Minimum Radius Ratio for Stability of Coordination Polyhedra

Polyhedron	Ligancy	Minimum Radius Ratio
Triangle	3	0.155
Tetrahedron	4	0.225
Octahedron	6	0.414
Cube	8	0.732
Cubo-octahedron	12	1.000

Table 8-2. Values of the Cation Ligancy with the Oxygen Ion

Ion	Radius Ratio	Predicted Ligancy	Observed Ligancy*	Bond Strength
B^{+3}	0.20	3 or 4	**3,4**	1 or 3/4
Be^{+2}	0.25	4	**4**	1/2
Li^{+1}	0.34	4	**4**	1/4
Si^{+4}	0.37	4	**4**,6	1
Al^{+3}	0.41	4 or 6	**4,5,6**	3/4 or 1/2
Ge^{+4}	0.43	4 or 6	**4**,6	1 or 1/2
Mg^{+2}	0.47	6	**6**	1/3
Na^{+1}	0.54	6	**6**,8	1/6
Ti^{+4}	0.55	6	**6**	2/3
Sc^{+3}	0.60	6	**6**	1/2
Zr^{+4}	0.62	6 or 8	**6**,8	2/3 or 1/2
Ca^{+2}	0.67	6 or 8	7,**8**,9	1/4
Ce^{+4}	0.72	6 or 8	**8**	1/2
K^{+1}	0.75	8	6,7,8,**9**,10,12	1/9
Cs^{+1}	0.96	12	**12**	1/12

* Bold values are those usually found.
Data from Reference P5

repulsive force becomes strong enough to prevent the anions from approaching closely to the cation, making the structure less stable than another structure with fewer anions about each cation. Table 8-1 shows the minimum radius ratio for the stability of various coordination polyhedra. These numbers predict that triangular coordination will occur for radius ratios of 0.155 to 0.225; tetrahedral coordination for radius ratios of 0.225 to 0.414; octahedral coordination for radius ratios 0.414 to 0.732; and cubic coordination for radius ratios 0.732 to 1.000. Table 8-2 gives the ligancy of various ions to the oxygen ion. It shows that empirical data on known compounds agrees very well with the radius ratio predictions. The values in bold are those usually found. The other values are observed only in a few crystals.

The ions with transition values of the radius ratio are especially interesting. The aluminum ion, for instance, forms oxygen tetrahedra in many aluminosilicates, including most ceramic coatings, but octahedra in others. It has ligancies 4 and 6 in sillimanite, 5 and 6 in andalucite, and 6 alone in syenite—all three stable minerals having the same composition Al_2SiO_5. Zirconium is octahedrally coordinated in most crystals, but it has an irregular eight coordination in zircon.

The third principle is that the structures that can be built from a given combination of cations and anions must obey the laws of electrostatic neutrality. In other words, in a stable ionic structure the valence of each anion, with changed sign, is exactly or nearly equal to the sum of the electrostatic bonds to it, as given in the last column of Table 8-2. For example, Si^{+4} with a bond strength of 1 and a valence of 4 will be tetrahedrally coordinated, while in the same material oxygen, with a valence of 2, will be bonded to two cations.

The fourth principle is that the coordination of a cation increases as the charge of the anion decreases, and decreases as the field strength increases.[R10] For example, in some materials, the fluoride ion coordination is higher than that of the oxide.

These four principles lead to the conclusion that a plot of the ionic radius of one cation versus that of a second cation in the same structure, which is called a structure field map, permits the determination of the probable structure of that material.[M27]

Table 8-3. Effective Ionic Radii for the Major Pigmenting Ions

Ion	Radius for Coordination Number (nm)		
	4	6	8
Al^{+3}	0.053	0.067	
Co^{+2}	0.071	0.0885	
Cr^{+3}		0.0755	
Cu^{+2}	0.076	0.087	
Fe^{+2}	0.077	0.092	
Fe^{+3}	0.063	0.0785	
Mg^{+2}	0.072	0.086	0.103
Mn^{+2}		0.097	0.107
Mn^{+3}		0.0785	
Mn^{+4}		0.068	
Ni^{+2}		0.083	
Pb^{+2}		0.132	0.145
Pr^{+3}		0.1137	0.128
Pr^{+4}		0.092	0.110
Sb^{+5}		0.075	
Sn^{+4}		0.083	
Ti^{+4}		0.0745	
V^{+4}		0.073	
V^{+5}	0.0495	0.068	
Zn^{+2}	0.074	0.089	0.104
Zr^{+4}		0.086	0.098

Data from reference M27.

Figure 8.12

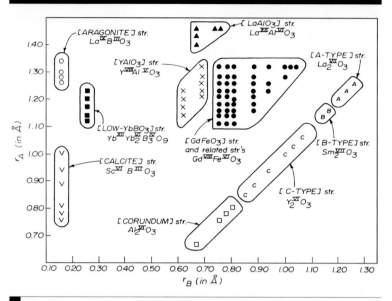

Structure field map of crystals with the $A^{+3}B^{+3}O_3$ stoichiometry.

Table 8-3 shows the effective ionic radii for the major pigmenting ions[E25] when they appear in tetrahedral, octahedral, or eight-fold coordination. The most striking conclusion from this table is that practically all of the pigmenting ions have radii between 0.075 and 0.095 nm. One may therefore conclude that crystal structures that accommodate ions in the range 0.07 to 0.10 nm will be the most likely to occur in a pigment structure.

Figure 8.12 is a structure field map for systems that crystallize in the $A^{+3}B^{+3}O_3$ stoichiometry. Examination of the area of interest indicates that the corundum structure may be of interest. In fact, the manganese alumina pinks, and some of the chrome alumina pinks, crystallize in that structure.

Figure 8.13 is a structure field map for systems which crystallize in the $A^{+4}B^{+4}O_4$ stoichiometry. The rutile structure is revealed as one of interest. Several pigment systems, such as those based on titanium dioxide and tin oxide, have this structure. Also indicated is a possibility that some materials having the zircon structure or the scheelite structure may be of interest. In both these structures, one of the ions would be of suitable size for a pigmenting ion, but the other would not. In practice, the zircon structure has been found to be of considerable value, while the scheelite structure has not been used so far.

Figure 8.14 is a structure field map for systems having the

Figure 8.13

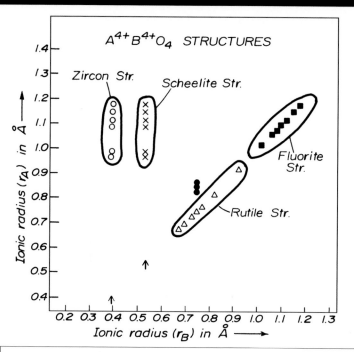

Structure field map of crystals with the $A^{+4}B^{+4}O_4$ stoichiometry.

Figure 8.14

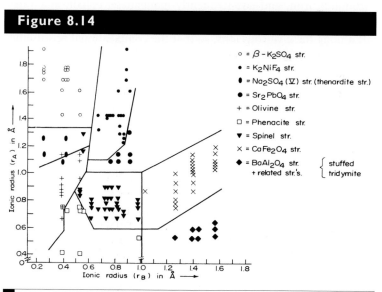

Structure field map of crystals with the AB_2O_4 stoichiometry.

AB_2O_4 stoichiometry. Examining the region of interest reveals a large number of compounds having the spinel structure. This system has found the widest use in the development of pigment systems. In addition, some materials having the olivine or phenacite structures may be of interest. Only one olivine, cobalt silicate, is currently used.

The spinel structure is the most common structure found in pigment systems. The model material is the mineral $MgAl_2O_4$. This mineral is cubic in structure, with a_o = 0.8083 nm. In this structure perfect MgO_4 tetrahedra share corners with slightly distorted AlO_6 octahedra. The unit cell has 32 anions and thus forms 64 tetrahedral interstices, of which 8 are occupied by cations, and 32 octahedral interstices, of which 16 are occupied by cations. Each oxygen ion is surrounded by four cations—three aluminum and one magnesium.

Although, as with all structures, there are definite ionic size relationships among the constituent ions that must be fulfilled, because these relationships are satisfied by the transition metal ions of the first period, the spinel structure is the most common of all the AB_2O_4 structures.

Several varieties of spinels can be made. Of these, the 3-to-2 spinels are probably the most common, the most typical, and the most important with respect to pigment systems. In the 3-to-2 spinels, the divalent ions may be magnesium, manganese, cobalt, nickel, copper, iron, and zinc. The trivalent ions can be aluminum, chromium, iron, and less frequently manganese, cobalt, and vanadium. Moreover, the spinels form an extensive series of mixed crystals among these various ions, so that the compositional possibilities are practically limitless. The pigments of this variety include most blacks, the cobalt aluminate blue, the cobalt-zinc-aluminum-chromium bluegreens, the chrome-aluminum-iron-zinc browns, and the majority of the chrome-alumina pinks.

The 2-to-4 spinels are also quite common, and a few of them are of interest as pigments. In this variety, the divalent ions can be magnesium, manganese, cobalt, nickel, copper, iron, or zinc. The tetravalent ions can be tin or titania. While these materials are not used as ceramic pigments, a nickel-zinc-cobalt titanate is used as a green pigment in paints.

The octahedral and tetrahedral interstices in spinels are of comparable size. Hence, the ions are arrayed over the available sites in accordance with their site preference energies.[M27] The octahedral site preference energies for some of the ions of interest are, in Kcal/mole: chromium III, +16.6; nickel II, +9.0; aluminum III, −2.5; iron II, −9.9; iron III, −13.3; and zinc II, −31.6. A more positive value for this number indicates preference for the octahedral sites, while a more negative number indicates preference for the tetrahedral sites. In some cases, this leads to unusual arrangements of the ions. For example, nickel ferrite is actually $Fe(FeNi)O_4$. Materials such as this are called inverse spinels.

The other crystal structure that is of particular importance for pigments is the zircon structure. The use of this structure, however, is different from that of the spinels. In the spinels, the color comes from the use of a transition metal ion as part of the chemical composition. In the case of zircon, however, the interest is in dispersing dopant ions in small concentrations within the structure of the model compound zirconium silicate.

The structure of zircon is tetragonal with a_o = 0.6616 nm and c_o = 0.6016 nm.[B2] It can be viewed as an array of anion complexes of SiO_4 in which are dispersed the zirconium cations. Since the ionic size of most coloring ions is 0.07 to 0.1 nm it may be assumed that most of the substitution occurs on the zirconium sites. The symmetry of the zirconium site in zircon is illustrated in Figure 8.15. The coordination is found to be eight-fold, with four Zr-O bonds 0.241 nm apart and four Zr-O bonds 0.205 nm. apart.

The optical effects of this strange symmetry have been worked out.[D4] It has been found that the four oxygens that are furthest from the zirconium ion act similarly to two oxygens located on the center line between the zirconium ion and the centroid of the two ions, to

Figure 8.15

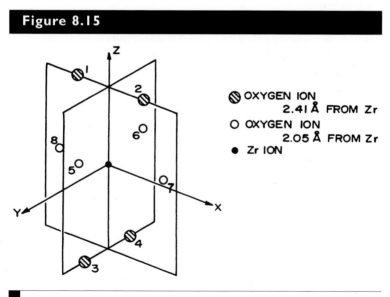

⊗ OXYGEN ION
    2.41 Å FROM Zr
○ OXYGEN ION
    2.05 Å FROM Zr
● Zr ION

Symmetry in the zircon structure.

give a pseudo-octahedral coordination. That is, referring to Figure 8.15, ions 1 and 2 act together as if there were one oxygen on the positive z axis at a distance from the zirconium ion equal to that of ions 5, 6, 7, and 8. The same is true for ions 3 and 4 acting like one oxygen ion on the negative z axis. Thus, while zirconium is an eight-fold coordinate in zircon, ions substituted for zirconium have a spectral effect not unlike that of an octahedrally coordinated ion.

The fact that all cations in the zircon structure are tetravalent leads to the fact that when vanadium is substituted for zirconium, it enters the lattice in the tetravalent state. For this reason, vanadium in zircon is blue. The ionic state of praseodymium in zircon is not well established. On the one hand, the yellow color would suggest a distorted version of the Pr^{+3} state, which is light yellow-green, rather than the Pr^{+4} state, which is usually found to be black (usually, because many praseodymium compounds are nonstoichiometric, which always leads to a black color). On the other hand, Pr^{+3} is probably too large to be accommodated in the zircon lattice, while the ionic size of Pr^{+4} is within the acceptable range of ionic size.

8.7 Oxide Pigments

Let's now examine some of the principal pigment systems. A wide variety of elements are available from which to choose in developing inorganic pigments. Furthermore, several crystalline systems are employed.

A systematic approach to the consideration of these materials has been developed by the Dry Color Manufacturers Association.[B11, D2] This approach classifies the 44 different pigment systems according to their principal colors and their crystal structures. This approach will be followed in discussing the major systems used in each color family. Of course, some crystalline systems and some pigmenting elements will appear in more than one family. On the other hand, certain colors, such as green and yellow, are obtained by several different systems. Table 8-4 lists the alternatives available for coloring ceramics. The details of their application are given in the subsections that follow.

8.7.1 Opacifiers (White pigments). Whiteness or opacity is introduced into ceramic coatings by adding a substance that disperses in the coating as discrete particles that scatter and reflect some of the incident light.[E27] In order to do this, the dispersed substance must have a refractive index that differs appreciably from that of the clear ceramic coating. The refractive index of most glasses is 1.5 to 1.6,

Table 8-4. Mixed-Metal Oxide Ceramic Pigments

Crystal Class, Name (Category)	CAS Registry Number	Chemical Formula	DCMA Number
Baddeleyite			
Zirconium vanadium yellow baddeleyite	68187-01-9	$(Zr,V)O_2$	1-01-4
Corundum/hematite			
Chrome alumina pink corundum	68187-27-9	$(Al,Cr)_2O_3$	3-03-5
Manganese alumina pink corundum	68176-99-2	$(Al,Mn)_2O_3$	3-04-5
Chromium green/black hematite	68909-79-5	Cr_2O_3	3-05-3
Iron brown hematite	68187-35-9	Fe_2O_3	3-06-7
Garnet			
Victoria green garnet	68553-01-5	$3CaO \cdot Cr_2O_3 \cdot 3SiO_2$	4-07-3
Olivine			
Cobalt silicate blue olivine	68187-40-6	Co_2SiO_4	5-08-2
Nickel silicate green olivine	68515-84-4	Ni_2SiO_4	5-45-3
Periclase			
Cobalt nickel gray periclase	68186-89-0	$(Co,Ni)O$	6-09-8
Phenacite			
Cobalt zinc silicate blue phenacite	68412-74-8	$(Co,Zn)_2SiO_4$	7-10-2
Pyrochlore			
Lead antimonate yellow pyrochlore	68187-20-2	$Pb_2Sb_2O_7$	10-14-4
Rutile/Cassiterite			
Nickel antimony titanium yellow rutile	71077-18-4	$(Ti,Ni,Sb)O_2$	11-15-4
Nickel niobium titanium yellow rutile	68611-43-8	$(Ti,Ni,Nb)O_2$	11-16-4
Chrome antimony titanium buff rutile	68186-90-3	$(Ti,Cr,Sb)O_2$	11-17-6

Table 8-4. Mixed-Metal Oxide Ceramic Pigments

Crystal Class, Name (Category)	CAS Registry Number	Chemical Formula	DCMA Number
Rutile/Cassiterite			
Chrome niobium titanium buff rutile	68611-42-7	$(Ti,Cr,Nb)O_2$	11-18-6
Chrome tungsten titanium buff rutile	68186-92-5	$(Ti,Cr,W)O_2$	11-19-6
Manganese antimony titanium buff rutile	68412-38-4	$(Ti,Mn,Sb)O_2$	11-20-6
Vanadium antimony titanium gray rutile	68187-00-8	$(Ti,V,Sb)O_2$	11-21-8
Tin vanadium yellow cassiterite	68186-93-6	$(Sn,V)O_2$	11-22-4
Chrome tin orchid cassiterite	68187-53-1	$(Sn,Cr)O_2$	11-23-5
Tin antimony gray cassiterite	68187-54-2	$(Sn,Sb)O_2$	11-24-8
Manganese chrome antimony titanium brown rutile	69991-68-0	$(Ti,Mn,Cr,Sb)O_2$	11-46-7
Manganese niobium titanium brown rutile	70248-09-8	$(Ti,Mn,Nb)O_2$	11-47-7
Sphene			
Chrome tin pink sphene	68187-12-2	$CaO.SnO_2 \cdot SiO_2 \cdot Cr$	12-25-8
Spinel			
Cobalt aluminate blue spinel	68186-86-7	$CoAl_2O_4$	13-26-2
Cobalt tin blue-gray spinel	68187-05-3	Co_2SnO_4	13-27-2
Cobalt zinc aluminate blue spinel	68186-87-8	$(Co,Zn)Al_2O_4$	13-28-2
Cobalt chromite bluegreen spinel	68187-11-1	$Co(Al,Cr)O_4$	13-29-2
Cobalt chromite green spinel	68187-49-5	$CoCr_2O_4$	13-30-3
Cobalt titanate green spinel	68186-85-6	Co_2TiO_4	13-31-3
Chrome alumina pink spinel	68201-65-0	$Zn(Al,Cr)_2O_4$	13-32-5
Iron chromite brown spinel	68187-09-7	$Fe(Fe,Cr)_2O_4$	13-33-7
Iron titanium brown spinel	68187-02-0	Fe_2TiO_4	13-34-7
Nickel ferrite brown spinel	68187-10-0	$NiFe_2O_4$	13-35-7
Zinc ferrite brown spinel	68187-31-9	$ZnFe_2O_4$	13-36-7
Zinc iron chromite brown spinel	68186-88-9	$(Zn,Fe)(Fe,Cr)_2O_4$	13-37-7
Copper chromite black spinel	68186-91-4	$CuCr_2O_4$	13-38-9
Iron cobalt black spinel	68187-50-8	$(Fe,Co)Fe_2O_4$	13-39-9
Iron cobalt chromite black spinel	68186-97-0	$(Co,Fe)(Fe,Cr)_2O_4$	13-40-9

Table 8-4. Mixed-Metal Oxide Ceramic Pigments

Crystal Class, Name (Category)	CAS Registry Number	Chemical Formula	DCMA Number
Spinel			
Manganese ferrite black spinel	68186-94-7	(Fe,Mn) (Fe, Mn)	13-31-9
Chrome iron manganese brown spinel	68555-06-6	(Fe,Mn) (Fe,Cr,Mn)$_2$O$_4$	13-48-7
Cobalt tin alumina blue spinel	71750-83-9	CoAl$_2$O$_4$/Co$_2$SnO$_4$	13-49-2
Chromium iron nickel black spinel	71631-15-7	(Ni,Fe) (Fe,Cr)$_2$O$_4$	13-50-7
Chromium manganese zinc brown spinel	71750-83-9	(Zn,Mn)Cr$_2$O$_4$	13-51-7
Zircon			
Zirconium vanadium blue zircon	68186-95-8	(Zr,V)SiO$_4$	14-42-2
Zirconium praseodymium yellow zircon	68187-15-5	(Zr,Pr)SiO$_4$	14-43-4
Zirconium iron pink zircon	68187-13-3	(Zr,Fe)SiO$_4$	14-44-5

and therefore the refractive indices of opacifiers must be either greater or less than this. As a practical matter, opacifiers of high refractive index are used. Some possibilities are tin oxide, with a refractive index of 2.04, zirconia, with a refractive index of 2.40, zircon, with a refractive index of 1.85, and titania, with a refractive index of 2.5 for anatase and 2.7 for rutile.

In glazes and other ceramic coatings fired at temperatures above 1000°C, zircon is the opacifier of choice.[B6, E27] It has a solubility of about 5% in many glazes at high temperature, and 2 to 3 percent at room temperature. A customary mill addition would be 6 to 10% zircon if color is also to be introduced, and 15% for a white. Thus, most opacified glazes contain both zircon that was placed in the mill and went through the firing process unchanged, and zircon that dissolved in the molten glaze during firing, but recrystallized on cooling.

The maximum opacity is given by that opacifier which has the finest particle size. Since this greater fineness is achieved by milling, the finer zircons are also the most expensive. On the other hand, zircon for smelting into frit is best when intermediate in size. The effectiveness of the zircon opacifiers can therefore be improved in partially or fully fritted glazes by melting some of the zircon into the frit.

Zirconia is seldom used as an opacifier because in most glazes it reacts with the silica in the glaze to form zircon.[J1] Hence, since zircon is much less expensive than zirconia, zircon is the opacifier used. Tin oxide is a more effective opacifier than any of the other possibilities because it has the lowest solubility—less than 1% in most glazes. However, the high price of tin oxide restricts its use to those special cases, such as with chrome-tin pinks, where it also enhances the effectiveness of the coloring pigments.

In porcelain enamels, and in glazes firing at less than 1000°C, titania in the anatase crystal form is the opacifying agent of choice.[E3, S8] Because it has the highest refractive index, titania is the most effective opacifying agent one can use. However, at a temperature of about 850°C, anatase inverts to rutile in silicates. Once inverted to rutile, titania crystals can grow rapidly to sizes that are no longer effective for opacification. Moreover, because the absorption edge of rutile is very close to the visible, as the rutile particles grow the absorption edge extends into the visible, leading to a pronounced cream color. Thus, while titania is a very effective opacifier at lower temperatures, it cannot be used above 1000°C.

The solubility of titania in molten silicates is around 8 to 10%. At room temperature, this solubility is reduced to around 5%. Thus, when using titania as an opacifier, substantial amounts, about 15% or more, must be used. An appreciable percentage of the opacifier will dissolve in the molten ceramic coating and recrystallize on cooling. In many titania-opacified porcelain enamels, all the titania dissolves in the frit and is recrystallized during the firing of the ceramic coating.

When a pastel color is required, one adds an opacifier plus a pigment to the ceramic coating. The compatibility of the pigment and opacifier is important. For example, zircon opacifier should be used with zircon or zirconia-based pigments. Chrome-tin pinks are stronger if some tin oxide opacifier is used. Titanium-based pigments used in enamels require titania opacifier.

8.7.2 Black and Gray Pigments. Black ceramic pigments are formed by the calcination of several oxides to form the spinel structure.[E20, V3] The formulation of blacks illustrates the wide flexibility of the spinel structure in incorporating various chemical entities. The divalent ion may be cobalt, manganese, nickel, iron, or copper. The trivalent ions may be iron, chromium, manganese, or aluminum. Table 8-4 lists five different black spinel pigments: copper chromite

Table 8-5. Typical Black Pigments

Oxide	Content (percent)						
	A	**B**	**C**	**D**	**E**	**F**	**G**
CoO	34.1	27.2	37.6	12.9	-	-	-
CuO	-	-	-	-	34.3	-	-
FeO	-	-	-	9.2	-	25.0	-
NiO	-	5.7	-	10.9	-	-	32.4
Al_2O_3	-	-	1.3	5.9	-	-	-
Cr_2O_3	31.9	30.8	-	27.3	65.7	75.0	33.0
Fe_2O_3	34.0	36.3	46.6	18.0	-	-	34.6
Mn_2O_3	-	-	14.5	15.8	-	-	-
Total	100.0	100.0	100.0	100.0	100.0	100.0	100.0

black spinel, iron cobalt black spinel, iron cobalt chromite black spinel, manganese ferrite black spinel, and chromium iron nickel black spinel.

The selection of a particular black pigment depends somewhat on the coating material with which the pigment is to be used. If care is not taken, the pigment may show a green, blue, or brown tint after firing. Of particular importance in this connection is the tendency of the glaze to attack the pigment and release cobalt. Thus, in some cases it is desirable to use a cobalt-free pigment.

Table 8-5 gives the formulae of some typical black pigments. Formula A is a typical cobalt-chrome-iron black. In some systems, however, it will have a slight greenish tint. In zinc-containing glazes, Formula B would be recommended. For a black with a slightly bluish tint, Formula C containing manganese and higher cobalt would be recommended. For a black with a brownish tint, one would recommend a complex formula like D. When a cobalt-free system is needed, Formulas E, F, or G can be considered. Formula E is a copper chromite that is suitable for use in coatings firing below 1000°C, such as porcelain enamels. Formula F is a mixed spinel-corundum system that is suitable for use in zinc-free coatings. This is the least expensive black on the market for use in coatings firing over 1000°C. However, if zinc oxide is present, it will react with the pigment to form a brown color. Formula G is a relatively new pigment developed to provide a cobalt-free system of general usefulness. It can be used with most glaze systems, and at all reasonable firing temperatures.

The appearance of a black in a glaze is shown in Figure 8.16. The dark tiles are a masstone with 2% pigment. The lighter tiles are

Figure 8.16

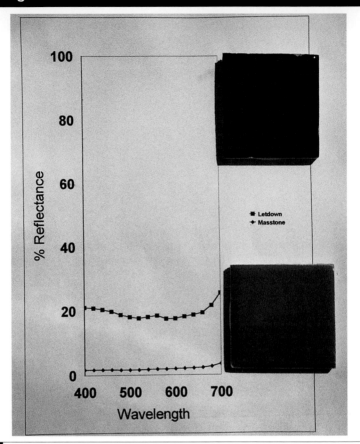

Spectral reflectance of a glaze with a black pigment: (a) masstone with 2% pigment (b) letdown with 1/2% pigment, 6.3% opacifier.

a letdown with 0.5% pigment and 6.3% opacifier. This figure also illustrates that the simplest way to get a gray is to dilute a black pigment with a white opacifier. This dilution must be done with great care to provide an even color, without specking. It is usually preferable to use a compound that has been formulated to give a gray color.

Figure 8.17 shows that more uniform results are obtained when a calcined pigment is used that is based upon zirconia or zircon, doped with the various ingredients of blacks such as cobalt, nickel, iron, and chromium oxides.

For certain special effects in underglaze decorations, it is possible to prepare a very beautiful deep gray color (Figure 8.18) by dispersing antimony oxide in tin oxide. The limitation on the use of

Figure 8.17

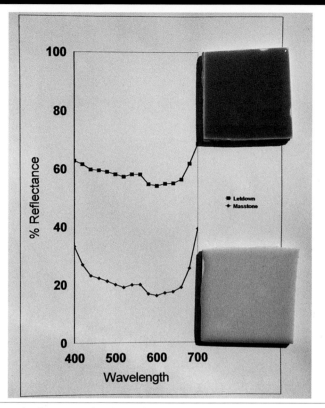

Spectral reflectance of a glaze with a zirconia gray pigment: (a) masstone with 2% pigment; (b) letdown with 1/2% pigment, 6.3% opacifier.

these materials is the high cost of the tin oxide, which limits their use to special effects.

An important point to note with grays is the many subtle shade variations that are possible. With appropriate blending of three or four carefully chosen pigments, many different shades are possible.

8.7.3 Blue Pigments. The traditional way to obtain blue in a ceramic coating is with cobalt, which has been used as a solution color since antiquity.[M9] Today, cobalt, as shown in Figure 8.19, may be reacted with alumina to produce the spinel cobalt aluminate, or with silica to produce the olivine structure cobalt silicate. The silicate involves the use of higher concentrations of cobalt, with only modestly stronger color.

At the lower temperatures encountered in porcelain enamels and glass colors, pigments based on cobalt continue to be fully satisfac-

Figure 8.18

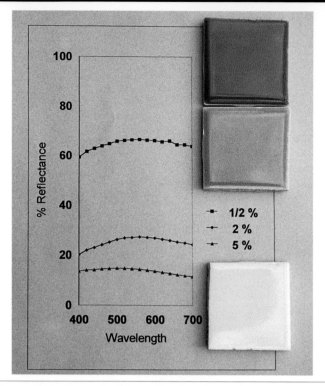

Spectral reflectance of a glaze with a tin antimony gray pigment: (a) masstone with 5% pigment; (b) masstone with 2% pigment; (c) letdown with 1/2% pigment, 6.3% opacifier.

tory both for stability and for tinting strength, which is quite high.[E29] At the higher firing temperatures encountered with ceramic glazes, however, difficulties arise from partial solution of the pigment, resulting in diffusion of the cobalt oxide in the glaze, giving a defect commonly called "cobalt bleeding." Thus, in glazes, the cobalt pigments have been largely replaced by pigments based on vanadium-doped zircon.

These pigments, which are illustrated on Figure 8.20, are less intense than the cobalt pigments and tend toward turquoise. Therefore, they are not applicable in all cases. Where they are applicable, they give vastly improved stability.

The zircon vanadium blue pigment is made by calcining a mixture of zirconia, silica, and vanadia in the stoichiometry of zircon, and in the presence of a mineralizer.[E6, E16] The latter materials, which are selected from the various halides and silicohalides, facilitate the transport of the silica during the reaction that forms the pigment. For the development of a strong blue color, it is necessary to retain the stoichiometry of zircon and to use such mineralizers as will facilitate the various transport processes and incorporate the optimum amount of vanadium into the zircon structure when it is formed.

With these pigments, it is generally best to use zircon for any opacification. It is also desirable to have some zircon in the glaze to promote the stability of the pigment.

8.7.4 Green Pigments. There are several ways to obtain green pigmentation in a ceramic coating.[H5] Five of the most important will be reviewed.

Historically, the basis of most green pigmentation was the

Figure 8.19

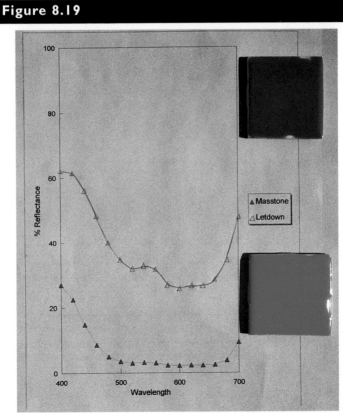

Spectral reflectance of a glaze with a cobalt blue pigment:
(a) masstone with 2% pigment; (b) letdown with 1/2% pigment, 6.3% opacifier.

Figure 8.20

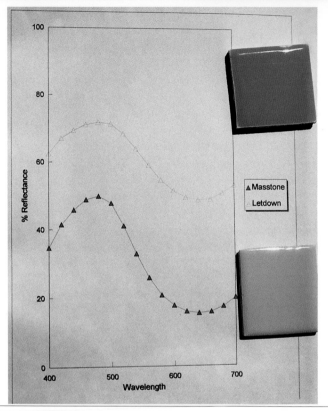

Spectral reflectance of a glaze with a zircon vanadium blue pigment:
(a) masstone with 2% pigment; (b) letdown with 1/2% pigment,
6.3% opacifier.

chromium ion. First, as shown in Figure 8.21, chromium III oxide itself can be used to produce a green color. This procedure, however, has a number of limitations. In the first place, there is some tendency for pure chromium oxide to fume or volatilize during the firing process, which leads to absorption into the refractory lining of the furnace used. Secondly, if tin-containing white pigments or pastel colors containing tin are also in the furnace, the chrome will react with the tin to form a pink coloration. Finally, the ceramic coating into which chromium oxide is placed must not contain zinc oxide, because zinc in the coating reacts with chromium oxide to produce an undesirable dirty brown color.

More satisfactory results are obtained if chromium oxide is used as part of a calcined pigment. One such system is the cobalt-zinc-alumina-chromite bluegreen pigments (Figure 8.22). These pigments

Figure 8.21

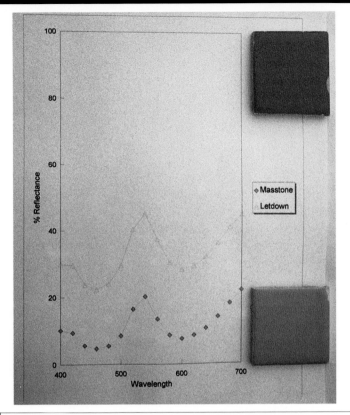

Spectral reflectance of a glaze with a chrome green pigment: (a) masstone with 2% pigment; (b) letdown with 1/2% pigment, 6.3% opacifier.

are spinels in which varying amounts of cobalt and zinc oxides appear in the tetrahedral sites and varying amounts of alumina and chromium oxide appear on the octahedral sites. By using higher amounts of chromium oxide and lower amounts of cobalt oxide, the greener pigments are obtained. Conversely, by lowering the amounts of chromium oxide and raising the amounts of cobalt oxide, shades from bluegreen to blue are obtained. These pigments should not be used in low concentrations because they give an undesirable dirty gray color.

The final type of chromium oxide–containing green color is the Victoria green shown in Figure 8.23. This material is prepared by calcining silica and a dichromate with calcium carbonate, to form the garnet structure. This pigment gives a beautiful bright green color, but is very transparent. It tends to blacken if applied too thinly. It is

149

Figure 8.22

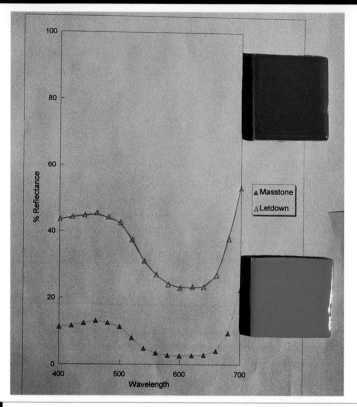

Spectral reflectance of a glaze with a cobalt chrome bluegreen pigment:
(a) masstone with 2% pigment; (b) letdown with 1/2% pigment,
6.3% opacifier.

not satisfactory for opaque glazes or pastel shades, for in letdown it
gives a gray cast. It can be used only in zinc oxide free coatings with
high calcium oxide content. In addition, this is a difficult pigment to
manufacture correctly, so the price is high.

Because of all the difficulties mentioned in the use of chromium-
containing pigments and because there is a definite limit to the bril-
liance of green pigments made with chromium oxide, many ceramic
glazes have been converted to pigments in the zircon system,[E4] as
shown in Figure 8.24. The cleanest, most stable greens are obtained
today by the use of blends of a zircon vanadium blue, which we
have already discussed, and a zircon praseodymium yellow, which
we will discuss shortly. The bright green shades are obtained from a
mixture of about two parts of the yellow pigment to one part of the
blue pigment.

Figure 8.23

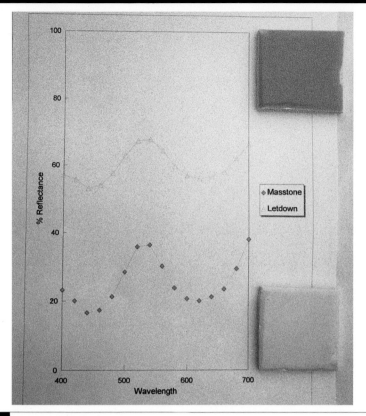

Spectral reflectance of a glaze with a Victoria green pigment: (a) masstone with 2% pigment; (b) letdown with 1/2% pigment, 6.3% opacifier.

The final green to be discussed is the use of copper compounds for low-temperature firing applications (Figure 8.25). The use of copper is of little interest to most industrial manufacturers, but it is of great interest to art potters because of the many subtle shades that can be obtained. This occurs because the pH of the glaze used has a particular effect on the colors obtained from copper. If the coating is alkaline, a turquoise blue color results, but if the coating is acidic, a beautiful green color results. The copper oxide dissolves in the coating, so a very transparent color is obtained. Copper oxide volatilizes above 1000°C, so it should not be used above that temperature.

Another limitation on the use of copper colors is that copper oxide renders any coating unsafe for contact with food or drink.[E12] Copper pigments should never be used on any article that may come in contact with food or drink.

Figure 8.24

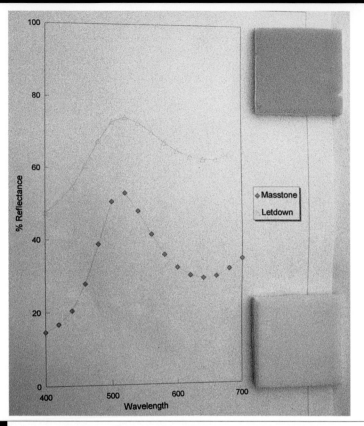

Spectral reflectance of a green glaze with mixed zircon praseodymium yellow and zircon vanadium blue pigments: (a) masstone with 2% pigment; (b) letdown with 1/2% pigment, 6.3% opacifier.

8.7.5 Yellow Pigments. Just as there are a number of systems for preparing green colors, there are also several systems for preparing a yellow ceramic color.[E29] In the case of yellows, however, there are valid technical and economic reasons for the use of a particular yellow pigment in a given application. The pigments of greatest tinting strength, the lead antimonate yellows and the chrome titania maples, do not have adequate resistance to molten ceramic coatings. Thus, other systems must be used if the firing temperature is above 1000°C.

For applications firing above 1000°C, the zirconia vanadia yellows are worthy of consideration. They are prepared by calcining zirconia with small amounts of vanadia[B7, S4](Figure 8.26). Small

Figure 8.25

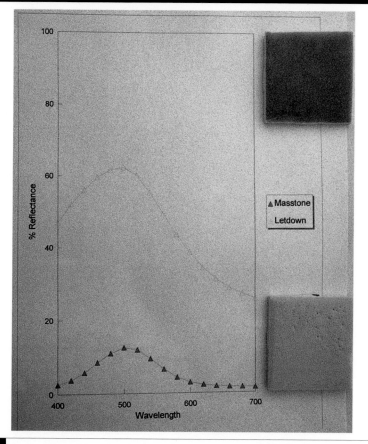

Spectral reflectance of a glaze with a copper oxide pigment: (a) masstone with 2% pigment; (b) letdown with 1/2% pigment, 6.3% opacifier.

amounts of titania and/or iron oxide may be used to alter the shade. In the absence of these latter materials, a lemon yellow shade is obtained. In their presence, an orange-yellow results. In ceramic coatings, zirconia vanadia yellows are usually weaker than tin vanadium yellows and muddier than zircon praseodymium yellows. However, they are economical pigments for use with a broad range of coatings fired above 1000°C.

Tin vanadium yellows (Figure 8.27) are prepared by introducing small amounts of vanadium oxide into the cassiterite structure of tin oxide.[R4] Tin vanadium yellows develop a strong yellow color in all ceramic coating compositions. They are very opaque pigments, requiring little further opacification. The primary deterrent to their

Figure 8.26

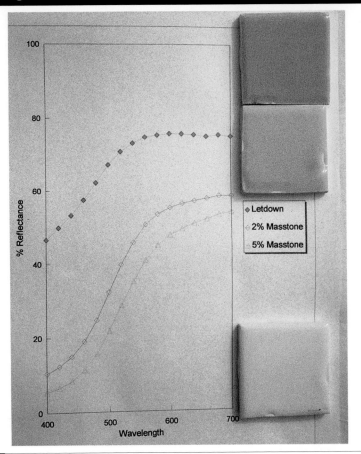

Spectral reflectance of a glaze with a zirconia vanadium yellow pigment: (a) masstone with 5 % pigment; (b) masstone with 2% pigment; (c) letdown with 1/2% pigment, 6.3% opacifier.

use is the very high cost of the tin oxide, which forms their major component. As a result, together with the improvement of the zircon praseodymium yellow, which we will discuss next, the use of this pigment is now minimal.

The zircon praseodymium yellow pigments (Figure 8.28) are formed by the calcination of about 5% praseodymium oxide with a stoichiometric mixture of zirconia and silica, and in the presence of a mineralizer.[E8, E16] The result is a bright yellow pigment. It is quite analogous to the zircon vanadium blue pigment in that the crystal structure is zircon. These pigments have excellent tinting strength in high-temperature coatings. They can be used in almost any ceramic

Figure 8.27

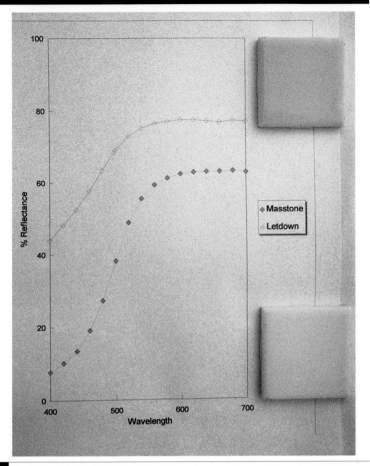

Spectral reflectance of a glaze with a tin vanadium yellow pigment: (a) masstone with 2% pigment; (b) letdown with 1/2% pigment, 6.3% opacifier.

coating, although preferably with zircon opacifiers. They blend well with other pigments, particularly with zircon- and zirconia-based pigments. They are finding increased usage for all applications in which the firing temperature exceeds 1000°C.

For lower-temperature applications, the tinting strength of the lead antimonate pigments is unsurpassed, except by the cadmium sulfoselenides, which will be discussed later, and which are very toxic and expensive. These pigments (Figure 8.29), which are often called Naples yellow, are very clean and bright, and have good covering power, requiring little or no opacifier. Their primary limitation is their instability above 1000°C, which leads to volatilization of the

Figure 8.28

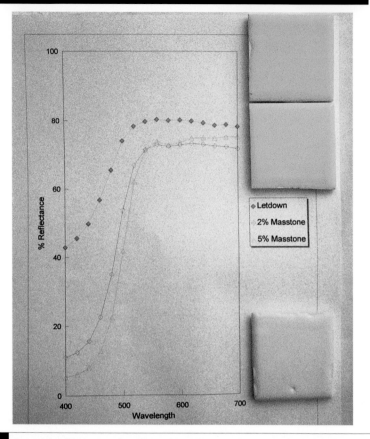

Spectral reflectance of a glaze with a zircon praseodymium yellow pigment: (a) masstone with 5% pigment; (b) masstone with 2% pigment; (c) letdown with 1/2% pigment, 6.3% opacifier.

antimony oxide. Substitutions of ceria, alumina, or tin oxide are sometimes made for a portion of the antimony oxide to improve stability, but these are just palliatives. Their use is pretty much limited to coatings such as porcelain enamels, which fire at lower temperatures.

One final orange-yellow pigment remains to be considered. A pigment is formed when chromium oxide is added to antimony oxide and titania to form a doped rutile.[E37] This material (Figure 8.30) gives an orange-yellow or maple shade useful at lower temperatures. It decomposes around 1000°C. It has substantial use in porcelain enamels, where it is the basis for such appliance colors as harvest and avocado.

Figure 8.29

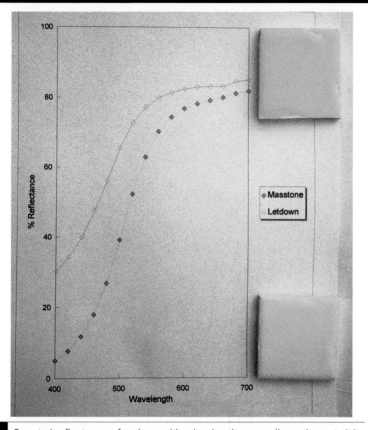

Spectral reflectance of a glaze with a lead antimony yellow pigment: (a) masstone with 2% pigment; (b) letdown with 1/2% pigment, 6.3% opacifier.

8.7.6 Brown Pigments. By far the most important brown pigments used in ceramic coatings today are the zinc-iron-chromite spinels,[M5, M23] shown in Figure 8.31. This family produces a wide palette of tan and brown shades, and it can be controlled with reasonable care to produce uniformity within the production variables existing in commercial plants. Within the spinel structure, the zinc oxide will be found on the tetrahedral sites, and the chromium oxide on the octahedral sites. The iron oxide will be distributed in such a way as to fulfill the requirements of the structure. As a result, adjusting the formula alters the shade. For example, minor additions of nickel oxide to this system produce a dark chocolate brown. The presence or absence of iron oxide on the tetrahedral site affects the yellowness of the shade. Because they are compara-

Figure 8.30

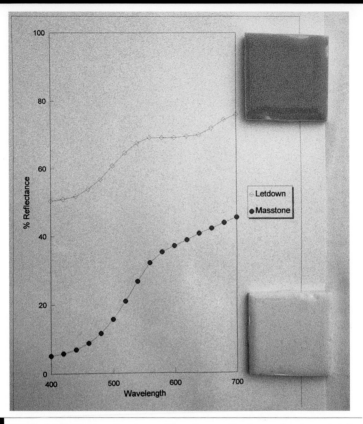

Spectral reflectance of a glaze with a chrome titania maple pigment: (a) masstone with 2% pigment; (b) letdown with 1/2% pigment, 6.3% opacifier.

tively low in price, these pigments are the browns selected for most applications.

Two systems closely related to the zinc-iron-chromites have been developed to improve the firing range and stability of brown pigments.[E27] The first of these is the zinc-iron-chrome-aluminate pigments shown in Figure 8.32. These are really hybrids of the zinc-iron-chromite brown and the chrome-alumina pink. They produce warm and orange-brown shades with improved firing stability. They must be used in coatings high in zinc oxide and alumina and low in calcia.

Another related pigment is the chrome-iron-tin brown, shown in Figure 8.33, and often called a tin tan. It must always be used in a zinc oxide–containing coating. The reason is that the pigment

Figure 8.31

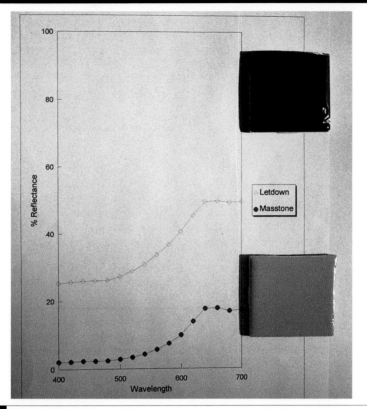

Spectral reflectance of a glaze with a chrome iron zinc brown pigment:
(a) masstone with 2% pigment; (b) letdown with 1/2% pigment,
6.3% opacifier.

requires zinc oxide from the coating to react during the firing process to produce a zinc-iron-chromite pigment. This pigment is characterized by excellent stability at low concentrations. Thus, it makes an excellent toner for some tan and beige shades, in blends with various pink pigments.

The final brown pigment to be considered is the iron manganese brown (Figure 8.34). This hematite pigment is the deep brown associated with electrical porcelain insulators and with artware and bean pots. In medium to light shades, the presence of manganese will often lead to a poor surface and unstable color. Hence, the use of this pigment is limited.

Figure 8.32

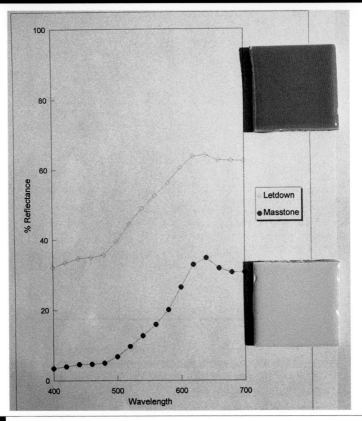

Spectral reflectance of a glaze with a chrome iron zinc alumina maple pigment: (a) masstone with 2% pigment; (b) letdown with 1/2% pigment, 6.3% opacifier.

8.7.7 Pink, Purple, and Maroon Pigments. Although true red is not available in oxide systems, pink, purple, brick red, and maroon shades are obtained in several ways.[E29] One such system is the chrome alumina pinks (Figure 8.35), which are similar in crystal structure and behavior to the zinc-iron-chromite browns, except for the absence of iron oxide.[H3] Chrome alumina pinks are combinations of zinc oxide, alumina, and chrome oxide. Depending on the concentration of zinc oxide, the structure may be either spinel or corundum. The latter is analogous to the ruby.

In general, a ceramic coating formulated for the use of a chrome alumina pink should be free of calcia, low in lead oxide and boron oxide, and with a surplus of zinc oxide and alumina. Sufficient zinc

Figure 8.33

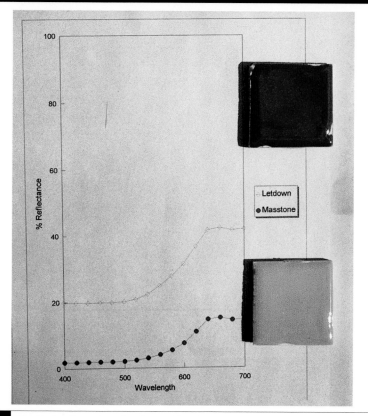

Spectral reflectance of a glaze with a tin tan pigment: (a) masstone with 2% pigment; (b) letdown with 1/2% pigment, 6.3% opacifier.

oxide must be present to prevent the glaze from attacking the pigment and removing zinc oxide from it.

A related, but somewhat stronger pink pigment is the manganese alumina pink, shown in Figure 8.36. This pigment is formulated by adding manganese oxide and phosphate to alumina. A very pure, clean pigment is obtained. It requires a zinc-free coating high in alumina. Unfortunately, the manufacture of this pigment involves the creation of some serious pollution problems. As a result, several manufacturers have stopped making it, so there is doubt about its continued availability.

The most stable pink pigment is the zircon-iron system, shown in Figure 8.37. This pigment is made by calcining a mixture of zirconia, silica, and iron oxide together with a stoichiometry to

Figure 8.34

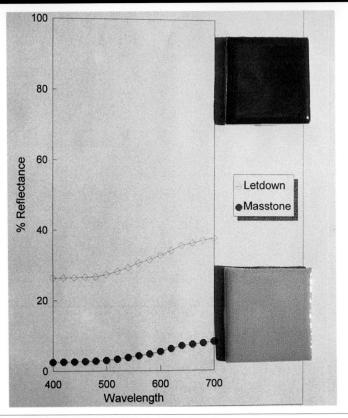

Spectral reflectance of a glaze with a iron manganese brown pigment: (a) masstone with 2% pigment; (b) letdown with 1/2% pigment, 6.3% opacifier.

produce zircon.[E16, E19] This pigment is sensitive to details of the manufacturing process, so one manufacturer's product might not duplicate another's.[L1] Shades extend from coral to pink. They are stable in all coating systems, but those without zinc oxide are bluer.

The final pink system, and the only one to produce purple and maroon shades as well as pinks, and the closest one can come to red in an oxide system, is the chrome-tin system. It can be defined as pigments that are produced by the calcination of mixtures of small amounts of chromium oxide with substantial amounts of tin oxide. In addition, most such materials have substantial amounts of silica and calcium oxide in the formulation.

The chemistry of these materials is very complex, and only recently has their chemical nature been worked out. If one mixes

Figure 8.35

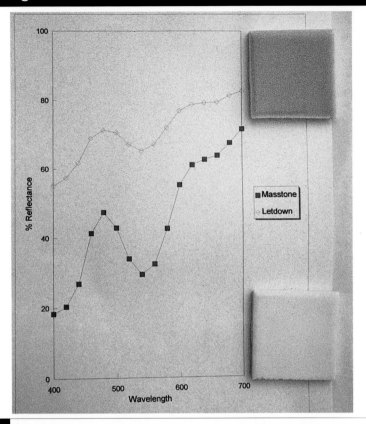

Spectral reflectance of a glaze with a chrome alumina pink pigment: (a) masstone with 2% pigment; (b) letdown with 1/2% pigment, 6.3% opacifier.

about 90 percent tin oxide with small amounts of chromium oxide, and either calcia or ceria together with boron oxide as a mineralizer, one obtains a purple or orchid-colored pigment (Figure 8.38). The crystal structure is cassiterite, and it can therefore be considered a solid solution of chromium oxide in tin oxide. While this is not the crystal structure of most chrome-tin pinks, residual amounts are present in almost all cases. It is this residual amount of chromium-doped tin oxide that gives most chrome-tin pinks a somewhat gray or purple overtone.

For most chrome-tin pinks, additions of substantial amounts of calcia and silica are required. Only in the presence of these materials can pink, red, or maroon shades be obtained (Figure 8.39). Here the crystal structure is tin sphene, in which chromium oxide is dissolved

Figure 8.36

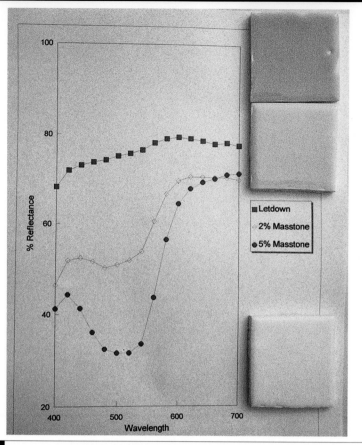

Spectral reflectance of a glaze with a manganese alumina pink pigment: (a) masstone with 5% pigment; (b) masstone with 2% pigment; (c) letdown with 1/2% pigment, 6.3% opacifier.

as an impurity.[E15] The color of this pigment depends to a great extent on the ratio of chromium oxide to tin oxide. Generally speaking, when the ratio is 1 to 5, the resulting color is green; when it is 1 to 15, the color is purple; when the ratio is 1 to 17, the color is red or maroon; and when it is 1 to 25, the color is pink. These pigments must be used in a coating low in zinc oxide, high in calcia. Some tin oxide should be used as an opacifier.

Figure 8.37

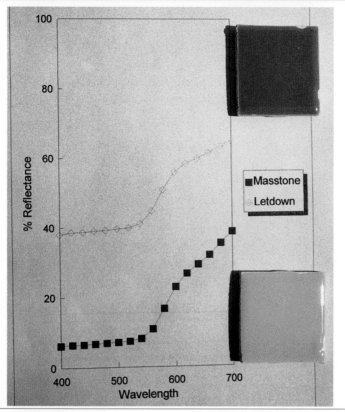

Spectral reflectance of a glaze with a zircon iron pink pigment: (a) masstone with 2% pigment; (b) letdown with 1/2% pigment, 6.3% opacifier.

8.8 Cadmium Sulfoselenide And Inclusion Pigments

Thus far we have examined only oxide pigments. Oxide pigments are preferred because they are more stable in the oxide environment of a molten silicate glaze. However, to date it has been impossible to obtain a bright red color using oxide pigments. Therefore, it has been necessary to use one nonoxide system—the cadmium sulfoselenide reds and yellows—to obtain that important part of color space.

The cadmium sulfoselenides are based upon solid solutions of cadmium selenide, cadmium sulfide, and/or zinc sulfide.[E23] They are made both as pure colors and as extended pigments containing

Figure 8.38

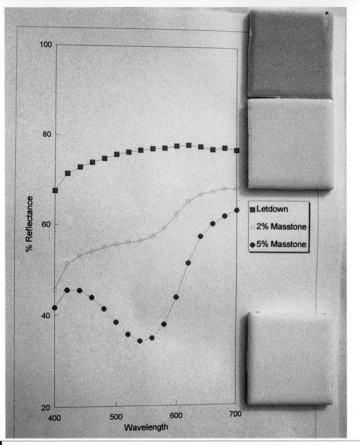

Spectral reflectance of a glaze with a chrome-tin orchid pigment: (a) masstone with 5% pigment; (b) masstone with 2% pigment; (c) letdown with 1/2% pigment, 6.3% opacifier.

barium sulfate. The latter group of pigments are called lithopones. They are much more widely used than the pure pigments. However, for ceramic use, the pure pigments are necessary.

The basic material, cadmium sulfide, may be either amorphous or crystalline. The crystalline form is dimorphous, and most processes produce some of both forms. The alpha modification is lemon yellow in color and hexagonal. The beta form is vermilion in color and cubic.

The synthetic pigment is produced by one of several related procedures:

Figure 8.39

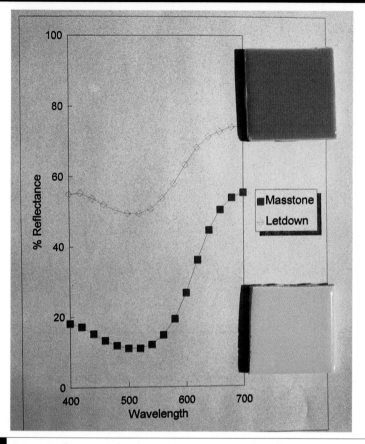

Spectral reflectance of a glaze with a chrome-tin pink pigment: (a) masstone with 2% pigment; (b) letdown with 1/2% pigment, 6.3% opacifier.

- Fuse cadmium oxide or cadmium carbonate with sulfur.
- Vaporize cadmium and sulfur in the absence of air.
- Melt sodium thiosulfate in its own water of crystallization, then add cadmium sulfate and calcine at 400 to 500°C.
- The best quality product is made by reacting an aqueous solution of cadmium sulfate or cadmium chloride with a solution of an alkaline metal sulfide. Zinc, selenium, or mercury may be added to the cadmium sulfide to produce color variations. After precipitation, the color is filtered, washed, and calcined in an inert atmosphere. The process requires very careful control of the precipitation and calcination steps, in order to obtain the desired color and physical properties.

Figure 8.40

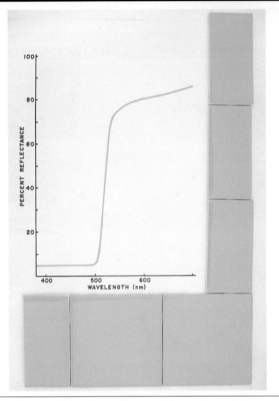

Spectral reflectance of a glaze with a cadmium yellow pigment.

The pure cadmium sulfoselenide colors come in a range of shades from primrose yellow, through yellow and orange, to red and maroon. Cadmium sulfide itself is a yellow to orange color, depending on details of its manufacture and the ratio of the alpha to beta forms of the crystal.

Figure 8.40 shows the primrose or light yellow color. It is produced by the precipitation of a small amount of zinc sulfide with the cadmium sulfide. This pigment has 90% cadmium sulfide, 10% zinc sulfide.

The orange, red, and maroon shades are made by incorporating increasing amounts of selenium compounds with the cadmium sulfide. For example, the orange pigment shown in Figure 8.41 has 79% cadmium sulfide and 19.5% cadmium selenide. The ratio of cadmium sulfide to cadmium selenide is about 4:1.

The red pigment shown in Figure 8.42 has 62.5% cadmium

Figure 8.41

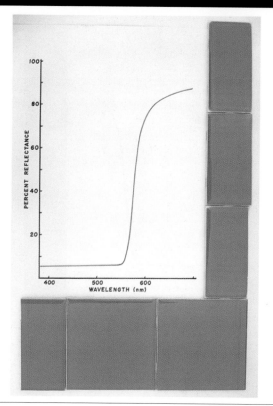

Spectral reflectance of a glaze with a cadmium orange pigment.

sulfide and 36.5% cadmium selenide. The ratio of cadmium sulfide to cadmium selenide is about 1.7:1.

A deeper red pigment shown in Figure 8.43 is formed from a mixture of 55.5% cadmium sulfide and 43.5% cadmium selenide. The ratio of cadmium sulfide to cadmium selenide is about 1.3:1.

A very deep red-maroon pigment shown in Figure 8.44 is manufactured from a mixture of 50.5% cadmium sulfide and 48% cadmium selenide. This shows the shade that occurs at a ratio of cadmium sulfide to cadmium selenide of 1:1.

By raising the concentration of cadmium selenide above that of cadmium sulfide, one can produce true maroon shades. However, these are rarely used in ceramics because they are not sufficiently different from chrome-tin pink pigments.

Cadmium sulfoselenide pigments require a glaze specially designed for this purpose. The glaze will contain only small amounts

Figure 8.42

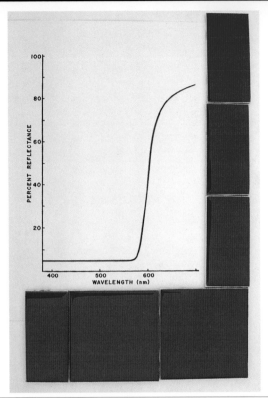

■ Spectral reflectance of a glaze with a cadmium light red pigment.

of lead oxide, since high lead fluxes react with the selenium in a cadmium sulfoselenide pigment to form lead selenide. It should be low in boron oxide and other aggressive fluxes. The glaze should also be low alkali. It should contain a few percent of cadmium oxide, so that its potential relative to cadmium in the pigment is reduced. It should be free of vigorous oxidizing agents such as nitrates, which oxidize the pigment, completely destroying the color.

The thermal resistance of these materials in firing is definitely limited. They can be fired to about 1000°C. Therefore, while these pigments can be used in glass colors, in porcelain enamels, and in low-temperature glazes fired up to cone 04, they cannot be used in higher-temperature applications.

The most serious problem with these pigments is their extreme toxicity. Cadmium and its compounds are poisons when ingested or inhaled.[53] They are also experimental carcinogens. Selenium

Figure 8.43

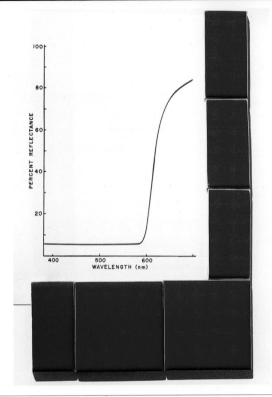

Spectral reflectance of a glaze with a cadmium deep red pigment.

compounds are also toxic. Hence, great care is required in the use of these pigments.

Moreover, while the cadmium sulfoselenide pigments have good resistance to alkali solutions, they have poor resistance to even dilute acids. Even relatively mild acids, such as food acids, will attack the pigment, releasing the highly toxic cadmium. For the latter reason, the cadmium sulfoselenide pigments should never be used in applications that may come in contact with food or drink. Even properly formulated ceramic coatings containing these pigments will usually fail the FDA compliance policy guidelines,[n7] so it is illegal to offer them for sale.

In order to extend the range of these colors, an inclusion pigment system has been developed.[D3] In this system, the cadmium sulfoselenide is incorporated in a clear zircon lattice during manufacture. In this way, the superior stability of zircon is imparted to the

Figure 8.44

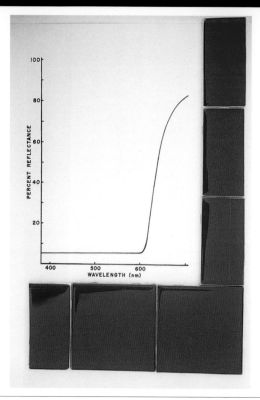

Spectral reflectance of a glaze with a cadmium maroon pigment.

pigment. One benefit of this procedure is that products are now available for use in tile glazes at cone 1, and even in sanitary ware glazes at cone 7. Another benefit is that the very toxic cadmium sulfoselenide is contained within a zircon lattice, making the pigment much safer to use.

However, the inclusion pigments are difficult and costly to make, and not all shades are available. The color palette extends from yellow through orange-red. Dark reds are not available.

8.9 Kubelka-Munk Theory for Color Matching

A major problem with all the color measurement systems discussed is that the color values obtained are not related in any completely systematic way to the concentrations of the pigments in the glaze.[E42, M24] Hence, it is difficult to use the color data to adjust the pigment concentrations in a glaze to get a desired result.

It has been suggested[M26] that an approach that does offer possibilities for relating the visible reflectance data of a glaze to reflectance data of the pigments in that glaze is the Kubelka-Munk theory.[K8] These authors showed that, at each frequency in the visible spectrum, each component of a formulation possesses a coefficient of absorption K, and a coefficient of scatter S, such that these coefficients, multiplied by the appropriate concentrations of the pigmenting materials, yield an equivalent coefficient for the overall formulation:[M12]

$$K_m = c_1 K_1 + c_2 K_2 + c_3 K_3 + \ldots + c_W K_W$$

$$S_m = c_1 S_1 + c_2 S_2 + c_3 K_3 + \ldots + c_W S_W$$

Here the c's are the concentrations of the coloring materials added to the formulation, and c_W is the concentration of the opacifier.

To use this theory, one needs a straightforward way to obtain these coefficients from measurable reflectance data. Fortunately, for any given material the ratio of these two coefficients is simply related to the reflectance of that material:

$$\frac{K}{S} = \frac{(1-r)^2}{2r}$$

In this equation, r is the reflectance measured with the specular component excluded. Many modern spectrometers can measure this quantity directly. However, if the spectrometer available can only measure total reflectance (specular included), the specular excluded can be estimated by:[S2]

$$r = \frac{R - k_1}{1 - k_1 - k_2(1 - R)}$$

where k_1 is the Fresnel reflection coefficient,[S2] which is 0.04 for ceramic surfaces, and k_2 is an empirical constant for which the value 0.4 has proven generally satisfactory.

$$r = \frac{R - 0.04}{0.96 - 0.4(1 - R)}$$

Thus, one can obtain the ratio of these two coefficients for any material directly from the reflectance data.

8.9.1 Formulating a Letdown Color.
Let us now consider a specific problem—the formulation of a pastel, or letdown color, by mixing a single pigment with an opacifier.[M26] One begins by preparing three samples: a masstone with only the pigment, no opacifier; a white, using the opacifier of choice, no pigment; and a letdown of known opacifier-to-pigment ratio. All three samples must be to the same total concentration (pigment plus opacifier). The reflectance of the three pieces is then measured, and for any frequency, the K/S values are calculated for the pigment, the opacifier, and the letdown. Inserting the first two equations into the equation for K/S, one can then write:

$$\frac{[K]}{[S]_{Ld}} = \frac{c_P K_P + c_W K_W}{c_P S_P + c_W S_W}$$

If the reasonable assumption that the opacifier is an effective scatterer is now made, so that one may set $S_W = 1$, it follows that:

$$S_P = \frac{[c_W]}{[c_P]} \frac{[(K/S)_{LD} - K_W]}{[(K/S)_P - (K/S)_{LD}]}$$

all the parameters of which are known quantities, as $K_W = (K/S)_W$, if $S_W = 1$. Once S_P is calculated, one can obtain K_P from:

$$K_P = \frac{[K]}{[S]_P} S_P$$

This method was successfully used to predict the color of a green glaze from the K_P and S_P values for the blue and the yellow pigments used in making the ceramic coating,[M25-26] as shown in Figure 8.45.

8.9.2 The effect of pigment concentration
can be examined if the requirement that the total concentration of opacifier plus pigments remains constant is removed. To do this, the effect of solubility of pigment and opacifier must be allowed for.[E44]

In a masstone, and in the measurement of the glaze with only opacifier, the values of the concentrations c_W and c_P, respectively, will be reduced by the extent of solubility. In a letdown, the situation is more complicated. The pigments and opacifier may not be attacked at the same rate. In the case of zircon opacifiers and zircon-based pigments, the opacifier is much more soluble than the

Figure 8.45

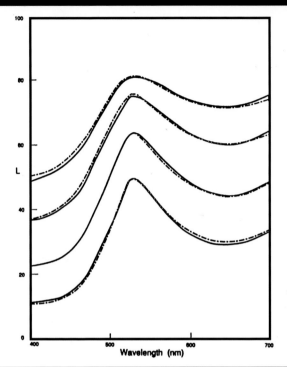

Spectral analysis of glazes containing 65% zircon praseodymium yellow, 35% zircon vanadium blue pigments, plus opacifier (a) solid line experimental data (b) dash line calculated from data on the components.

pigments. A principal reason is that the particle size of the pigments is usually much larger than that of the opacifier. For example, milled zircon opacifiers have mean sizes of 1 to 3 microns. By contrast, zircon pigments have mean sizes of 8 to 15 microns. Therefore, one would expect most of the attack to be on the opacifier. This hypothesis will be examined experimentally.

In this more general case, the effective concentrations are related to the added concentrations by:

$$C_W = C_{WA} - fS_N$$

$$C_P = C_{PA} - (1 - f)S_N$$

where c_{WA} and c_{PA} are the concentrations of opacifier and pigment, respectively, added to the glaze; S_N is the net solubility, and f is the fraction of the solubility satisfied by the opacifier.

175

Figure 8.46

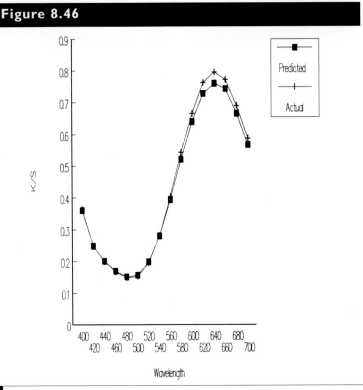

Comparison of predicted and actual color for glazes with a 5%, five-to-one loading of opacifier and a blue pigment.

This approach was examined for typical examples of the triaxial zircon colors added to opacifier and a single base glaze at five different concentrations from 5% to 18% of pigment plus opacifier.[E44] The values of the solubility parameters were then optimized, using the criteria that the S_p values for a given pigment should be independent of the pigment concentration in the glaze, or the letdown ratio, and the K_p values should be independent of the letdown ratio. The degree of correspondence between the calculated and experimental data are illustrated in Figure 8.46.

The "best" values obtained were 1.45% for the solubility and 1 for the fraction contributed by the opacifier. The latter value indicates that the opacifier serves as a complete "sacrificial lamb," protecting the pigment from attack by the glaze. The base glaze has 1.29 wt.% zircon. Added to the 1.45% solubility, this yields a total zircon solubility of 2.74 wt.%, which agrees with literature values for most glazes.

Part III
Processing of Ceramic Coatings

Chapter 9
Milling

Glaze or enamel preparation involves the production of a finely ground and intimate mixture of the raw materials selected, so that all parts of the batch that might be sampled have the same properties. Although there are ways to apply coatings in the dry state that are becoming increasingly important for porcelain enamels, most sectors of the ceramic and related industries use a dispersion of the ground raw materials suspended in water, or occasionally alcohol. This mixture, called a slip, may consist of water and the glaze ingredients (see Chapters 4–6), including the various additives (see Chapter 7) and pigments (see Chapter 8).

The usual manufacturing processes involve mixing the ingredients, particle size reduction, dispersion in water, removal of unwanted materials, and the addition of minor amounts of additives to modify the properties of the slip. The first three of these processes are carried out together by wet grinding.[T1]

Grinding as a method of ceramic coating preparation is the pulverization of the raw materials by impact and abrasion. The machinery most often used is a tumbling mill comprising a rotating cylinder partly filled with freely moving, impact resistant shapes. In the laboratory, a mill rack is used to turn a porcelain jar, which serves as the rotating cylinder. On a production scale, the container is an integral part of the machine, which is called a ball mill. As the cylinder turns, the particles to be ground are struck hard blows and are abraded against each other and against nearby hard surfaces.

An alternate method of energizing the mill is to vibrate it rather than rotate it. This type of equipment is called a vibroenergy mill.

Ball milling is the most commonly used industrial method for preparing ceramic coating slips. Ball mills are closed cylindrical vessels (aside from their lockable loading/discharging ports) that rotate about a horizontal central axis. Sizes range from one-quart laboratory mills to production mills capable of holding tons of slip. Production mills are usually built of metal but lined with an abrasion-resistant material. To bring about the size reduction, ball mills contain spheres or cylinders. The combination of mill lining and grinding media is such that the action of one on the other does not produce significant contamination of the slip.

Particle size reduction results from the cascading action of the media on the grains or lumps of coating batch as the mill rotates. Even under optimum conditions, ball milling is energy inefficient. It is therefore important to control such factors as will improve the grinding efficiency. Some of these factors are:[T1]

- type of mill lining
- type and size of grinding media
- weight and ratio of grinding media, coating components, and water in the mill
- mill speed
- particle size of the feed
- consistency and hardness of the feed

The mill lining will tend to be eroded by the action of the mill contents, leading to contamination of the slip. Hence, the lining material must have good resistance to abrasion by the grinding media and the coating constituents. Some contamination is unavoidable. The most common linings are silica, porcelain, or alumina. Contamination of ceramic coatings with fragments of these materials is not generally serious, because these oxide components are already part of the coating formulation. Rubber linings are gaining in popularity because, in combination with high-density media, they can lead to reductions in the milling time to a given particle size. These linings have good wear resistance and reduce noise level during operation.

The factors that influence the choice of grinding media are density and shape, homogeneity and freedom from voids, impact and abrasion resistance, and toughness. In wet ball milling, the density of the media relative to the density of the slip is an important factor in determining the rate of particle size reduction. The greater the density of the media relative to the slip, the faster the milling will proceed for slips of a given viscosity.

Slips with optimum viscosity for milling have densities of 1.6 to 2.5 g/cc, depending on the density of the coating components. A suitable density is 1.6 g/cc for slips free of lead oxide, barium oxide, etc., up to 2.5 g/cc for a lead bisilicate coating.

Some typical densities for grinding media are:

flint pebbles	2.5 to 2.6 g/cc
porcelain	2.3 to 2.6 g/cc
steatite	2.6 to 2.8 g/cc
high-density alumina	3.3 to 4.6 g/cc

The advantage of alumina grinding media is apparent. They are more expensive, however, so the other media are still used in some applications.

The selection of grinding media should also take into account the mill lining, as the goal is for the media to mill the charge, and not the mill lining.

When balls are used instead of cylinders, it is customary to use up to three different sizes, with the diameter difference no greater than three times. Large balls work effectively in the initial stages of grinding, when there may be some large particles in the product. Later in the milling process, the smaller balls are most effective.

The average size of the media should also be related to the size of the coating material. A coarser feed requires larger balls or cylinders. However, for powdered materials up to one ton capacity, one-half- to one-inch balls or cylinders should suffice.

In wet ball milling, the mill loading quantities must be closely controlled.[F3] Experience has shown that for best results, the grinding media and intervening voids should occupy about 55% of the mill volume. The media should occupy this volume regardless of the mill size or the type of media used. The dry batch charge should occupy 11 to 18% of the total mill volume. Within this range, it depends on the type of media. A greater product charge can be tolerated when high-density media are used. This is because of the higher momentum they attain during the milling process. The amount of water charged has a significant effect on the grinding efficiency. For pseudospherical particles, approximately equal quantities by volume of water and dry batch usually lead to good grinding. By weight, this is about 1 part water to 2 to 2.5 parts dry batch. When clays are present in the batch, more water will be required to counteract the increased viscosity resulting from the presence of the clay. Other types of suspending agents may have a similar effect. Hence, water usually ends up being about 50 to 55% of the total slip volume.

If too much water is added to the mill, the particles of the dry batch charge tend to escape from the abrading surfaces of the media, being washed away from impact by the water. When too little water is added to the mill, the highly viscous slip degrades the particle size reduction process because the media impacts are smothered in a coating of viscous slip. Hence, the specific gravity of the slip developed during milling is an important parameter.

A suitable gravity for the slip depends on the specific gravity of the dry batch charged. For a leadless system of mean specific gravity 2.5, one can use 33% water, 67% solids. For a high lead oxide system of mean specific gravity 4.5, one should use 21% water, 79% solids.

Another important variable is mill speed.[A1] As the mill rotates, the contents, under the influence of gravitational, centrifugal, and frictional forces, move to some extent relative to the mill lining. Figure 9.1 illustrates the relevant effects. At very low rotational speeds (Figure 9.1d), the media and coating components remain at the bottom of the mill, as gravitational forces predominate. Little, if any grinding of the dry batch would occur, but wear of the lining would occur.

At the other extreme (Figure 9.1a), if the mill speed is much too fast, centrifugal forces drive the contents outward onto the mill lining, where they remain stationary relative to the lining. Because there

Figure 9.1

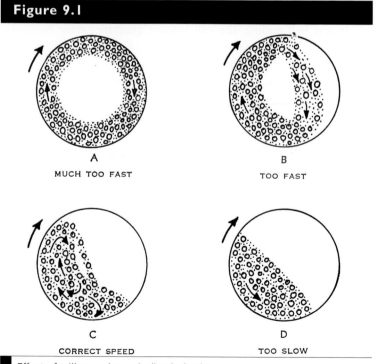

A
MUCH TOO FAST

B
TOO FAST

C
CORRECT SPEED

D
TOO SLOW

Effect of mill speed on grinding behavior.

is no relative motion between the media and charge, there is no impact or abrasion, and hence no particle size reduction occurs. The lowest mill speed at which this condition occurs is called the critical mill speed. It can be estimated from:

Critical Speed (RPM) = 21 to $30/(D)^{1/2}$

where D is the mill diameter in meters.

Experience has shown that a mill speed approximately 60% of the critical speed gives the best results (Figure 9.1c). At this speed the dry batch materials and the grinding media are carried upward by frictional forces in the mill to the correct height before cascading down onto the underlying material. Particle size reduction then occurs by attrition, as the media, coated with slip, tumble over each other.

At a slightly higher rotational speed (Figure 9.1b), the charge is carried too high on the circumference of the mill before collapsing. This inefficient condition is called cascading. It leads to high rates of media wear, and hence product contamination. The ideal angle between the horizontal and the point where the grinding media leave the mill lining is $45°$.

The linear speed of the mill casing for a given speed of rotation is greater for mills of larger diameter. Hence, larger mills operate at slower speeds than do small mills.

Wearing of the mill lining and the grinding media can be minimized, but it cannot be eliminated. Therefore, action is required to counter the effects of the wear. As the mill wears, its volume increases. An increase in the volume of 10 to 20% can readily occur. This increase must be alleviated by an increase in the media charge. Wearing of the grinding media results in a reduction in their size. Ultimately, the size of the smallest media may decrease to the point at which they will be abraded by the larger media. Such overly small media must be removed. Periodic (three to four times per year) inspection of mill lining and grinding media are necessary to maintain optimum conditions.

While wet grinding in ball mills is the principal technique used for grinding ceramic coating slips, there are other means available. Dry grinding is used when a milled coating material is to be transported a long distance, or when it is to be applied dry by such processes as electrostatic dry powder, flame spraying, or fluidized bed techniques. In addition, for ceramic coatings that exhibit appreciable solubility in water, production by dry grinding eliminates problems that arise from the presence of soluble species in the slip.

Much of what has been said about wet milling applies also to dry grinding. There are small differences. Media loading is usually reduced slightly—to 45 to 50% of the mill volume.

Vibroenergy mills have found some use, particularly in sanitary ware coating. They can be used for both wet and dry milling. High-frequency vibration forces are produced by the use of out-of-balance weights attached to a shaft and driven by an electric motor.

In a horizontal vibration mill, the grinding media and intervening voids should occupy 85 to 90% of the mill volume. The charge occupies 100 to 120% of that void volume. In this type of mill, circular motion of the grinding media gives optimum results. Hence, spherical grinding media are preferred. The number of size-reducing impacts is greater than that achieved in ball milling, although the intensity of the impacts is reduced. However, the outcome is faster grinding, together with excellent mixing.

Continuous operation of vibration mills is possible, and classification can be added without difficulty.

For all types of mills, some mill operating parameters are important. To prevent cross-contamination, colored and white coatings are ground in separate mills. Leadless and lead-based coatings are separately processed for the same reason. When limits on the number of mills prevent the separation of all coating slips into separate mills, the mills must be thoroughly cleaned. Cleaning of a mill can be as little as washing out with water, or it can involve grinding a mill out with an innocuous material. Silica is often used.

Usually, all ingredients are added to a mill before milling begins. However, in milling high-frit slips, the frit may be separately ground before adding the other ingredients.

Grinding times average 6 to 18 hours in production-scale ball mills. In the laboratory, milling times of one to two hours are usually satisfactory. In vibroenergy mills, 90 minutes would be a typical grinding time.

Particle size measurement is the ultimate control on milling operations. When a suitable size is prepared, the milled slip is removed from the mill. It can be run from the mill by gravity or pumped into storage tanks to await application. To remove any coarse fragments, it is customary to dump the slip through a 40 or 60 mesh screen, and through magnets to remove any tramp iron oxide. If the slip is too viscous, much of it will adhere to the grinding media and will not come out. Adding of a little extra water will usually control the problem.

All real powdered materials have a range of sizes. Even so-called monosized materials occur in a range of sizes—the range is merely narrower than most. Hence, all particle size measurements report a range or distribution of sizes. Moreover, different measurement techniques report different distributions. Some methods give a weight or volume distribution of sizes, while others report a distribution of weights or volumes. Laser dispersion or sedimentation-based instruments yield a distribution of sizes on a volume or weight basis. On the other hand, equipment like sieves, where one weighs the material on each sieve, yields a distribution of weights. These are not the same. Sieve data is $w_i/W = n_i d_i^3/\Sigma n_i d_i^3$, while the laser dispersion and sedimentation methods report n_i/N on a weight/volume interval basis.

There is no single accepted way to measure particle size, and no single method is applicable to all situations. In part, the method chosen is determined by the size range. Coarse sizes, above 100 microns, are readily handled by screens. Intermediate sizes—1 to 300 microns—are best handled by laser dispersion or sensing zone techniques. Submicron particles from 0.1 to 1 micron are usually examined by sedimentation techniques. The very finest sizes—below 0.1 micron—can only be assessed by electron microscopic techniques.

Another complication arises if one examines a non-pseudo spherical particle. What is being measured? This problem occurs in studying the particle size of clay, which is platelike. The various techniques report some kind of equivalent diameter. This figure may have little or nothing to do with the physical dimensions of these non-pseudospherical particles.

Chapter 10
Application Techniques

By the time one is ready to apply a ceramic coating to a substrate, much value has been added to each component. Hence, the application process must be straightforward and foolproof, minimizing errors that lead to waste. The method must be reproducible, economical, and flexible.[T1]

For each coating application, there is an optimum application thickness. In most cases the goal is the thinnest coating that will give a smooth, uniform coverage. For most applications, this works out to between 6 and 40 mils (0.15–1 mm) wet, or 3 to 20 mils (0.075–0.5 mm) dry. Thinner coatings can sometimes be used for electronic applications that involve very smooth substrate surfaces. Substrate smoothness is a major parameter in determining minimum coating thicknesses. The requirement for uniform coating is a total of at least 3 mils over the highest point on the substrate surface. Ceramic coatings do not easily flow and heal across thin or starved patches, or level over irregularities such as ripples or runs in the coating. Color in the glaze accentuates these effects. On the other hand, it is much easier to add thickness when required than it is to reduce thickness, short of cleaning the ware and starting over.

The application technique selected is one of the most important decisions the coatings engineer makes. Important criteria in this selection are:[T1]

- type of ware—in particular, the body roughness
- shape and size of ware
- throughput required
- energy and labor costs
- space available

In the sections that follow, the major application techniques will be examined with respect to these criteria.

10.1 Dipping

Dipping is a simple, efficient, rapid technique, requiring little capital equipment.[F2,T1] The ware are simply immersed in a bucket or tub of glaze. Water from the glaze slip enters the porous ware, leaving behind a film of glaze particles. Success in dipping, however, depends in large part on the operator's experience.

In this operation, the ware is immersed in the coating slip, moved around in a controlled way, withdrawn, and allowed to drain and dry. The equipment is very simple. It can be as little as a receiving tank or tub large enough to contain a depth of slip sufficient to permit the dipper to immerse the ware freely.

The dipping technique depends upon the size and shape of the ware.[G4] Holloware are first filled rapidly to the brim and poured out, to coat the inside. Both holloware and small flatware are lightly held by the foot and rim and completely immersed in the slip for a few seconds, with a gentle to and fro agitation, and then brought out at an angle, twisted to shake off surplus glaze, and allowed to drain. In production operations, dipping tongs are used, which hold the ware securely at three points. The whole operation takes only a few seconds; a time that must be closely controlled. After dipping, the finger or tong marks where the piece was held are touched up.

Flatware with a diameter greater than a hand's span are gripped by the fingers and a wire hook on the dipper's thumb. The ware is immersed, removed from the slip, shaken to remove excess slip, and set down to drain. Immediately, any bare spots are touched up with a finger wetted with coating material.

Speed of application is a critical variable in a dipping operation.[F2,G4] The longer the ware is immersed, the thicker the coating, but the absorption of water by the body, and hence the rate of coating buildup, steadily decreases as time increases. Moreover, if the walls are allowed to reach saturation, the adherence of the coating will be reduced.

The surface texture of the fired glaze is affected by many interrelated factors:[T1]
- slip density
- slip viscosity
- thixotropy of the slip
- particle size of the solids in the slip
- porosity of the ware
- thickness of the ware
- ware temperature
- immersion time
- slip additives
- operator skill

Of these several parameters, the last, operator skill, is paramount.

Coatings for porous ware must have a lower slip density than coatings for semivitreous or vitreous ware.[T1] Typical ranges include 1.4 g/cc for porous ware, to 1.7 g/cc for semiporous bisque ware, to densities of 1.7 to 1.9 for vitreous ware.

By the use of expert systems, there have been attempts to mechanize the dipping process. However, the complex motions needed for good dipping practice make it difficult to simulate. The one place where mechanization is successful is in coating the insides of holloware. The ware is inverted and placed over a bubbler of glaze slip.

10.2 Spraying

Spraying is a process in which a coating slip is broken down to a cloud of fine particles that are transferred to the substrate by either pneumatic, mechanical, or electrical forces.[T1] The advantages of spraying include the simplicity and portability of equipment, speed of operation, ease of process control, and the ability to fully automate the process.[P1]

The method requires a gun, a container or feed mechanism, an impelling agency, and a properly designed hood or booth maintained under negative pressure.[T1] Spraying requires less slip quantity than dipping. Thick or thin coatings can be applied to substrates of varying porosity. Large or intricate shapes can be uniformly coated. Loss of slip by overspray is a limitation to the method. In commercial-sized operations, the overspray is collected, adjusted, and recycled.

In air spraying—the most common type—the equipment needed is a spray gun, a compressor, and a spray booth. The slip flows through a control orifice or nozzle in the spray gun, where it meets a stream of pressurized air. This air stream disrupts the flow of liquid into a myriad of fine particles. The flow of slip and air is controlled by a trigger, and the volume of slip is regulated by the size of the nozzle. The nozzle aperture is generally larger in diameter for viscous ceramic coatings. Also, as the aperture wears, the flow rate and the spray pattern change. Hence, if abrasive materials such as ceramics are to be coated, wear-resistant nozzles are fitted.

When adjusted properly, the spray pattern will be a uniform strip made by the passage of a circular spray over the ware.[A1] Other patterns indicate either damage to the nozzle, or, more commonly, a lack of sufficient cleaning of the nozzle passages. These passages should be cleaned at least once daily.

There are three types of feed, whose usefulness depends on the application.[T1]

1. Gravity feed is better used for laboratory operations than for production. From a small cup attached to the gun, the slip flows to the nozzle. The rate of flow depends on the viscosity of the slip.
2. In suction feed, the nozzle is supplied from a cup attached to the gun, from which the slip is sucked.
3. A pressurized feed is the preferred option with the most viscous slips. Slip is positively fed to the nozzle, usually from a separate container set below the level of the gun.

The quality of the fired ceramic coating can be related to the uniformity of the sprayed surface on the ware as it enters the kiln. Factors that affect the uniformity of the sprayed surface originate partly in the slip, partly in the application process. All are interrelated. The factors include:

- slip density
- slip viscosity
- thixotropy of the slip
- fineness of grind of the coating material
- air pressure
- air flow rate
- coating feed rate
- nozzle aperture
- operator expertise
- substrate porosity
- substrate temperature
- number and position of spray guns

Two types of coating finish can be produced: wet spray and dry spray.[F2,T1] This refers to the amount of water retained by the atomized spray as it hits the substrate. A dry spray is produced by increasing the air rate or reducing the flow of slip to the nozzle. A high-density or high-viscosity slip tends to produce a dry surface. This technique produces dry, powdery coating deposits whose roughness and porosity mean that care is required in application, and higher firing temperatures are needed to completely fire out the coating. Also, dry spraying requires a glaze that melts and seals over several cones (i.e., 100–200°C) below the top glazing temperature. This technique is most useful when one needs a thick coating without cracking, or needs to cover underglaze colors without special hardening-on techniques.

Coatings applied by a wet application have smooth surface texture before firing. A high gloss develops at a lower firing temperature, and with less temperature difference between the seal-over temperature and the top glazing temperature. Unless care is taken, however, the coating may sag or ripple. Changes in the nozzle size and atomizing air will change the efficiency of fine droplet production.

Spraying lends itself to high-volume automated production systems. The articles are continuously fed to a wire belt and through a preheat tunnel before the coating is applied from a battery of angled spray guns, such that the underside is first coated, followed by the top surface of the ware.

Coating reclaim is essential for automated systems. What is reclaimed is:

- slip caught by rear baffles or curtains within the booth
- overspray transported by air currents to adjacent dust control equipment
- washings from cleaning operations

Whenever one has a conductive substrate, the surface quality and the uniformity of coating can be improved by using the electrostatic spray coating technique.[M8,T1] Loss of coating to overspray is also greatly reduced.

In an electrostatic spray system, the slip reaches the applicator gun from a pressurized stock container through a regulator. Droplets are produced either by air atomization or by centrifugal force from a sharp-edged rotating surface. The drops acquire a high negative charge and, because like-charged particles repel, the droplets are dispersed as a fine mist. At the same time they are driven forward to the grounded substrate, following the lines of force. Hence, coating material can reach the underside of the ware, and full edge coverage is achieved, as a homogeneous cloud develops around the ware.

There is a back-spray effect from particles rebounding from the ware. On impact, particles lose their charge. On rebounding, they become recharged enough to travel back to the spray equipment. Placing a ring of ionizers, called a Faraday cage, around the gun eliminates this effect.

The environment in an electrostatic spray booth plays an important role in the success of the method. Temperature and relative humidity are maintained within narrow limits. Hence, expensive auxiliary equipment is one limitation of this technique.

After deposition by an electrostatic process, the coating acts as a membrane for the movement of the entrapped media (water) in which the solid was suspended. This electro-osmosis results in a tight compaction of the coating particles. Hence, when properly run, an electrostatic spray line can produce high-quality ceramic coatings.

10.3 Waterfall or Bell Coating

Ceramic tiles require only one face to be glazed, but often with a very thin, smooth coating. This suggests the waterfall, or curtain technique[T1] (see Figure 10.1). A continuous feed of tiles is carried on parallel tracks of stranded wire or rubber belt under a curtain of fluid slip. The slip continuously circulates in the machine. It flows from an overlying reservoir onto a device shaped like a squashed bell. The bell spreads the stream of slip into a controlled curtain. The ware passes rapidly through the curtain of slip. The portion of the curtain not adhered to the ware passes to a lower sump, from which it is pumped through a filter back to the upper reservoir.

As the leading edge of the tile enters the waterfall, the slip flows across the horizontal surface uniformly, and only the face of the tile is coated. The traverse speed of the tile, the density of the slip, and the porosity of the body control the thickness of the coating retained on the tile. To limit the occurrence of bare spots or thinly glazed areas, multiple waterfalls are often used. Also, the coating varies from the leading to the trailing edge. Hence, the tiles are often turned $180°$ between passes under the waterfall.

Figure 10.1

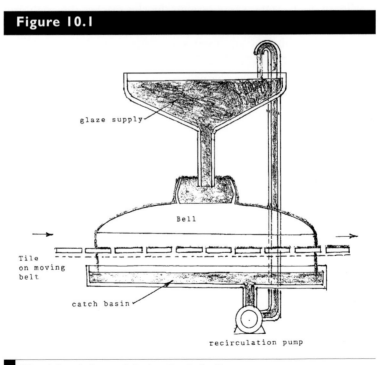

glaze supply

Bell

Tile
on moving
belt

catch basin

recirculation pump

Waterfall technique of glazing tiles (ref. n2).

192

10.4 Dry Glazing

Dry glazing involves the scattering over a liquid base glaze of a mix of partly transparent and partly white crushed frits.[B12] The glass frit grains stick to the wet, liquid surface of the raw tiles. These semi-adhered granules are then fixed with an organic binder of CMC in water, or covered with a minor application of wet glaze. During firing, the glaze and frit grains melt into each other. This produces a surface with a fine granite appearance. It is usually very hard, compact, and abrasion resistant.

The frit grains can be fed by bucket elevator, by small belt conveyors, or by pneumatic circulation. They are fed to a grain distributor, which has a homogenizer with blades, allowing the material to flow evenly over a vibrating screen, scattering the grains over the tiles.

Many decorative effects may be achieved by varying the choice of frit and their size distribution. Often, multiple coats offer further flexibility in design.

10.5 Discing

In centrifugal glazing, or discing, slip is transported mechanically to a rotating atomizer. The slip is then passed through a hollow spindle onto a set of rotating discs, spaced slightly apart. Centrifugal force throws off the coating slip into a fan of droplets. The technique reduces or eliminates the need for compressed air, as for spraying. While this method can produce a variety of surfaces, its primary use is in producing textured coatings and spatters. It is another method for creating a granite effect.

10.6 Painting

The hand painting of ware is still practiced by a number of smaller manufacturers, as well as by studio potters.[F2] A fully loaded soft brush is used in order to prevent smearing as the glaze is applied. A binder or glycerine is mixed with the glaze slip, to promote a smoother brushing action and a more uniform film. Nevertheless, it is usually necessary to apply two or three coats to avoid unevenness and bare spots. The principal limitations of the method are its labor intensiveness, and the difficulty of eliminating streakiness and brush marks.

10.7 Dry Application Techniques

There are a few techniques of application that don't use a water-based slip. One used in the tile industry is called monopressatura.[B12] This term refers to a single pressing-glazing technique in which the glaze and body are pressed together in a specially designed hydraulic press. A principal advantage of this technique is the elimination of a separate glazing line. The glazes produced by this technique have a strong interface and a reduced microbubble structure. This normally yields improved hardness and abrasion resistance. The glazes usually have a textured or granite effect and are 1 to 2 mm in thickness.

Flame spraying can be used to apply vitreous coatings in the molten state to heat-sensitive or massive substrates.[T1] In flame spraying, the coating material is melted and projected as heated particles onto the substrate, where it instantaneously solidifies as a coating. The smoothness of such coatings leaves a lot to be desired, and a hermetic coating (one that liquids cannot bypass) is next to impossible, so the usefulness of flame spraying is very limited.

There are also a couple of techniques for applying ceramic coatings as dry powders.

To coat cast iron bathtubs, hot castings are coated by sifting dry powder over them.[A1,M8] On contact, the coating material melts and adheres, but requires reheating of the ware for a smooth surface finish. Operator skill is essential to obtain a uniform coating. Recently, there have been successful efforts to accomplish this task with robots. Expert systems analysis is used to program the robots to duplicate the manipulations of a skilled coater.

The most important dry method, and the method most recently introduced, is dry electrostatic application.[M8] This technique was first developed for organic paints. The technique involves charging individual coating particles at a high voltage and then spraying them toward the substrate.

For purposes of charging, a paint particle has two advantages: its very high resistance—10^{16-18} for paint, versus 10^{6-8} for vitreous material—and its lower density—1.1 for paint, versus 2.5 for ceramic.

Hence, a charged organic particle will be attracted to a grounded substrate and will adhere to it without loss of charge. A ceramic particle will be deposited on the workpiece, but it will lose its charge and fall off. A solution to this problem has been found in encapsulating ground frit in an organic silane, to simulate the electrical properties of organic powders.

After dry grinding of the frit down to 30 microns, the powder is dried and then injected with up to 0.5% of encapsulant. This coated material is suspended in a fluidized bed container from which it is transported to special electrostatic powder guns for low-pressure application, using a potential of up to 100 kV. The deposited coating is fragile compared to other application methods, so the transfer to the firing kiln is difficult.

Spray plant manufacturers are now offering complete recirculating electrostatic powder spray machines, claiming 95 to 98% efficiency of powder usage. Optimum conditions of temperature and humidity are recommended, to be controlled within narrow limits, such as 40 to 50% humidity with temperature at 20 to 25°C.

Chapter 11
Decoration

Throughout history, aesthetics has been an important part of the appeal of ceramic products. One aspect of aesthetic appeal is color, which was discussed in Chapter 8. Another aspect is texture, or a deliberately uneven surface. Some of the application methods discussed in Chapter 10 yield texture. A third opportunity for improving the appearance is decoration, the application of color or colors as a pattern or picture, which is the subject of this chapter.

There are five places where color can be applied to a glazed ceramic article: as a body stain, as an engobe, as an underglaze color, as a colored glaze, or as an overglaze or glass color.

The use of a body stain refers to a pigment added to the body formulation itself. While this method is sometimes an economical way to color a product, it does not lend itself to the application of a pattern or picture.

An engobe may be described as the application of a ceramic pigment to the surface of a raw body.[n1] This method has the advantage of concentrating the expensive pigment in a coating layer instead of throughout the body. Like body stains, however, it also does not lend itself to the application of a pattern or picture.

By contrast with engobes, underglaze decorating is the application of color to a bisque body. It is a technique used primarily for the application of patterns and pictures, particularly in the tableware industry. In colored glazes, or in glaze decorating, the pigment is dispersed in the glaze itself. This method is restricted to applications where multiple glaze layers are applied, as in the tile industry.

Finally, there are overglazes or glass colors, which are applied to the already formed and sometimes fired glaze, as an overcoat to yield a pattern or picture.

There are some important differences that determine the

selection of the technique for decoration. First, an underglaze color or an in glaze color must be stable to glost fire while in contact with the molten glaze. By contrast, while some overglaze decorations are applied over the green glaze and fired with it, other overglazes, as well as all glass colors, are applied and then fired only at temperatures of 550 to 800°C. One important result of this lower firing temperature is the sharper detail that is possible with the various printing methods and with decalcomania.

Moreover, the range of colors and effects that can be obtained is directly related to this thermal stability.[E28] Some colors, such as the bright reds, can only be obtained in overglaze decoration. Thus, while a full palette of colors is possible in overglaze decoration, in underglaze the palette is somewhat limited.

The durability of a decoration in service, with respect to both chemicals and abrasion, will depend largely on the distance between the outer surface of the ware and the decoration. Therefore, overglaze decorations are distinctly inferior to in glaze and underglaze decorations with respect to durability in service.

11.1 Media

Before a pigment can be used for decoration, it must first be dispersed into an appropriate medium. In addition to the pigments, a decorating medium may contain vitreous fluxing materials to bond the pigment to the ware. It will also contain an organic or water-based vehicle to enable it to be applied.

11.1.1 Underglaze media may contain, in addition to the pigments, components of the glaze or the body to facilitate bonding to the substrate at the glost firing. These are all dispersed in a viscous organic resin-vehicle mix that may be either organic or water based. Some of the resins used are linseed oil, turpentine, Canada balsam, and synthetic resins such as formaldehydes, alkyds, polystyrene, vinyl acrylics, and stearates.[R1]

A good underglaze medium must be suited to rapid color application by the desired method of decorating. Then it must burn off readily in the hardening-on or glost firing and leave the final pigment and glaze undisturbed.

11.1.2 Overglaze colors and glass colors are prepared by milling the pigments with appropriate vitreous fluxes.[W4] If the decoration is to be fired along with the glaze, the flux may be similar in composition to the glaze. With glass colors, and with ceramic decorations that are to be fired at 550 to 800°C, the fluxes will be very low melting glasses, often containing high lead oxide concentrations. The pigment content in these formulations may be as low as 5%, or it may be quite high, depending on the strength of the desired color. However, in order to maintain the softening temperature and the thermal expansion of the system, the pigment is rarely above 40%.

The flux-color mixture is formulated so that it will soften enough in the decorating kiln to form a tight, glassy bond with the underlying glass or glaze. In many cases, it is expected that the pigment-flux mixture will sink into the softened glaze during the decorating fire. In this way, substantial improvement in the durability of the coating can be achieved.

The flux materials for overglaze colors and glass colors are usually high in lead oxide and boron oxide and low in alumina. If they are not properly handled, severe durability problems can result. Moreover, most of these materials are not safe for use in contact with food or drink. Therefore, good design dictates that overglaze decorations should not be used in direct contact with food or drink. Instead, they should be placed on the outside of the ware, where they can be seen but cannot come in contact with the contents.

In this connection, it should be pointed out that a modest increase in the firing temperature can substantially improve the durability of an overglaze flux. Through the addition of silica and alumina to the flux, substantial improvement in the metal release and resistance to dish washing is achieved.

11.1.3 The milling process for the homogenization of a decorating medium is carried out in an organic mixture appropriate to the application. Conventional mixtures are liquid at room temperature and have been milled into a paste form using a squeegee oil.[C10] These media can be applied without heating, but they must be dried thoroughly after each color application if multicolor decorations are required.

Vendors of overglaze decorations and glass colors can also supply conventional media in ultraviolet curable mixtures.[Y3] Ultraviolet radiation transforms a liquid coating into a solid one instantaneously on exposure. Hence, these media offer a number of advantages over squeegee oil media. These include faster drying times, reduced energy and equipment costs, less space required, faster line speeds, and reduced solvent emissions.

Formerly, all overglaze inks were of these kinds. Today, however, their use is limited mainly to single-color applications and the application of decalcomania.

11.1.4 Today, multicolor direct application uses thermo-plastic inks, which are commonly called hot-melt enamels.[C10] In these products, the ceramic components are dispersed in a thermoplastic that is solid at room temperature but becomes fluid when heated. When these enamels are applied to a room-temperature substrate, they harden on contact, so they can be overcoated with a different color immediately, eliminating the need for drying between color applications. As many as seven colors can be sequentially applied without intervening drying.

Some advantages of using hot-melt enamels, in addition to the ability to make multicolor decorations, include minimization of misprints; greater ease in producing fine detail and sharp lines; enamels that are supplied ready-to-use, with no on-site mixing required; cleaning of equipment reduced, because there is no volatilization of medium to smear the decoration; and greater flexibility of design, as wraparound decorations and overlapping colors are possible. The disadvantages are mostly related to the necessity of heating the coating material for application. As a result, equipment parts in contact with the medium will have somewhat reduced life. Changeover between decorating jobs will be somewhat more involved, as the equipment is more complex.

11.2 Choosing a Method of Decoration

There are a number of techniques for applying decorations. They include lining and banding; hand painting; spraying; the several printing processes (copper plate printing, transfer or pad printing, and screen printing); the application of decalcomania; and finally, stamping. The selection of an appropriate technique depends first on the size and shape of the substrate, then on the details of the decoration itself.

Some questions that are relevant to the choice of a decoration method include the following: Is one color to be applied, or several? Is the decoration a line drawing, areas of solid color of uniform strength, or is it a picture involving halftones? How large is the decoration? Is it to be applied to a flat surface, to the outside of a cylinder, or to a complex surface? Let us now consider the characteristics of each of these techniques for the application of decorations, and, in particular, how the answers to these questions dictate an appropriate decorating method.

11.3 Lining and Banding

Let's begin with lining and banding (see Figure 11.1). This is a high production rate and relatively low-cost technique applicable to any article that is in some way circular about an axis. Bottles and ceramic holloware are typical examples of articles appropriate for lining and banding. Possible line widths vary from very fine up to one-quarter inch, and they can be applied either by hand or by machine.

In the hand-lining operation, the operator must exercise great skill not only in the application of the color to the ware, but also in blending the organic medium with the color.[59] This is done by working the two together with a spatula on a glass plate. Small additions of turpentine are made to increase the drying rate of the organic medium. Control of the oil-to-pigment ratio and the resin-to-turpentine ratio is very difficult and subject to wide fluctuations, which cause great variations in the quality of the end product. In this method the article is mounted in such a way that it can be revolved about its axis. An armrest is arranged above or beside the ware so that one's hand can be kept steady while applying the band.

The basic process of hand banding was mechanized in two steps. In the first step, equipment was developed for holding the ware while it was banded by hand. In the second step, equipment was developed that does the entire job mechanically.[E1] Machines are available that

Figure 11.1

Plate with a decoration applied by banding.

can operate at speeds of up to 600 linear inches per minute, although for difficult shapes their speed must be reduced substantially.

With automatic equipment, variations in banding are reduced. A prepared color mixture is used with a fixed pigment-to-resin-to-vehicle ratio. For higher speeds, the thermoplastic or hot-melt mixtures can be used. The mixture may also contain a wetting agent to retard settling out of the pigment. Even with automated equipment, however, applying bands over one-quarter inch wide requires a great deal of skill in machine alignment to insure a uniform color application. It is often necessary to resort to spraying the color when wide bands of high quality are desired.

11.4 Hand Painting

It may surprise you to learn that freehand painting of ceramics (see Figure 11.2) is still a commercially viable process, and not just in very low wage countries. The process consists of filling in printed outlines or of copying a standard pattern using a brush and colors suspended in appropriate media.[S9,R1] The materials used do not differ appreciably from those used in lining and banding, being mixtures of pigment, resin, and vehicle. Therefore, the same high level of skill is required here in mixing colors in order to obtain materials of appropriate consistency.

Figure 11.2

Plate with a hand-painted decoration.

11.5 Spraying

While spraying is widely used for glaze application, in the tableware industry it also finds application in decoration.[59] By the use of various masking techniques, it is possible to apply anything from narrow bands up to a full rim spray. Color may also be spattered on by an adjustment of the spray gun. Simple patterns may also be sprayed on by the use of stencils.

This method is primarily limited by the fact that it is relatively expensive, as the ware must pass through several operations. The color is prepared by grinding to a suitable consistency in a medium that may be either oil or water based. This medium may be any of a number of low-viscosity mixtures such as linseed oil, turpentine, or varnish. Solid-colored sprays are applied wet to yield a smooth fired color.

11.6 Printing

There are several processes based on the technology of the printing industry, which range from century-old copper plate printing to the latest silk screening methods. The steps in a printing process include the preparation of an oil-color mixture and using this mixture to make a print, which in turn is applied to the ware. Three such processes will be discussed: copper plate printing; copper plate and gelatin pad printing, often called transfer printing; and finally, silk screening.

11.6.1 Copper plate printing is the traditional technique.[59] In this method, a copper plate is engraved or etched with the design. This engraving is then filled with ceramic printing ink, which is heated to obtain the desired fluidity and transferred from the engraving to a piece of fine tissue paper. The design, which is now transferred from the engraving to the paper, is used as a transfer to be applied to the ceramic article. Because of the stickiness of the oil-color mixture, the design will fasten itself tenaciously to the bisque ware, and the paper may then be removed by soaking the article in water.

A most important part of this printing process is the mixing of the color and medium. The ratio of oil to color must be varied with the type of color being used. The mixture is placed in a reservoir above printing machine rollers and fed in horizontally to the heated rollers. The amount of pigment that adheres to the tissue paper is controlled by doctor blades. The printed patterns are then cut out and placed face down on the ware. The transfer is then rubbed down with a brush containing a soap solution. Finally, the ware is put in a water bath and the tissue paper is removed. After drying, the ware is ready for glazing.

11.6.2 The printing process has been highly automated with the transfer printing process.[S1] With this technique, a solid convex pad of silicone rubber (formerly gelatin) is lowered onto an inked engraving while under pressure. The pad is deformed and picks up the ink trace from the engraving. The gelatin pad is then lowered onto the ware, and the design is transferred to the ceramic article. The advantages of this machine are substantial. The use of paper, and the accompanying operations of rubbing down, washing off, and drying are completely eliminated. Whereas copper plate printing requires skilled workers, this machine can be worked by relatively unskilled labor. The output of one machine is about 4 to 6 pieces per minute.

The transfer printing machine uses a medium that is quite different from that used in copper plate printing.[R1] A medium for this machine must have good dispersion, a controllable drying rate, and a controllable viscosity. It is only with the introduction of the thermoplastic or hot-melt media that this technique has become economically feasible. With such media, multicolor decorations can be applied by successive pads without intervening drying.

This machine can handle flatware, and even bowls, but it is not suitable for holloware. Thus, in the tableware industry it is necessary to match the colors printed by this method with the colors applied by a method suitable for holloware.

11.6.3 Silk screening, or more correctly screen process printing, is a stencil operation in which the stencil is supported by a mesh fabric.[D8] The design is printed by drawing a rubber blade or squeegee over the stencil, which is filled with ceramic ink. This forces the ink through the open areas of the stencil and deposits it on the ceramic surface. This process has advantages over the other printing processes in the speed and relative low cost of preparation of screens. Compared to decalcomania, it has the advantage of being able to deposit thicker layers. The principal limitation on the process is that it is restricted largely to flat surfaces. Hence, its greatest use is in decorating tile. Plates and other flatware can also be silk screened. In general, all line designs are suitable for screen printing; halftone effects are practical, but they require considerable care and skill in the preparation and handling of the screens. Figure 11.3 illustrates the complex decorations now possible with the best practice.

Figure 11.3

Advanced decoration by screen printing (courtesy of Esmalglass).

Originally of silk, the fabric normally used today for the screens used in screen printing are made of nylon or metal cloth of about 125 to 150 meshes per inch.[L2] The fabric is stretched evenly over specially designed metal frames. There are a number of methods for applying the design to the prepared screen. These include hand cutting, direct stencil, and photographic techniques.[S9] Today, the preferred method is photographic. This method takes advantage of the light sensitivity of potassium dichromate in combination with various colloid materials. This method offers the advantages of speed and perfect reproduction. After the screen is treated with the colloid photosensitized by potassium dichromate, light is allowed to impinge on it through the negative of the design, and the unexposed soluble parts of the coating are then washed away, leaving the open pores for the screening operation.

The quality of the screen printing equipment is an important consideration.[Y3] Screen printers have a number of moving parts that are subject to conditions that create wear and tear. Yet, reliability and repeatability are important to a successful operation. Hence, it rarely pays to use less than the most durable equipment available.

As with the other printing processes, conventional squeegee oil-based media require drying and hardening-on before further processing. Ultraviolet-cured media speed up the drying process.[Y3] However, increasingly, thermoplastic hot-melt media are used that harden instantaneously without drying.

Figure 11.4

Plate with decalcomania.

11.7 Decalcomania

Decoration with decalcomania (see Figure 11.4) is a two-step process—the manufacture of the paper transfer or decal, followed by the decoration of the ware. In the United States, most decalcomania are manufactured by specialty firms and sold to the user.

Underglaze decalcomania are used extensively in the tableware industry in order to achieve multicolor effects. They are particularly appropriate for halftone effects.

The manufacture of decalcomania is done by lithographic or silk screen processes.[59] The first step in preparing polychrome transfers is to analyze the artist's design for the decoration and to decide how many colorants will be required. The breakdown into separate colors is done photographically, using colored filters in front of the camera, and color film in it. The color separation negatives are developed, dried, and then used to make a positive on light-sensitive lithographic plates or silk screens.

The primary difficulty in making decals is obtaining a high enough volume of pigment to give adequate color strength after firing. The usual solution is to grind as much pigment as possible into the decal varnish. Then, after printing, more pigment is dusted onto the wet print. The excess color is brushed off and the decal cleaned thoroughly.

The printing of decals is carried out under closely controlled humidity conditions, to prevent cracking of the organic medium. When the decal is completed, it is usually stored in a humidity-controlled area. Often a clear varnish is printed over the pattern to protect it in handling.

The current method of decal application includes the use of solvent-mount decals. These decals are printed on duplex paper, so it is necessary to strip off the backing sheet. The decalcomania is then soaked in a solution to soften it, so that it sticks to the ware. A sponge or squeegee is then used to obtain close contact between the decal and the ware. After drying, the paper backing is removed with a damp sponge.

This method can be automated. However, automatic application has not been widely accepted because the rate is not faster than the hand technique.

The problems in using decalcomania are primarily those of good housekeeping.[D9] Dirty sponges or water, greasy fingers, and the use of sponging water from dark colors on lighter colors all result in a blurred pattern. Great care is required to insure that good adhesion between the ceramic color and the bisque ware is obtained.

11.8 Stamping

The process of stamping underglaze patterns involves the application of a monochromatic decoration by a rubber stamp, usually mounted on a soft rubber backing (see Figure 11.5). This highly

Figure 11.5

A backstamp.

automated, low-cost process has long been used for back stamping, less extensively for actual decoration.

A varnish similar to that used for printing is ground with the underglaze color and placed on a glass or steel plate.[59] The rubber stamp is pressed against the color plate, picking up the color. The stamp is then pressed against the ware while the color is being rerolled on the plate. This procedure can be highly mechanized; operations up to 8,000 pieces per shift are possible with one machine.

Chapter 12
Firing

Following the application of the glaze and the decorations, the ware is dried and prepared for firing, to convert the dried particles to a smooth, vitreous coating. This is accomplished by firing the ware at cone 06 to cone 10 (1050 to 1250°C) in a kiln.

The first decision to be made is how to support the ware while the coating is molten. For flatware coated on only one side, such as most tile, this is simply a matter of placing it with the coated side up. Other shapes are not so simple.

One approach, used for sanitary ware and some tableware, is to remove any coating material from the base, or foot of the ware.[R1] This is also called dry footing. The sanitary ware and holloware are then placed directly on refractory shelves of the kiln. Plates and saucers are assembled into open setters called cranks, which enable a stack of ware to be fired at one place on the refractory shelf.

An alternate approach, used by some tableware manufacturers, is to support the ware on its underside by various refractory metal pins. This procedure has the advantage of allowing the foot of the ware to be glazed. However, the downside is that after the firing, the ware will show pin marks. These pin marks can be made less visible by polishing, but they cannot be completely eradicated.

Porcelain enameled parts are usually hung on hooks attached to moving chains.[M7] The hook passes through a hole punched through a flange or similar unexposed part of the ware.

The kilns used for firing coated ceramics come in two basic types: intermittent or periodic kilns, and continuous or tunnel kilns. The kilns for firing porcelain enamels are almost always of the continuous type.

12.1 Intermittent Kilns

With intermittent or periodic kilns, the ware is placed in the kilns when they are cold and is then heated up on a predetermined time-temperature schedule to a selected maximum temperature.[R1] This temperature is usually held for a certain period (up to 3 hours) called the soak. After the soak, the heat source can be reduced or shut off, and the ware allowed to cool in the furnace until it is cool enough to be removed. Figure 12.1 illustrates a typical kiln firing schedule.

Several technical advances in recent years have significantly improved the performance of intermittent kilns, so that in many cases they can provide as high quality a firing as a continuous kiln. One improvement is low mass insulation, which increases the maximum rate-of-change of kiln temperature that can be achieved. A more significant change is the use of modern electronic controls. Within the limitation of the maximum rate-of-change, modern electronic controls permit almost infinite variation of the time-temperature profile to achieve optimum results.

With production-scale equipment, the production rate is increased by using a kiln with two kiln cars, mounted on a track

Figure 12.1

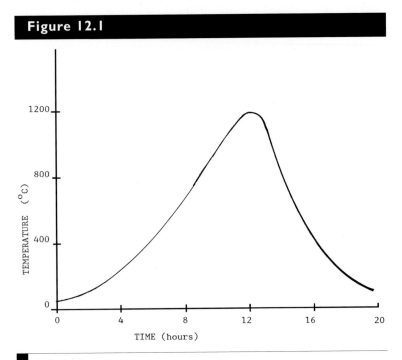

Typical firing curve.

passing through the kiln shell. In this way, a load is set while the kiln is running. At the appropriate time, the kiln is opened, the car with the fired load removed on one side, and then the car with the new load placed in the kiln from the other side, and the kiln restarted.

Intermittent kilns can be fired by either gas or electricity. Most small kilns are electrically fired. On the other hand, in North America, most production-sized kilns are gas fired, for reasons of fuel cost.

12.2 Continuous Kilns

In a continuous kiln, ware is passed through a kiln in which a temperature profile has been previously established, and is maintained unaltered while the ware is passing through. The time-temperature profile is determined by the rate at which the ware passes through the kiln.

In a traditional high-thermal-mass tunnel kiln, the ware is placed on kiln cars that run on rails through the tunnel. They are designed so that the car wheels and the rails are protected from the heat of the firing zone. Most tunnel kilns are straight, but some are circular or U-shaped. The circular kilns have a short open section between the exit and entry ports, where the ware is unloaded and new ware loaded.

In kilns where the top temperature is less than 900°C, metal chains or belts can be used to hold the ware instead of kiln cars. Metal chains are characteristic of the kilns used to fire porcelain enamels, while belts are characteristic of tableware decorator kilns.

For flat shapes such as tile, ware can be passed through a continuous kiln, while supported on slowly (a few RPM) rotating silicon carbide rods. These kilns are called roller-hearth kilns. As is discussed in section 12.4, the roller-hearth kiln lends itself to fast firing, which is its principal application. While used primarily for firing tile, the roller-hearth kiln has been adapted to the firing of tableware by using refractory slabs, called bats, as supports.

In North America, most continuous kilns are gas fired, for reasons of fuel cost.

12.3 Comparison of Intermittent and Continuous Kilns

One advantage of continuous kilns over intermittent kilns is in fuel consumption.[R1] In a continuous kiln, some of the hot air given off the fired ware in the cooling zone is fed to the preheating zone to heat the incoming ware. With gas-fired kilns, the hot air is also fed to the burners as secondary air, thus further increasing fuel efficiency.

Another advantage of continuous kilns is lower maintenance costs. In a continuous kiln, the interior walls and roof of the kiln are maintained at the same temperature for extended periods, and, hence, do not suffer the thermal shock that the interiors of intermittent kilns do.

The quality of ware from a well-designed continuous kiln will generally be somewhat better than from a well-designed intermittent kiln.[R1] One reason is that it is easier to obtain the same temperature-time profile for ware fired at different times. Another reason is that it is practical to design a continuous kiln for minimal side-to-side and top-to-bottom thermal variation. Of course, it is possible to get a higher-quality ware from a well-designed intermittent kiln than from a poorly designed or maintained continuous kiln. Moreover, the advent of modern electronic controls has substantially reduced the quality differences by making it easier to obtain a consistent thermal profile from firing to firing in an intermittent kiln.

Flexibility is the great advantage of intermittent kilns. A continuous kiln determines the whole production line output. Leaving gaps in the setting of a continuous kiln when there is a lack of orders is not only uneconomical, but it can also lead to uneven heating and imperfectly fired ware. The same problem arises if the speed of travel through the kiln is varied.

Thus, a continuous kiln governs the whole factory's scheduling It cannot be adapted to allow for a variation in demand for the product. Shutting down a high-thermal-mass tunnel kiln takes days or even weeks, and is thus impractical for any but the most severe problems. During vacations or holidays it continues to operate.

By contrast, adjusting intermittent kilns for order flow is easy. If there are fewer orders, fewer firings are run. If demand exceeds capacity, kilns are run every day, and additional kilns can often be added without excessive capital cost.

A related flexibility is in the scheduling of labor. A continuous kiln requires an operator 24 hours a day, 7 days a week. With careful scheduling, an intermittent kiln can be operated during normal working hours.

Another advantage of intermittent kilns is that they take up much less floor space than continuous kilns of the same capacity.

Finally, the capital cost of an intermittent kiln is generally less than that of a continuous kiln of the same capacity. In addition, the minimum kiln capacity for economic operation is much lower for intermittent kilns.

12.4 Fast Firing

Two of the major costs in kiln operation are the capital cost of installing the kiln and the wage cost of the operators. Both of these costs are insensitive to the throughput of the kiln. The third major operating cost, fuel, is only partially related to throughput, because a significant portion of the fuel is used to heat the kiln itself, rather than the ware. Thus, an economic analysis of kiln operation quickly leads to the conclusion that the higher the throughput, the lower the cost per unit of production. Hence, for a number of years, ceramic engineers have sought ways to reduce firing time and thus increase the throughput of the kilns.

The maximum rate of temperature change that ceramic ware can withstand depends on the shape of the ware and the mechanical strength of the body. Thus, fast firing has been most applicable to tile, where cold-to-cold elapsed times have been reduced to as little as 30 minutes, and 45 minutes is common. For tableware, where the shapes are diverse and sometimes more fragile, six hours cold-to-cold is the fastest so far. For the larger shapes of sanitary ware, the fastest results are 12 to 15 hours cold-to-cold.

For the fast firing of tile, the roller-hearth kilns described in section 12.2 have become standard. The ware passes through a roller-hearth kiln in a single layer. This creates the option of automating the loading and unloading of the kiln, which further reduces costs.

12.5 Firing Conditions

For reasons that are partly historic, partly economic, and partly related to the properties of the product, the whiteware industries have largely settled on a firing condition that most companies use for their glost fire. In part, the selection relates to the decision of whether to operate a single-fire or a two-fire process. In a single-fire operation, the ware is made (occasionally for tableware fired at a low temperature to remove volatiles), coated, and then both body and coating are fired to maturity at the same time. In a two-fire operation, the body is made and fired to maturity before coating. The coating is matured in a second firing at a lower temperature than the firing that matured the body.

As one might expect, a single-fire process is lower in cost. A two-fire process is easier to control for consistent high-quality ware free of defects.

The kilns for sanitary ware are fired to 1180 to 1250°C for 12 to 30 hours, to achieve a cone 8 to a cone 10 in a single-fire process.

Stoneware is single-fired to 1170 to 1200°C for 6 to 8 hours, to achieve a cone 6 or 7. Hotel and restaurant china is two-fired. The glost fire is 1160 to 1180°C for 6 to 18 hours to achieve a cone 4. Vitreous floor tile is a single-fire operation at 1170 to 1250°C for 30 to 60 minutes to achieve cone 3 to 5. Most other tiles, including wall tile, are single-fired at 1130 to 1140°C for 30 to 45 minutes to achieve cone 1. Fine china and some artware are two-fired. The glost fire is 1050 to 1100°C for 6 to 18 hours to achieve cone 03 to 01. Hobbyware and some artware are glost fired at 1000°C for 2 to 15 hours to achieve a cone 06.

Chapter 13
Defects and Their Control

This chapter will present an overview of defects in ceramic whiteware glazes, their occurrence, and their elimination. We will cover bubble defects, surface texture, crazing and peeling, specking, and crawling or tearing.

13.1 Bubble Defects

Glazes and frits are capable of retaining substantial quantities of the gases that originate in the vitrification process.[T1] Some of this gas is held in solution; the rest is aggregated as bubbles of varying sizes.

All glazes contain some bubbles.[E32] Many of the smaller bubbles have little or no effect on the glaze quality and can be ignored, particularly if they are separated from the external surface of the glaze. However, when they get larger and/or closer to the surface, they will disturb the surface and become a problem.

Bubble defects are very common in all glazes, but especially in leadless glazes.[P1] Lead oxide is a very reactive substance that promotes the accelerated elimination of the gas produced during the firing of the glaze. Hence, when lead oxide is not present, attention must be given to minimizing the production of gas and eliminating that which does occur.

The gases that fill bubbles come from one or more of the following sources:

1. Air from the space between the particles of glaze in the dried, but unfired glaze layer. In a dried but unfired glaze, upwards of 40 percent of the green glaze volume will be empty space arising from the evaporation of the water from the glaze slip during drying.[R5]

2. Air entrapped in the glaze slip. Air may also be trapped in a glaze due to excessive additions of wetting agents, or too much agitation of the slip before application.

3. The decomposition of glaze components. The use of carbonates, clays, talc, fluorides, and organic compounds will result in gas evolution when these materials decompose during firing.[L3] In addition, residual crystalline material, particularly quartz, serves as an anchor promoting the retention of this gas.[D7]

4. The breakdown of glaze contaminants. Contaminants that can cause gas include rust from processing equipment, and silicon carbide, which is used in some kiln furniture.

5. The breakdown of organic binders.

6. Water vapor entrapped by rapid melting and sealing of the glaze. This is a particular problem for fast-fire operations. Some water is not released until the temperature exceeds 500°C, where many glazes begin to fuse.[T1]

7. Inadequate drying of the body and engobe, if used. This is a particular problem for single-fire operations, and for automatic glaze lines, where an engobe application may be followed immediately by the glazing application.[J2] It can also occur with porous, bisque-fired bodies.

8. Water trapped in frit. Most frits contain 0.1 to 0.3% of trapped water.[R3] It has been detected by infrared spectroscopy, and is thought to be the result of the tetrahedral structure of water resembling that of glass.

The gases that come from these various sources either remain in solution in the coating or they coalesce, rise to the surface, and burst. This is the process called fining. The factors that affect the rate at which bubbles grow, rise, and burst include:

1. Glaze composition, in particular components such as whiting that introduce large quantities of gases, and those such as alkalis that increase the glaze viscosity at the melting temperature.

2. Glaze viscosity. In a fluid glaze, bubbles can coalesce and grow. The rate of rise to the glaze surface increases rapidly as the bubble size increases.[D10] In a high-viscosity system, bubbles find it difficult to coalesce and grow.

3. Glaze surface tension. This property affects the ability of bubbles to burst once they reach the glaze surface. It also affects the ability of the glaze to heal over and smooth out the crater left after a bubble bursts.

4. The thickness of the glaze layer. There is a directly proportional relationship between the bubble diameter and the

glaze thickness. In addition, the thicker the glaze, the longer it takes for a bubble to reach the surface, where it can be eliminated. Moreover, as the glaze thickness increases above a critical thickness, the number of bubbles increases with thickness.[B10]

5. Furnace atmosphere. A stagnant atmosphere will develop a saturation of the volatile constituents of a glaze, impeding further volatilization.[M6]

The largest bubble defects are conventionally termed *blisters*. Smaller bubbles are called *pinholes*. The terms *eggshell* and *orange peel* refer to surfaces with many pinholes.

Blisters are usually large bubbles close to the surface of the glaze that destroy the smoothness of the glaze surface. If the bubbles burst, but sufficient time is not given to heal them over before the glaze solidifies, the small open craters also appear as blisters.

To prevent blistering, one or more of the following procedures are usually recommended:[T1]

1. Eliminate, or at least reduce, the amounts of those constituents that give off gas during the firing process.[L3]

2. Minimize the use of those mill additions that release gas or water vapor during the firing process.

3. Reduce the thickness of the glaze layer. A thinner glaze layer will facilitate the passage of gas to the glaze surface and will promote smaller bubbles.

4. Make sure that the glazed ware is thoroughly dried before firing.

5. Change the firing cycle to reduce the rate of temperature rise in the early stages of firing—up to about 650°C. This increases the time available for the gases to pass through the glaze layer before it heals over.

6. Reduce the highest temperature reached in the glost fire. Many blisters are caused by overfiring.

7. Increase the maturing temperature of the glaze.

Dimples and pinholes in glazes (see Figure 13.1) are smaller but more common bubble defects. They are often traces of where bubbles have burst and only partially healed.

Pinholing is a very frustrating defect to correct. The suppression of bubble formation and eruption requires various responses. Some of the key factors in the prevention of pinholing are:

1. The glaze composition may be such that the glaze is sealing over at too low a temperature. As a result, there is insufficient time for gas to escape.[L3] This is a particularly important consideration for fast-fire operations. Moreover, a very

Figure 13.1

Tiles with pinholes.

low-melting glaze is usually too reactive with the substrate surface.

2. Poor frit quality. Unmelted inclusions in frits are one source of bubbles. Frits used for leadless glazes must be thoroughly melted to eliminate inclusions.

3. Soluble vanadium salts are a notorious source of dimples. All vanadium-containing pigments must be washed to remove unreacted vanadium before they are used in a glaze.[E27]

4. When a properly formulated glaze still exhibits a pinholed surface, then the application technique must be examined. Pinholing can be caused in spray application by holding the spray gun too close to the ware, or by using excessive air pressure. It can develop if a second spray coat is applied before the first coat is thoroughly dry.

Let's now examine some of these approaches to the elimination of bubble defects in greater detail. First, it has been noted that some raw materials give off large quantities of gas as they decompose.[L3] Table 13-1 lists the decomposition temperatures of selected glaze raw materials, and the extent of the weight loss accompanying the decomposition. When possible, a raw material substitution can eliminate this major source of bubble defects.

The higher the temperature at which the gas comes off, the more

Table 13-1. Decomposition of Selected Raw Materials

Material	Decomposition Temperature (°C)	Product	Wt% Loss
alumina hydrate	250	alumina	35
clay	500–650	metakaolin	14
dolomite	800	CaO, MgO	48
whiting	850–900	CaO	44
talc	1000	$MgSiO_3$	7
strontium carbonate	1200–1300	SrO	30
barium carbonate	1300–1400	BaO	22

(from refs. G5 and I1)

important it is to eliminate that raw material. Hence, the first recommendation is to avoid using strontium or barium carbonates directly as raw materials. Instead, obtain strontium or barium values from appropriate frits. A more important recommendation here is to eliminate talc from the glaze formula. Talc loses its water of hydration at approximately 1000°C, well above the temperature at which the glaze melts. If more magnesia is required in the glaze formula than is provided as impurity in other raw materials, there are several suitable frits available.

Table 13-2. Melting of Glaze Raw Materials and Decomposition Products

Raw Material	Melting Temperature* (°C)
alumina	>1300
BaO	>1300
CaO	>1300
feldspar	1170
frits	700–1000
MgO	>1300
$MgSiO_3$	1200
metakaolin	>1300
nepheline syenite	1100
silica	>1300
ZnO	>1300
zircon	>1300

At temperatures greater than 1300°C, the material dissolves in most glazes instead of melting.
(from ref. A1)

Another recommendation is to replace calcium carbonate (whiting) with wollastonite, with a suitable adjustment of the silica content. Calcium carbonate loses 44% of its weight at about 900°C, which is near the glaze melting temperature in many cases.

Adjusting the glaze formula so as to raise the seal-over temperature will also yield dividends in reduced bubble defects. Table 13-2 lists some of the principal glaze raw materials and decomposition products. The seal-over temperature is increased by reducing the amounts of low-melting raw materials. Hence, proper frit selection is very important here, as the frits are the first ingredients to melt in many glazes. Table 6-2 gives the formulations and melting temperatures of several of the most common leadless frits. While there are exceptions, in general terms, seal-over temperature increases when the concentrations of boron oxide and the alkalis in a frit are minimized, and the concentrations of calcia, magnesia, and zinc oxide, when used, are increased.

Proper selection of mill additives can also reduce the tendency to gassing. The voids in a glaze left by the evaporation of the water in the glaze slip can amount to over 40% of the available space.[R5] As shown in Figure 7.1, the use of deflocculants can substantially reduce this void space. Deflocculated slips settle in an efficient manner to give a dense coating, while a flocculated slip produces a coating with much more void space.

In summary, the reduction or, preferably, the elimination of bubble defects in leadless glazes involves a number of changes to the formulation and processing of the glaze.

The steps in formulation include changes to increase the seal-over temperature, proper raw material selection to minimize volatiles, and the use of mill additives such as deflocculants. Alkali and B_2O_3 contents are minimized, while alkaline earths are increased. Talc is avoided, and whiting is replaced by wollastonite.

The changes to the processing include proper application technique, minimal glaze thickness consistent with good surface, complete drying before firing, and firing at an optimum firing temperature, and on an optimum firing schedule, that allows sufficient time for gases to escape before the glaze seals over.

Before leaving bubble defects, we will discuss a related gassing problem. Under microscopic examination, it often appears as a miniature crater, with a center that descends into the body, and it often contains a dark speck. In aggravated cases, a chip of the glaze may have delaminated and fallen off. Often, the sides of the crater or the chip in the glaze are not perpendicular to the glaze surface.

This is a body problem. The usual source is organic material trapped under the surface of the body that does not vaporize until high temperatures are reached in the firing, and the glaze has sealed over. Due to the high driving force, when the material does vaporize, it does so explosively, creating the observed crater.

This problem can be addressed by examining the choice of body raw materials, to find materials that do not create this problem. It can also be addressed by raising the seal-over temperature of the glaze, as we have discussed.

13.2 Surface Texture

Figure 13.2

Surface texture refers to a lack of smoothness of the surface of a glaze (see Figure 13.2). It exhibits irregularities on the scale of one-tenth to one-quarter of an inch.

These irregularities may arise from one or more causes. Excessive viscosity at the firing temperature of the glaze, or inadequate firing temperature and duration, can lead to this defect.[S14] Surface texture can also result from the bubble defects that have just been discussed, or their craters.[E36] It can result from improper application, as many glazes will not smooth out a rough application.

Glazed tile with many defects, poor surface.

At the highest temperatures of the glaze firing process, the glaze must have a sufficiently low viscosity that it will flow out smoothly and evenly, to equally cover all substrate surfaces.[E36] Gases must be allowed to escape, and the surface smoothed over at the places where the gas bubbles burst. The alkaline earths (and MgO and ZnO) impart a lower melt viscosity to a glaze and increase the flow of the glaze over the substrate surface, provided the firing temperature is above the 1100°C necessary to dissolve these constituents.

The presence in the glaze of constituents that do not dissolve at the glaze firing temperature aggravate this problem. For example, the solubility of zirconia at firing temperatures is limited to about 5 wt % in most glazes.[E27] To be effective, most ceramic pigments must not dissolve in the glaze during firing.

The application process can make a large difference in the smoothness of the fired glaze. Leadless glazes, in particular, have a limited ability to flow at the firing temperatures. Hence, application processes such as the waterfall that yield a smooth application are better able to yield a smooth fired glaze. Additives such as deflocculants that promote a dense laydown of the green glaze particles will improve the surface smoothness.

Figure 13.3

Bowl with crazed glaze.

13.3 Crazing and Peeling

Crazing appears as a pattern of cracks in a glaze extending from the outer surface of the glaze to the glaze-body interface (see Figure 13.3). This defect is caused by a mismatch between the thermal expansion coefficients of the glaze and the body.[T1] This mismatch induces stresses in both the glaze and the body as the glazed body is cooled to room temperature after firing.

A related effect is called peeling or shivering. While a moderate compression of a glaze, with corresponding tensile forces in the body, can be tolerated, at a larger mismatch in thermal expansion compression is generated in the glaze that can exceed the strength of adhesion between the glaze and the substrate. This yields a stress-relieving fracture at the interface. Usually, this occurs at corners of the ware and results in apparent chipping of the glaze. Hence, it is common to attribute glaze chipping at corners to shivering.

Figure 13.4 illustrates a defect initially ascribed to peeling based on appearance. A detailed analysis of these stress-induced defects will be found in Chapter 15. Applying that analysis, the defect in Figure 13.4 was found to actually be the result of multiple crazing.

This discussion is limited to the methods used to control crazing and peeling. The actions that are taken to improve crazing resistance include:[T1]

1. Reducing the thermal expansion coefficient of the glaze, until it is less than that of the body.
2. Increasing the setting point of the glaze, as higher firing glazes are usually lower in thermal expansion than softer glazes.
3. Decreasing the thickness of the applied coating, as thin coatings can sometimes avoid developing enough stress to induce crazing.
4. Increasing the thermal expansion coefficient of the body until it exceeds that of the glaze.

Figure 13.4

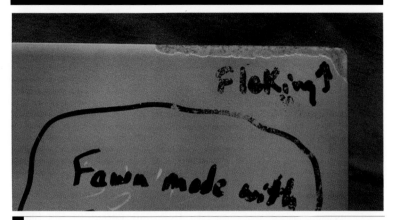

Glazed tile showing what looks like peeling, but actually is crazing through an underlayer.

5. Increasing the flux content of the body, as most fluxing oxides have higher thermal expansion coefficients than do the more refractory oxides.

6. Grinding the quartz or flint in the body more finely, so as to reduce the incidence of free silica in the fired body.

In the rare cases in which shivering or peeling is observed, these changes should be reversed.

One final problem needs to be mentioned, that of delayed crazing (see Figure 13.5). When a porous body is used, it may be rehydrolyzed in service, lowering the body expansion, and hence exposing the coating to tensile forces that may lead to crazing.[D8] Hence, even a properly fit glaze-body system may show crazing after exposure to moisture for a considerable period. Fortunately, this does not occur for fully vitreous bodies.

Figure 13.5

Plate with delayed crazing.

13.4 Specking

A speck is a discrete particle of unreacted or unwanted material in a glaze[E39]

Figure 13.6

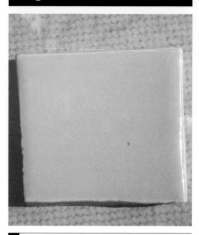

A speck in a tile glaze.

(see Figure 13.6). Many specks are dark particles, but an intrusive white particle in a clear glaze is also a speck. This same speck in an opaque white glaze could be ignored.

Although there are several causes of specking, the fault is usually caused by contamination by extraneous material, often iron containing. There are several sources of these contaminants.

Impurities in the raw materials can pass into the glaze. Clays in particular often have substantial impurities of iron and titania.

The wear of milling and other process equipment may introduce specks. Mills and mill media must be monitored for wear, and defective parts removed.

Cleanliness of the glaze application area is very important. Ware must be clean when glazed. Particular care is required in handling pigments to see that stray pigment particles do not get into glazes.[E28] It is important to remember that every pigment is a contaminant for every other pigment!

The atmosphere in the firing kiln must be regulated to see that specks are not deposited on the ware as it passes through.

13.5 Crawling and Tearing

When crawling or tearing occurs, irregularly shaped areas that are either unglazed or partially glazed mar the uniformity of the fired glaze[E39] (see Figure 13.7). The defect can range from a small exposed area of substrate to beading of the glaze, where it has formed globular islands of different sizes and shapes. The factors affecting this defect include

Figure 13.7

Tile with crawling defect.

glaze surface tension, the bond strength between the green glaze and the substrate, the shrinkage of the green glaze during drying, and the green strength of the glaze.[T1,S14]

One cause of crawling is a lack of wetting of the body by the glaze—that is, the absence of bonding between the glaze and the body. Any condition that leads to poor adhesion will promote crawling or tearing. Oil stains and/or dust on the surface of the ware keep the glaze from developing a bond with the body. Therefore, biscuit ware should be handled as little as possible and stored under dust-free conditions. In single-fire operations, soluble salts from the body can accumulate on the substrate surface. These salts can lift the glaze away from the body, leading to crawling.

Another cause of tearing is excessive or rapid shrinkage of the glaze during drying. The drying conditions must be adjusted so that fractures of the weak green glaze do not occur. Unfortunately, many drying cracks are so small that they cannot be seen before firing. During firing, the material on either side of the crack pulls back due to surface tension, opening up a tear. Shrinkage problems can also arise from applying a second wet glaze layer before the first layer is thoroughly dry.

There are several approaches to the elimination of tearing or crawling defects:

1. First, keep the clay content of the glaze as low as is consistent with proper slip suspension. Avoid the use of ball clays and other highly plastic ingredients, except in small quantities. These plastic ingredients promote crawling. This is an important difference between glazes and bodies. In bodies, greater ease of forming suggests maximizing the plastic constituents; in glazes, tearing limits the plastic content to that required for slip suspension.

2. Avoid overgrinding the glaze slip. A finer particle size increases surface tension, and with it, the tendency to crawl.

3. Minimize the quantity of opacifiers used. Opacifiers promote crawling.

4. When using zinc oxide in the mill formulation, use only material precalcined at 900 to 950°C. Zinc oxide that is also granulated is preferred. This will minimize the formation of hydroxide gels on the surfaces of the zinc oxide particles, which lead to crawling.[R7]

5. Keep the glaze thickness to the minimum consistent with good coverage. Thicker glazes are more apt to crawl or tear. The minimum glaze thickness is a function of the smoothness of the substrate surface. You need about 3 mils of glaze

over the highest point on the substrate surface. Thus, some very smooth electronic ceramic bodies can be successfully glazed with only 3 or 4 mils of coating thickness, while some coarse artware bodies may require 10 to 12 mils of coating thickness for adequate coverage.

6. The tendency to tear or crawl can be ameliorated by adding a small amount of a binder to the glaze.[R5] This stiffens the green coating, preventing cracks that would become tears on firing. In extreme cases, a very small amount of a low-foam wetting agent can also be added.

13.6 Metal Marking

While glazes cannot be readily cut, with hard metals they can be scratched and/or or metal marked.[55] The drawing of a stainless steel knife across a ceramic glazed dinner plate can sometimes result in a scratch. More often, it results in a mark on the plate, which may or may not be readily removable from the glaze surface (see Figure 13.8).

The ease of metal marking and/or scratching varies between glazes. Leadless stoneware matte glazes are the easiest glazes to mark, but they are also the easiest to clean. White opacified leadless glazes vary greatly in their ease of marking, but they are the hardest

Figure 13.8

Plates with knife markings.

glazes to remove metal marks from. Leadless gloss glazes are more difficult to metal mark, probably due to their greater smoothness. All leadless glazes are generally resistant to scratching.

The presence of crystalline zircon opacifier in a glaze drastically increases the incidence of metal marking.[C2] Nonopacified gloss glazes show high metal marking resistance. Opacified gloss glazes suffer from crack formation around zircon particles that protrude from the glaze surface. This crack formation leads to metal deposition in and around the cracks, resulting in severe and permanent metal marks.

Fine china and other lead glazes are similar to gloss leadless glazes for metal marking. The great problem with lead glazes is that they are readily scratched.[S5]

These results correlate with the relative hardness of the glaze, zircon, and the metal marker. When the metal is harder than the glaze, the principal result is scratching. When the glaze is harder than the metal, the only result is metal marking. Protruding zircon particles also cause metal marking. These problems are minimized when the hardness of the glaze resembles that of the stainless steel knife.

Part IV
Coating Properties

Chapter 14
Adherence

A ceramic coating must not only act as a protective and aesthetically pleasing surface, but it must also bond effectively to its substrate. Particularly when the substrate is a very different kind of material, as for example a metal in the case of a porcelain enamel, this is not a trivial consideration. Therefore, this chapter will discuss some experiments which have provided an understanding of the requirements for effective adherence of a coating to a substrate.[P2]

To understand adherence, one must focus on the interface between the coating and the substrate. In the case of a porcelain enamel, there is on one side a metal substrate, usually a piece of steel, and on the other side a vitreous ceramic coating. These studies[P2] indicate that for proper adherence, it is necessary to develop a continuous electronic structure or chemical bond across the interfacial area. This continuity is realized when both the enamel coating and the substrate metal are saturated at the interface with an oxide of the metal, resulting in a transition oxide–like layer. This oxide must be one that, when in solution in the glass, will not be reduced by the metal. For iron and steel substrates, this oxide is FeO.

The nature of, and conditions at, the interface are all-important to adequate adherence. For the purposes of this discussion we will not be concerned with the problems associated with strains caused by thermal expansion mismatches. Those will be discussed in Chapter 15. For this discussion, we will assume that such problems are under control.

This discussion will also not be concerned with the mechanical contribution to adherence realized by creating a highly irregular interface by abrasion or etching of the substrate surface. Surface roughness generally improves adherence by creating a greater contact area. But it is of little value if the chemical bond is weak.[K4]

A chemical bond means that there is a continuity of the electronic structure across the interface, as well as a continuity of the atomic structure. To realize this continuity of atomic and electronic structure, a transition layer or zone is needed that is compatible or in equilibrium with both the metal substrate and the glass coating at the interface.[P2] This transition zone must include at least a monomolecular layer of the oxide of the metal between the metal and glass, and it is retained in processing only when both the metal and the glass at the interface are saturated with this metal oxide.

Figure 14.1 shows schematic models of atoms at the interface when an oxide layer is present and when it is absent. When present (Figure 14.1a), a layer of metal atoms must exist between the bulk metal and oxide that has both metallic and ionic-covalent characteristics, and a shared layer of oxygen ions between the oxide and glass. Thus, there is a cross-sectional continuity of the chemical bond across the transition zone.

Although a discrete oxide layer, as shown in Figure 14.1, satisfies the requirements for a continuous zone of chemical bonding, it is normally undesirable. Such macroscopic oxide layers are weak,

Figure 14.1

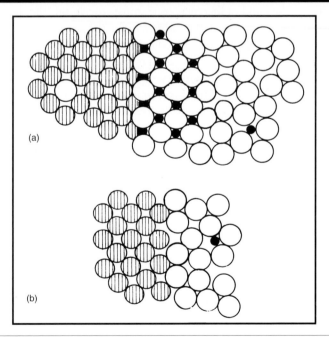

Schematic atomic representations of cross sections across the interface (a) when the oxide layer is present and (b) when no oxide layer is present.

Figure 14.2

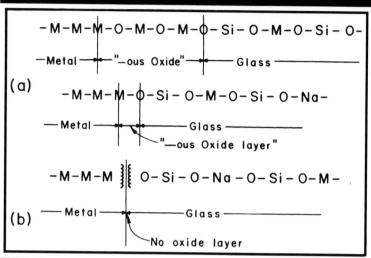

Schematic representations of transition zones through metal-glass interfaces, showing conditions for chemical and van der Waals types of bonding: (a) chemical bonding with and without discrete intermediate oxide layer; (b) van der Waals type of bonding.

resulting in a flaking off of the coating. A modification is required, which will be discussed shortly.

The absence of a metal oxide is also undesirable, as indicated in Figure 14.1*b*. Here the glass comes in direct contact with the metal without an intermediate oxide layer. This results in atomic continuity, but not electronic continuity; a van der Waals type of bond is all that is possible, which is considerably weaker than a chemical bond.

Figure 14.2 illustrates the solution to the problem. It shows in the second line of (part *a*) that only a monomolecular layer of the oxide is required for electronic continuity. It is this monomolecular layer that avoids the weakness associated with a bulk oxide layer, as in Figure 14.1*a*, or the weak van der Waals bonding associated with no electronic continuity, as in Figure 14.1*b*.

Thermodynamically, equilibrium compositions across the interfacial zone occur when the oxide has equal chemical potential over the zone.[B8,P2] This occurs when both the metal and the glass coating at the interface are saturated with the metal oxide.

Since most commercial enameling requires the heating of the substrate in air, a scale is formed on the substrate during the heatup period before the coating sinters to a continuous mass. Figure 14.3 represents the condition when a glass with no dissolved metal oxide

Figure 14.3

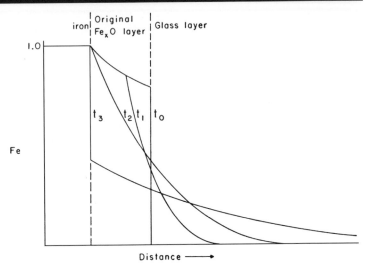

Schematic of the change in activity of iron oxide versus distance across the interfacial zone of a system containing a starting oxide layer after heating at a given temperature for a number of times.

is sealed to a metal with an oxide scale at time t_0. As soon as the glass fuses, it attacks the scale and dissolves the saturation amount of metal oxide. At the same time, the oxide diffuses into the bulk glass, as the driving force is for the whole system to move toward equilibrium. The solution reaction is faster than the diffusion flux, so the interfacial glass composition remains saturated as long as oxide remains, as represented by times t_1 and t_2.

Should the oxide layer be completely dissolved, the diffusion process would continue, resulting in a drop in the oxide activity at the interface, as represented by times t_3 and t_4. Hence, bonding would be reduced. Chemical bonding is maximized when the activity of the oxide is 1 because both the coating and the substrate are saturated with the oxide.

The practical problem is then one of maintaining oxide saturation at the interface, preferably by maintaining a monomolecular layer of the oxide. When the scale is dissolved, this maintenance of saturation can only be achieved by chemical reactions that oxidize the metal and introduce the metal cation in sufficient quantities into the glass at the interface.

For many years it has been known that additions to the ceramic coating formulation of certain easily reducible ions, such as cobalt oxide, nickel oxide, and copper oxide, result in improved adherence between the glass coating and the metal. These oxides, particularly cobalt oxide, contribute substantially to the attainment and stabilization of the saturation of both the substrate and the coating with the oxide of the metal. In the first place, once the initial oxide scale is removed, the presence of an easily reduced oxide, such as cobalt oxide, in the ceramic coating facilitates the dissolution of the substrate in the coating until saturation is achieved. For a coating containing cobalt oxide, the reaction would be:[B9,P2]

$$Fe + CoO(glass) = FeO(glass) + Co$$

The free energy for this reaction is -9 kcal/mole at 1000°C. NiO– and CuO in the glass can also be reduced when the glass is in contact with iron.

The effect of this reaction is illustrated in Figure 14.4. It shows the concentration profiles as revealed by electron microprobe that formed when a sodium disilicate glass with 4.8% CoO added was heated in air at 950°C for 10 minutes in contact with Armco iron that had been preoxidized to form about a 2-micron-thick oxide layer. This specimen showed no weight gain. Hence, the profiles in the glass are the result of the solution of the oxide on the metal and the redox reaction just written. The drop in SiO_2 and Na_2O content at the interface are due to the initial dissolution of the oxide layer.

Figure 14.4

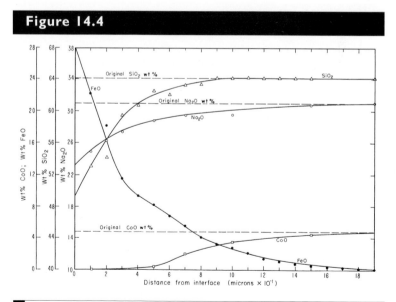

Diffusion profiles of a glass-iron composite heated at 950°C in an alumina crucible for 10 minutes.

The subsequent introduction of iron is due primarily to the reduction of cobalt oxide.

After saturation is initially achieved, further reaction can result in the deposition of cobalt metal, first as a layer at the interface and then as dendrites at the surface of the metal extending into the coating. Figure 14.5 is a photomicrograph of some dendrites grown in the same glass coating on iron after a treatment of 950°C for 3 hours.

An analysis of dendrites from several enamels by electron microprobe indicates that their composition is determined by the adherence oxide composition in the glass at the point and time of precipitation. The compositions of the dendrites show that the amounts of cobalt, nickel, copper, and iron are variable; the dendrites close to the interface where the iron oxide content in the glass is the highest are richest in iron. The mechanism for dendrite formation is illustrated schematically in Figure 14.6. It is based on a galvanic cell type of reaction. A circuit is established with the electrons that are released by iron going into the glass moving along the dendrite and reducing cobalt ions as they deposit in the dendrite. The circuit is completed as the resulting negative holes move toward the iron substrate and provide a site for the ferrous cations.

Figure 14.5

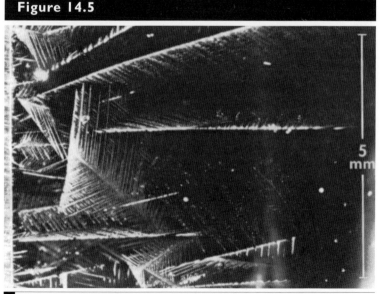

Dendrites growing from the interface between cobalt and glass with cobalt oxide after three hours at 950°C.

Figure 14.6

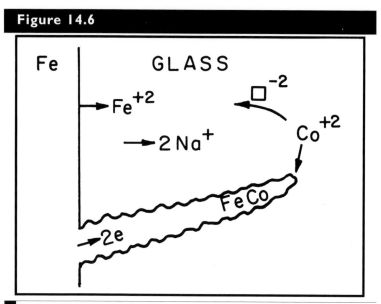

Schematic representation of dendrite formation.

Thus the adherence oxides play a critical role in creating and maintaining the saturation at the interface between the substrate and the coating. They appear to play a role in three of these types of reactions. In addition to their participation in the redox reaction resulting in the formation of dendrites, they enhance atmospheric oxidation of the substrate. Also, by precipitation and alloying with the iron at the interface, they enhance the type of redox reaction in which sodium is released.

Another technique that is often used in enameling to improve adherence is the application of a nickel flash to the substrate prior to enameling.[B8] This nickel flash acts in a similar manner to increase the reaction rate between the substrate and the ceramic coating by performing a similar function of enhancing the sodium-forming redox reaction. The sodium vapor, upon diffusing into the glass from the interface, subsequently undergoes reactions similar to those described for the substrate iron at favorable sites in the enamel layer.

Development of an interfacial bonding region has also been shown for coatings on ceramic substrates.[T1] Figure 14.7 shows the development of an interfacial bonding zone in an all-fritted lead borosilicate glaze applied to a bone china body. When examined in cross section with a scanning electron microscope, three distinct regions are noted. In addition to the glaze and the body, an intermediate bonding zone can be seen in the illustration of a transverse polished section of the system (upper left). The other five photographs are element distribution images for the same area. These images show the relative concentration and distribution of Si, Al, P, Ca, and Pb through the body-buffer-glaze interface.

In Figure 14.7, the density of the white dots indicates the abundance of a particular element. From the images we see that there is much phosphorus in the body and little in the glaze. In the phosphorus scan, the interface resembles the body. On the other hand, we observe substantial diffusion of lead into the body.

The Al trace shows a significant steady decrease through the glaze. Detailed measurements show a decrease of nearly 20% from the interface to the surface. A similar examination for silica shows the reverse trend, with a difference of about 5% from surface to interface.

These measurements indicate the same need for a continuity of electronic and atomic structure across the interface. This is the most important criterion for the development of adherence between a coating and its substrate.

Figure 14.7

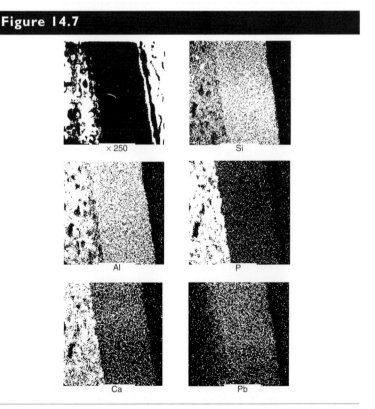

Elemental distributions at a glaze interface (a) view of the interface at the same magnification (250x) (b) Si (c) Al (d) P (e) Ca (f) Pb.

Chapter 15
Coating Fit

Vitreous coatings are brittle materials. As is characteristic of brittle materials, while they are very strong in compression, they are subject to ready failure in tension.[E36] When a ceramic coating is subjected to tensile stresses in excess of its ultimate tensile strength, it develops a characteristic fracture pattern called crazing. The reverse case, in which a glaze with a low expansion develops excessive compression, results in tensile failure of the body or the glaze-body interface, a condition called shivering or peeling.

Satisfactory ceramic coatings must not craze, shiver, or peel, either in manufacture or subsequently in service. A coating that meets these requirements is said to fit. To fit, a ceramic coating must have a thermal expansion that is modestly, but not excessively, lower than that of the substrate to which it is fused, over the temperature range from the temperature at which the vitreous coating cannot relieve stress by viscous flow (the set point) to room temperature.

15.1 Measurement of Thermal Expansion

To examine fit, we need information on the thermal expansion of the coating material and the substrate. Such information is obtained from a fused silica dilatometer, shown schematically in Figure 15.1. A previously fired specimen of the coating or the body is heated at a controlled linear rate in a fused silica tube furnace. In the furnace are a fused silica rod and a fused silica tube, differing in length by 1.000 or 2.000 inches at room temperature. The specimen is placed end-to-end with the rod. The rod and specimen are then placed inside the tube. The positions of the open end of the tube and the rod are carefully compared by means of a linear variable differential transformer. As the coefficient of thermal expansion of

Figure 15.1

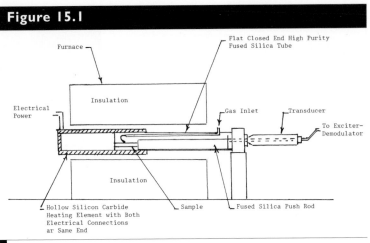

Flat Closed End High Purity
Fused Silica Tube

Furnace

Insulation

Electrical
Power

Gas Inlet

Transducer

To Exciter-
Demodulator

Insulation

Hollow Silicon Carbide
Heating Element with Both
Electrical Connections
ar Same End

Sample

Fused Silica Push Rod

Schematic of a fused silica dilatometer.

fused silica is low, and is known, the relative change in position of the tube and the rod is caused by the expansion of the specimen.

The specimens are rods 1.000 or 2.000 inches in length with the ends polished flat and parallel. The other dimensions are not critical, being rods or bars of about 1/4 to 3/8 in. in cross section. They have been fired to the schedule at which the product is to be fired.

The information obtained is fed to a strip chart recorder or a computer, yielding curves such as that shown in Figure 15.2. From the straight section of the curve is calculated the coefficient of thermal expansion normally reported. It is the coefficient in the equation:

$$l_T = l_O(1 + \alpha t)$$

With one exception, the temperature range over which the coefficient is determined is arbitrary. In the United States, it is conventional to report the coefficient over the range 50 to 350°C. The one exception is that the lower limit should be at least 20°C above room temperature. The reason is that until the linkages in the apparatus fully engage, the measurements may be inaccurate.

15.2 Stresses on Cooling a Fused-On Coating

The thermal expansion data on the body and the coating permit consideration of coating fit.[E35] Stress in a coating layer develops as the result of a differential thermal expansion between the coating and the substrate as they cool from the "setting" temperature to

Figure 15.2

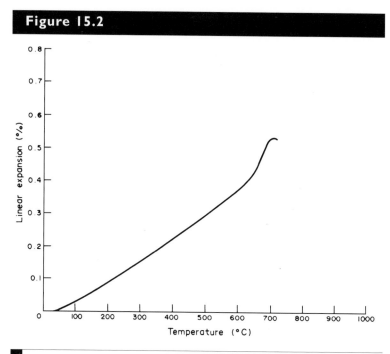

Typical thermal expansion data.

room temperature. The magnitude and sign of the stress will determine whether the coating will craze, be serviceable, or shiver.

Consider, as in Figure 15.3, a ceramic body coated with a glaze at high temperature, with the glaze-forming reactions complete. At the firing temperature, the two components have the same dimension, and any previous size change has been accommodated by viscous flow in the glaze. As the ware moves through the cooling cycle, the glaze begins to solidify until a temperature is reached where the two parts, solid glaze and body, are rigidly bonded.

At this point, the effect of any differences in the linear coefficients of thermal expansion of the glaze and of the substrate will appear. The dilatometer test measures the coefficient on heating, while stress in glaze-body systems develops on cooling. However, provided one has used previously fired samples, and has not exceeded the temperature at which they were fired, the expansion coefficients can be assumed to be reversible.

This discussion will focus on the effect of different coefficients, ignoring for a moment the shape of the curves and any after-expansion of the body. If the coefficients are equal, both glaze and body will contract in unison, so no strain will be generated.

But suppose that the thermal expansion of the glaze is less than

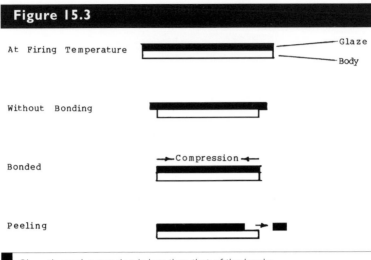

Figure 15.3

At Firing Temperature — Glaze / Body

Without Bonding

Bonded — Compression

Peeling

Glaze thermal expansion is less than that of the body.

that of the body (Figure 15.3). If the two layers were not constrained by their interfacial adhesion, they would contract at different rates. The action of sealing the two together forces them to be equal in length. Thus, stress develops in both components. With further cooling, the substrate will try to contract more than the glaze. But at the end of the cooling cycle, the final lengths must be equal. As a result, the glaze will be compressed and the substrate will be permanently in tension. The tensile strength exerted by the glaze could be great enough to bend the substrate if only one side of the body is glazed, as with tile.

However, in most cases at moderate differences, this condition can be tolerated, as the greater thickness of the body compared to the glaze will spread the stress enough that the body can withstand it. In some instances this is deliberately done to increase the overall mechanical strength of the product.[B1] At larger mismatch, however, excessive compression is generated in the glaze. This can be greater than the strength of adhesion between the glaze and the substrate. This yields a stress-relieving fracture at the interface known as shivering or peeling. Usually, this occurs at corners of the ware, and it results in apparent chipping of the glaze. Hence, it is common to attribute all glaze chipping at corners to shivering.

On the other hand, when the thermal expansion of the glaze is greater than that of the substrate, as shown in Figure 15.4, the glaze will try to contract more than the body.[E35] Again, the final lengths of the two parts must be the same, so the glaze will compress the substrate. It must therefore carry a balancing tensile stress.

Figure 15.4

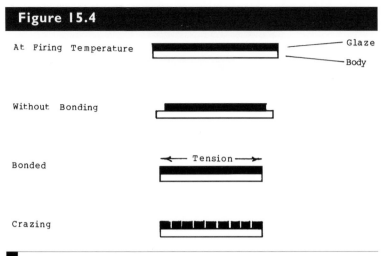

At Firing Temperature — Glaze / Body

Without Bonding

Bonded — Tension →

Crazing

Glaze thermal expansion is greater than that of the body.

Unfortunately, glass is less able to withstand tensile forces than compressive forces. Thus, even when the thermal mismatch is quite small, the glaze fails in tension. The resulting fracture pattern is called crazing.

Let us now consider the more complex case where an engobe has been applied to a substrate, and then a glaze applied over the engobe. In this situation a considerably more complex stress pattern results from the glost firing. Instead of just one coating on the substrate, there are two. There are also two interfaces to be considered—the body-engobe interface and the engobe-glaze interface. A further complication is that many engobes do not fully vitrify during firing, and they may have lower internal stress limits than the interfacial stress limits at the two interfaces.

In this situation, if all three parts have the same thermal expansion, there is no strain. If the engobe has the same thermal expansion as either the glaze or the body, the analysis reduces to the two-part problem already discussed. However, in the more common case, the body, engobe, and glaze all have different thermal expansion behavior.

When the body, engobe, and glaze have different thermal expansions, there are four possible combinations to be considered. They are:

1. The expansion of the glaze is greater than that of the engobe, which is greater than that of the body.

2. The expansion of the glaze is greater than that of the engobe, but the expansion of the engobe is less than that of the body.

Figure 15.5

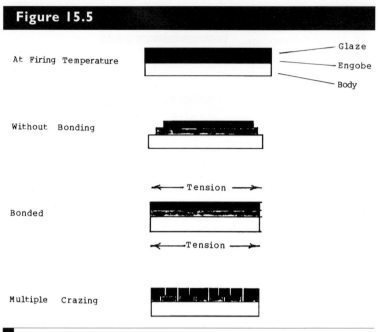

At Firing Temperature — Glaze, Engobe, Body

Without Bonding

Bonded — Tension → ← Tension →

Multiple Crazing

> Glaze thermal expansion is greater than engobe thermal expansion; engobe thermal expansion is greater than body thermal expansion.

3. The expansion of the glaze is less than that of the engobe, but the expansion of the engobe is greater than that of the body.

4. The expansion of the glaze is less than that of the engobe, which is less than that of the body.

The first combination, shown in Figure 15.5, is an amplification of the undesirable situation shown in Figure 15.4. On cooling, the glaze will try to contract more than the engobe, which will try to contract more than the body. But the final lengths of the three parts must be the same, so the glaze will compress the engobe, which in turn will compress the body. They must therefore carry balancing tensile stresses. Since neither the engobe nor the glaze can withstand tensile forces, multiple crazing results. In addition, since many engobes are weak in mechanical strength, some chipping at the edges can also occur.

In the second possible combination, shown in Figure 15.6, the thermal expansion of the engobe is less than that of the body. Hence, it will try to contract less than the body. This places the engobe in compression, the body in tension. Due to the greater thickness of the body, this can be tolerated, providing the difference in thermal expansion is not too great.

Figure 15.6

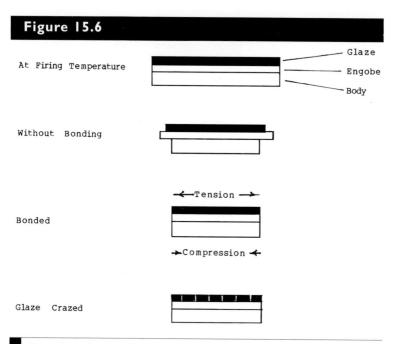

At Firing Temperature — Glaze / Engobe / Body

Without Bonding

Bonded — ◄─Tension─► / ►Compression◄

Glaze Crazed

> Glaze thermal expansion is greater than engobe thermal expansion (although it may be less than body thermal expansion); engobe thermal expansion is less than body thermal expansion.

However, the thermal expansion of the glaze is greater than that of the engobe. Hence, the glaze will try to contract more than the engobe. As the final lengths of the three parts must be the same, the glaze will compress the engobe. It must therefore carry a balancing tensile stress. Crazing of the glaze is the result.

It is very important to note that this crazing may occur even when the thermal expansion of the glaze is less than that of the body. Each of the two interfaces must be considered separately when analyzing the potential for crazing. If the glaze expansion exceeds that of the engobe to which it is bonded, it does not matter whether or not it is less than that of the body.

The third combination, shown in Figure 15.7, is very interesting, and it is one that occurs quite often because many engobes are mixtures of the body materials with fluxes. Here, the thermal expansion of the glaze is less than that of the engobe, and in most cases, less than that of the substrate as well. The action of sealing the glaze to the engobe forces them to be equal in length. As a result, the glaze will be compressed and the engobe will be stressed in tension.

However, the engobe's thermal expansion is greater than that of the body. Thus, the engobe will try to contract more than the body. Again,

Figure 15.7

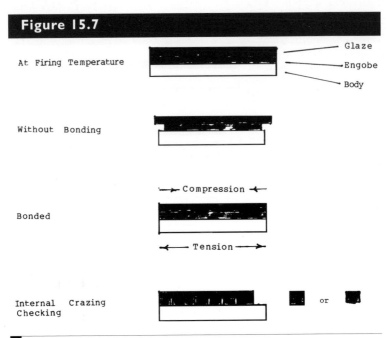

At Firing Temperature

Glaze
Engobe
Body

Without Bonding

Compression

Bonded

Tension

Internal Crazing
Checking

or

Glaze thermal expansion is less than engobe thermal expansion and body thermal expansion; engobe thermal expansion is greater than body thermal expansion.

the final lengths of the two parts must be the same, so the engobe will compress the body, and must therefore carry a balancing tensile stress. Hence, the effect of both the glaze and the body on the engobe is to create tensile forces. Fractures in the engobe can be expected.

What is the visible effect of this condition? In a transparent glaze, the cracks in the engobe may be visible, but in an opaque glaze, one might expect that the glaze will conceal the problem, and the ware will be usable. In the interior of the ware, that is the case. On the edges, it is not. Chipping is observed (see Figure 13.4). The chips may fracture at the engobe-body interface, or through the engobe. Where the chip fractures depends on the relative strengths of the engobe-body bonds and the engobe-engobe bonds.

Thus, in this case, a defect occurs that is traditionally associated with peeling. But the cause is in fact a crazing problem. When an engobe is used as well as a glaze, it is not possible to automatically associate chipping with a peeling problem. Again, in these three-layer systems, it is important to consider the two interfaces separately.

In the last case, shown in Figure 15.8, the glaze is lower in thermal expansion than the engobe, which in turn is lower in thermal

Figure 15.8

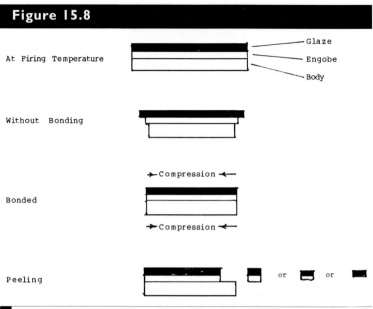

At Firing Temperature — Glaze / Engobe / Body

Without Bonding

Compression

Bonded

Compression

Peeling   or   or

Glaze thermal expansion is less than engobe thermal expansion; engobe thermal expansion is less than body thermal expansion.

expansion than the body. If the three layers were not constrained by their interfacial adhesion, the glaze would contract less than the engobe, which would contract less than the body. The action of sealing them together forces them to be equal in dimension. Thus, the glaze will be compressed by the engobe. The engobe will be stressed in tension by the glaze, but will be compressed by the body. In most cases, these effects will cancel out. The substrate will be permanently stressed in tension.

At moderate differences, this condition can be tolerated, as the greater thickness of the body relative to the glaze and engobe will serve to spread the stress enough that the body can withstand it. At larger mismatch, however, excessive compression is generated in the glaze. This can be greater than the strength of adhesion at one or the other of the interfaces. This yields the stress-relieving fracture at the interface known as shivering or peeling.

Thus, the analysis of thermal mismatches in coated whitewares having engobes under the glaze is not as simple and straightforward as is the simple glaze-body interaction. The stresses induced at each interface must be separately considered. For example, quite often chipping is not the result of peeling. Instead, it is caused by the opposite problem of crazing in one of the two coatings, usually the engobe.

Figure 15.9

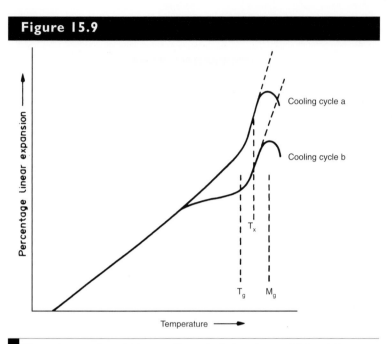

Thermal expansion of (a) normally cooled glaze bar and (b) rapidly cooled glaze bar.

15.3 Analysis of Thermally Induced Stress

This section will consider how to use thermal expansion curves to analyze coating fit.[T1] Figure 15.9 shows typical percentage linear expansion curves on the same glaze specimen bars when they are cooled slowly and cooled rapidly from the firing temperature. Some 20 to 50°C above the glass transition temperature (T_g), the curve reaches a maximum. This is the temperature at which the sag rate of the specimen due to viscous flow equals the expansion rate. This point, which occurs at a viscosity of about $10^{7.7}$ poise, is called the dilatometric softening point M_g.

This is one of the fixed points on an expansion curve that is of interest for determining coating fit. Another is the glass transition temperature T_g. Customarily, this is taken to be the intercept of the straight lines drawn through the two straight sections of the expansion curve.

The third point is the set point T_x, which is the temperature at which stress begins to develop in a real-time cooling situation. That is, when the coating is above its softening point, all stress will be relieved by viscous motion in the coating. But as the body cools down, a new condition develops from temperature T_x. At T_x the coating begins to behave as a solid, so any stress induced in the coating from this temperature down will remain. Continued cooling below T_x creates strain in the coating-body system that is proportional to the differential contraction of the coating and body from T_x to room temperature.

There is no generally accepted way to obtain T_x from the expansion curve, except that it is agreed that T_x lies between T_g and M_g. However, provided that the same decision is made every time, a meaningful picture can be developed. Therefore, let us select for the set point the midpoint between T_g and M_g:

$$T_x = (M_g + T_g)/2$$

To analyze for fit, one draws the expansion curves for the coating and the body to the same scale, and slides the graph for the coating over that for the body until they coincide at T_x. Thus, the origin of the coating expansion curve is displaced by an amount equal to the contraction mismatch at room temperature.

This is illustrated in Figure 15.10 for the behavior of three glazes when they are applied to the same body. The set points are 660°C for the normal-expansion glaze, 670°C for the low-expansion glaze, and 620°C for the high-expansion glaze. In each case, the glaze expansion curve has been slid vertically until the curve crosses the body curve at the set point.

The curve marked *normal expansion* is that of a glaze designed for this body and known to give good service. Notice that the two curves remain close to each other at all temperatures between T_x and room temperature. This reflects the equation for stress in a coating. For a thin coating on an infinite slab, as with a tile, for instance.[K5]

$$S_g = E(T_x - T)(\alpha_g - \alpha_s)(1 - 3j + 6j^2)$$

and:

$$S_s = E(T_x - T)(\alpha_s - \alpha_s)(1 - 3j + 6j^2)$$

where j is the ratio of glaze to body thickness. For a cylindrical body, such as a cup, the corresponding expressions are:

$$S_g = [E/(1 - \mu)](T_x - T)(\alpha_g - \alpha_s)[A_s/A]$$

and:

$$S_s = [E/(1 - \mu)](T_x - T)(\alpha_s - \alpha_g)[A_g/A]$$

where A, A_g and A_s are the cross-sectional areas of the whole piece, the coating, and the body, respectively.

For a normal coating operation, one is looking for a small

Figure 15.10

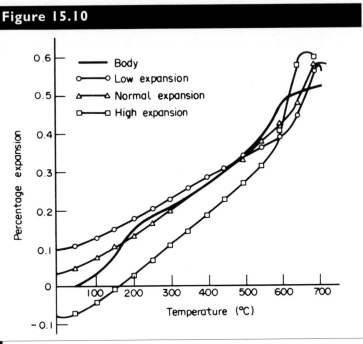

Thermal expansion curves repositioned to demonstrate glaze-body fit.

negative (compressive) stress in the coating, balanced by tensile stress spread over the larger cross section of the body.[T1] Remember that brittle materials like ceramics are much stronger in compression than in tension.

The curve marked *low expansion* in Figure 15.10 is one that would apply to a compression glaze on this body. Both the compressive stress on the coating and the tensile stress on the substrate increase by the greater difference in expansion coefficient. This type of coating would be used in applications that will see thermal shock, such as cooking ware or range tops.

The curve marked *high expansion* is an example of a situation that will usually lead to crazing. The higher expansion of the glaze than the body leads to positive (tensile) stress on the coating, balanced by compressive stress on the body. Experience has shown that the mismatch shown here is about 3 to 4 times what can be tolerated in a vitreous body, and about 1.5 times what can be tolerated in a porous body.

If a coating partially crystallizes on cooling, the expansion coefficient of the glass-crystalline system will be altered, sometimes drastically. For randomly oriented small crystals, the expansion of the

Table 15-1. Thermal Expansion Factors

Oxide	Factor	Oxide	Factor	Oxide	Factor
Li_2O	5.0	Al_2O_3	0.42	V_2O_5	5.9
Na_2O	16.9	B_2O_3	0.0	Cr_2O_3	5.1
K_2O	15.2	SiO_2	0.15	MnO	2.2
CaO	4.0	TiO_2	4.1	Fe_2O_3	4.0
MgO	1.35	ZrO_2	4.1	CoO	4.4
SrO	4.0	MoO_3	4.0	NiO	4.0
BaO	4.2	Sb_2O_3	3.6	CuO	2.2
ZnO	2.1	SnO_2	2.0	La_2O_3	4.0
PbO	3.2	WO_3	3.6	Nd_2O_3	4.0
CdO	4.0	P_2O_5	2.0	Pr_6O_{11}	4.0
				CeO_2	4.0

To obtain the cubic thermal expansion coefficient, multiply each oxide weight percent by its factor, and sum. To obtain the linear thermal expansion coefficient, divide the cubic thermal expansion coefficient by 3.

composite will be an average of that of the crystals and the residual glass. It is particularly important in these cases to see that the specimen used to measure expansion is fired on the same schedule as the material to be used.

In this discussion, it has been assumed that a sharp discontinuity exists between the coating and the substrate. In many cases there is substantial interaction between coating and substrate, producing an intermediate reaction or buffer layer. In most cases, this layer will have an expansion rate between those of the coating and substrate, and it will spread out the stress. Hence, the calculation of fit based on a sharp discontinuity is usually a conservative assumption. The exception is the case where a different crystal phase occurs in the boundary layer.

15.4 Prediction of Thermal Expansion Coefficients

Thermal expansion is a bulk property and is therefore a linear function of the composition of a material.[E36] Hence, a set of factors can be developed to calculate a thermal expansion coefficient, and several will be found in the literature.[A1,S12] The set that the author uses will be found in Table 15-1. As with all such calculations, the thermal expansion coefficients obtained by calculation are only modestly accurate. However, a calculation that indicates that the thermal expansion of one coating is lower than that of another coating is highly accurate.

An examination of Table 15-1 shows that the alkalis contribute to high thermal expansion, while boron oxide and silica make the least contribution to thermal expansions.[512]

The thermal expansion coefficients of ceramic bodies vary from 8 to $9 \times 10^{-6}/°C$ down to below $5 \times 10^{-6}/°C$. At the high end of this range, little accommodation for expansion will be required. At the low end, thermal expansion may be the most difficult property to allow for.

Chapter 16
Chemical Durability

A major reason for using vitreous materials for coatings is their potential for chemical resistance in service.[E30] Among the many products that have a vitreous coating for chemical resistance in service are chemical reactors, dental crowns, tableware and hotel china, food and beverage containers, stove tops, wall and floor tiles, washing machine baskets, and water heater linings.

These products are expected to withstand prolonged exposure to various corrosive liquids, especially water. They must not lose their gloss or change color, pit, or permit penetration of the liquid. The superiority of vitreous coatings for such service is indicated by examples of glazed pottery made several thousand years ago, which still exhibit a glossy surface. Water heater linings are expected to last 10 to 20 years while constantly exposed to 140°F water. Hotel china is expected to survive several daily washings in hot alkaline water without loss of gloss or other damage to the appearance of the surface.

Nevertheless, all vitreous surfaces are affected to some extent by contact with water, acid, or alkaline liquids. At the other extreme from the durable examples just cited are the sodium silicates, or water glass, which dissolve readily in water. In addition, even otherwise durable glass coatings are readily attacked by hydrofluoric acid.

Chemical resistance is an important parameter in the usefulness of most glass coatings. Chemical attack can alter the appearance of glass surfaces in several ways. A common effect is loss of gloss. Occasionally, pitting of the surface occurs. Commonly, the development of layers of reaction product is visible to the naked eye. Liquids stored in glazed vessels can become contaminated with elements extracted from the ceramic coating. Hence, it is important to inquire into the nature of the interaction between liquids and silicate glass surfaces and to develop coatings that minimize corrosion effects. That is the objective of this chapter.

16.1 Corrosion Processes

When a glass coating is brought into contact with an aqueous solution, alkali ions are usually extracted into the solution in preference to silica and the other constituents of the glass.[P4] An alkali-deficient leached layer is formed on the glass surface. The thickness of these silica-rich films, and probably their compactness, varies with the composition of the glass and, for the same glass, with the test conditions of time, temperature, and solution pH. Generally, a poorly durable material will develop a thicker film. The film thickness will be limited by the rate at which it is, in turn, corroded by the solution.

16.1.1 Ion Exchange. The first of these reactions can be viewed as an ion exchange, in which an entity from the solution, which will be called a "proton," penetrates the network, replacing an alkali ion, which escapes to the solution.[E18]

$$H^+_{solution} + Me^+O--Si_{glass} \rightarrow H^+O--Si_{glass} + Me^+_{solution}$$

Understand that what has been called the attacking "proton" is probably a hydrate thereof, as H^+ is not energetically favored in solution.[E46] Fortunately, this complication is basically irrelevant to the critical phenomena in durability.

As H^+ ions replace Me^+ ions, a surface film develops that resembles vitreous silica or silica gel and has different properties than the parent glass.[E30] This film swells, acts as a barrier to further reaction, and decreases diffusion rates into and out of the surfaces, thereby inhibiting further attack.[D1,P4,R2,T3] Studies have shown this to be the principal mode of attack in acidic and neutral media.

16.1.2 Hydroxyl Attack. The presence of alkali ions in the solution tends to raise the pH to the point at which the silica-rich layer can itself be attacked by hydroxyl ions:[E18]

$$Si-O-Si_{glass} + Me^+OH^-_{solution} \rightarrow Si-OH_{glass} + Si-O^-Me^+_{glass}$$

This latter reaction is autocatalytic, as the open oxygen can interact with another water molecule to regenerate the hydroxyl ion, which is then available for a repeat reaction:

$$Si-O^-_{glass} + HOH \rightarrow Si-OH_{glass} + OH^-_{solution}$$

Hydroxyl attack is strongly dependent on the concentration of alkali ions available in the solution, and hence on the pH. In alkali silicates, the transition between the region where hydroxyl attack predominates and where the ion exchange process predominates is rather sharp, between pH values 9 and 10.[B4] In more durable glasses, the transition between the regions of ion exchange and hydroxyl attack is more gradual. In some of the very durable hot water tank enamels the transition pH is 4.[E21] Hence, the rate of ion exchange is more sensitive to glass composition than is the rate of hydroxyl attack.[E30]

16.2 Kinetics Of Corrosion

For the ion exchange process, studies such as that shown in Figure 16.1 demonstrate that the rate of alkali extraction varies linearly with the square root of time at short times and at low temperatures.[P4] This graph plots the weight of Na_2O extracted under dynamic conditions and very low surface area/volume of solution (SA/V) against the square root of time for the early stages of extraction. By contrast, Figure 16.2, which shows data for longer periods of time, demonstrates that the rate of alkali extraction approaches a

Figure 16.1

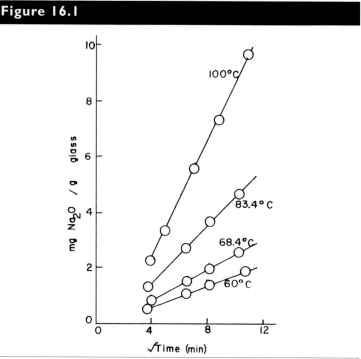

Short-time water leaching of $15Na_2O$, $85SiO_2$ glass (ref. P4).

Figure 16.2

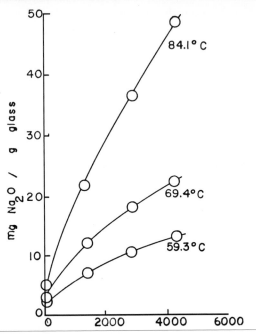

Long-time water leaching of $15Na_2O$, $85SiO_2$ glass (ref. P4).

linear time dependence under conditions of longer time and higher temperature.

This sort of extraction behavior can be represented by a rate equation of the form:

$$Q = at^{1/2} + bt$$

where t is the time and a and b are constants. This equation has a limiting slope 0.5 as time approaches 0 and 1 as time approaches infinity. Over limited times, approximately linear plots of log Q versus log t would be expected,[E18] with slopes varying between 0.5 and 1.

In mineral acids, the increased concentration of "protons" increases the rate of the diffusion-controlled ion exchange process. In many cases only this process is observed. In alkaline media the rate of ion exchange decreases, and the rate of the linear dissolution process increases until it is the only process observed.

These effects are illustrated[E21] by the data shown in Figure 16.3, which plots the weight loss due to leaching of a hot water tank porcelain enamel at 93 to 104°C. A systematic reduction in corrosion rate is noted as the pH is increased from less than 1 for the

Figure 16.3

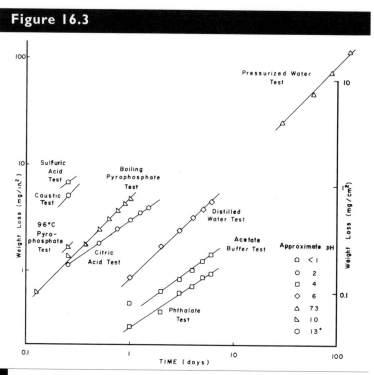

Weight loss data at 93–104°C for a hot water tank enamel (ref E36).

5% sulfuric acid test to 2 for the 5% citric acid test, to 4 for the phthalate test. The slopes of these curves are about 0.6, as one would expect for an ion exchange–dominated corrosion.

As the pH is further increased, the corrosion rate is increased. From the phthalate test, one proceeds to the distilled water tests at pH 7, to the pyrophosphate tests at pH 10, to the caustic tests at pH values greater than 13. Here the slopes of the curves are about 0.9, as would be expected for a process dominated by bulk dissolution.

Figure 16.4 shows some data on the same hot water tank enamel discussed previously, corroded at 65 to 66°C. Again, the slope is near 0.5 for the citric acid test, while it is near 1 for tests in alkaline media. Of course, rates are much lower at this lower temperature.

The curves drawn through the data points on these two figures were obtained by fitting the data to:

$$\log N_i = H\log t - E(1000/T) + F - GpH$$

for the ion exchange process, and:

$$\log N_d = A\log t - B(1000/T) + C + D(100/pH^2)$$

Figure 16.4

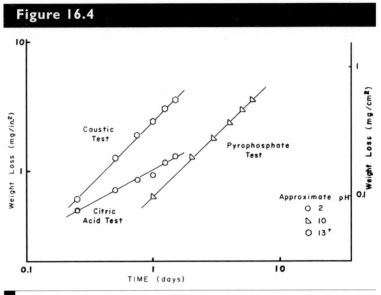

Weight loss data at 65–66°C for a hot water tank enamel (ref. E21).

for the dissolution process. *A* through *H* are constants determined by the least squares fitting procedure. The total measured weight loss is:

$$N = N_i + N_d$$

These equations demonstrate that the principal factors influencing the corrosion rate of a glass coating are time, temperature, and pH. Generally, these three parameters alone can account for better than 90% of the observed rates.

One consequence of the pH sensitivity of glass corrosion is that exposure to water vapor produces a different corrosion pattern than exposure to liquid water.[C6] Water vapor deposited on a vitreous surface rapidly increases in pH, due to the high SA/V ratio, leading rapidly to a zone where hydroxyl attack predominates. This rise in pH occurs much more slowly when the volume of liquid is larger.

While time, temperature, and pH are the principal factors governing the attack of liquids on glass, there are some secondary effects.[E22] The ions in the attacking solution may form complexes which reduce the activity of the solution. Other ions may interact chemically with hydrous silica ions on the surface of the glass coating. Figure 16.5 compares the weight loss of a hot water tank enamel due to attack by "pure" water with attack due to solutions buffered with citrate and acetate anions. Figure 16.6 shows similar data for maleate, phosphate, and succinate anions. A variation of as much as a factor of 2 is observed in the six solutions between the least aggressive (acetate) and the most aggressive (maleate). These anions have formed complex ions in solution that increase or decrease the solubility of a glass coating.

16.3 Corrosion by Hydrofluoric Acid

Hydrofluoric acid is a special case.[T1] It attacks readily all silicate glass structures. So strong is the attack by HF that it is used as an etchant for glass surfaces. In the presence of hydrofluoric acid or acidic fluorides, silicofluoride ions are formed according to the following equation:

$$SiO_2 + 6HF = SiF_6^{-2} + 2H_2O + 2H^+$$

These silicofluoride ions are slightly soluble, so mineral acids are used in etching processes to hasten the removal of the silicofluorides. Hydrofluoric acid also attacks the glass structure directly:

$$Si-O-Si_{glass} + H^+F^-_{solution} \rightarrow Si\text{-}OH_{glass} + Si^+F^-_{solution}$$

Even acid-resistant glass coatings are attacked, and a mixture of two parts HCl and one part HF gives rapid surface removal of glass coatings.[E30]

Figure 16.5

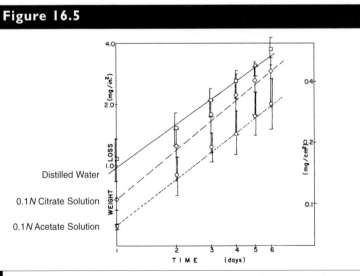

Weight loss from corrosion of a hot water tank enamel in water and in buffered media (ref. E22).

Figure 16.6

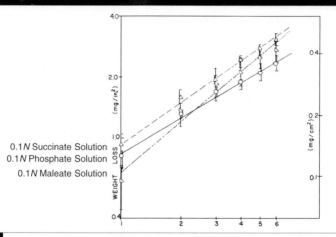

0.1 *N* Succinate Solution
0.1 *N* Phosphate Solution
0.1 *N* Maleate Solution

Weight loss from corrosion of a hot water tank enamel in three buffered media (ref. E22).

16.4 Effect of Coating Composition

The rate of extraction of ions from any glass coating is determined by the coating's overall composition, and by the extraction process that is at work.[E12,E14]

16.4.1 Resistance to Ion Exchange.
As one might expect, the rate of release of alkali ions from the coating by the ion exchange process increases with increasing alkali content.[M16] But this is only the first effect. Usually, K_2O is more soluble than Na_2O, which is more soluble than Li_2O. Mixtures of alkalis are usually less soluble than a single alkali.[D5,I2]

Additions of alkaline earth ions decrease coating durability, but much less so than alkalis.[M16] Hence, substituting alkaline earth for alkali on a mole-for-mole basis will appear to improve durability. The effect of ZnO on acid resistance is somewhat ambiguous. Its solubility is less than that of alkalis or alkaline earths, but more than that of SiO_2 or similar oxides. Additions of CdO lower the durability.

The effect of PbO additions on acid resistance varies with the presence of other ions. For example, in lead-alkali silicates the total modifier content (PbO + alkalis) is directly proportional to the amount of modifier extracted.[Y2]

Additions of alumina are especially beneficial in increasing acid resistance.[I2,M16,S12] The only circumstances in which alumina is not beneficial occur when large amounts are used, sufficient to force some Al^{+3} from 4 to 6 coordination. Additions of SiO_2, TiO_2 and ZrO_2 also improve acid durability.

Up to 12% B_2O_3 improves the durability of alkali silicate glasses.[M16] In most other circumstances, however, the addition of B_2O_3 drastically lowers the acid resistance. Only the alkalis lower durability more than B_2O_3.[M19] Additions of P_2O_5 and F, which interrupt the silicate network of the coating, also drastically lower the acid durability.

A parameter that correlates all these findings regarding ion exchange durability is:[E12,E14]

$$FM = Good/(Bad)^{1/2}$$

where FM is a figure of merit for a glass, expressed in terms of the molar concentrations of its constituents:

$$Good = 2(Al_2O_3) + (SiO_2) + (TiO_2) + (ZrO_2) + (SnO_2)$$

$$Bad = 2[(Li_2O) + (Na_2O) + (K_2O) + (B_2O_3) + (P_2O_5)] + (MgO)$$
$$+(CaO) + (SrO) + (BaO) + (F) + (ZnO) + (PbO)$$

The development of this parameter is discussed in the treatment of lead release that follows. For the moment, let us consider what it tells us about ion exchange durability. Most important is the observation that all components of a glass contribute to its durability, not just the constituents that are extracted. The oxides in this relationship are expressed as single ion concentrations, reflecting the ionic nature of this process. Note that the only desirable constituents are the refractory components of the glass matrix. All of the modifier ions, as well as B_2O_3 and P_2O_5, are deleterious. Hence, the problem in formulating durable coatings is to balance the durability requirements against the ease of forming the coating in the firing process.

The one limitation on this correlation is when the coating is subject to phase separation.[E12] Many glass coatings, particularly those containing B_2O_3 and alkaline earths, exhibit phase separation, either on a macroscale or on a microscale. In such a case, one of the phases will usually be high in SiO_2, the other in alkali or alkaline earth borate.[M15] If the borate phase is interconnected, it will determine the coating's durability. Even when it is not interconnected, the presence in the coating surface of a phase of low chemical durability may result in pitting.

16.4.2 Resistance to Hydroxyl Attack and Stability Diagrams.
Alkaline durability is a very different phenomenon from ion exchange durability. It has already been noted that alkaline durability involves corrosion of the silica structure itself.

Figure 16.7 is a stability diagram for silica in aqueous solution.[P4] It is a plot of the activity (which is related to the concentration, and approaches concentration at low values) of silicate species in water as a function of pH. The data are derived from thermodynamic calculations, and they indicate the driving force for the removal of silica from a glass exposed to water. The lower the thermodynamic activity of any soluble species, the better the coating durability. The activity of soluble silicate species such as $HSiO_3^-$, and SiO_3^{-2} is negligibly small below pH 9, and only becomes appreciable at pH 12. Hence, it is not surprising that there are very few materials that will improve the alkaline durability of a silicate-based glass coating.

Figure 16.8 shows a corresponding stability diagram for ZnO. Below pH 7, zinc oxide is a deleterious material, because the activity of Zn^{+2} exceeds that of the glass. In the alkaline region, however, it is an interesting material. The isoactivity points for $HZnO_2$ and ZnO_2 are near pH 13. Hence, ZnO can be a desirable addition in the pH 9 to 12 range.

Figure 16.9 shows a stability diagram for PbO. Below pH 7, lead oxide is soluble as Pb^{+2}, and to a much lesser extent, as $PbOH^+$. In the alkaline region, however, the solubility of $HPbO_3$ becomes significant only above pH 14. PbO thus improves alkaline durability, while at the same time it decreases ion exchange durability.

By contrast, Figure 16.10 shows the stability diagram for Al_2O_3. The soluble alumina species found here are Al^{+3} below pH 3.2 and

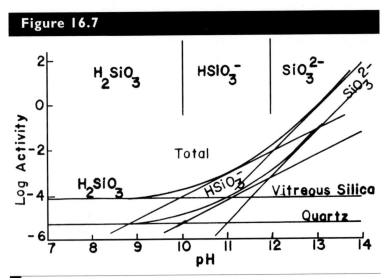

Figure 16.7

Stability diagram of quartz and vitreous silica in aqueous solution at 25°C and various pH (ref. P4).

Figure 16.8

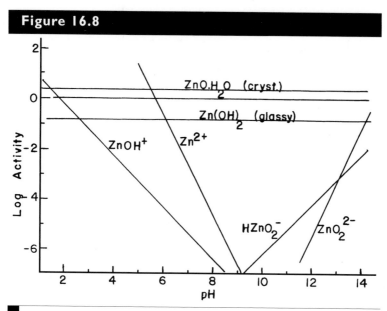

Stability diagram of zinc oxide in aqueous solution at 25°C and various pH (ref. P4).

AlO_2^- above pH 11. Hence, while alumina is desirable for improving ion exchange durability, it is only helpful for alkaline durability in the pH range from 7 to 10.

Figure 16.11 shows why zirconia is widely known to improve the durability of silicate glasses more than any other element. Even small concentrations (2%) yield significant improvements in both ion exchange and alkaline durability. Figure 16.11 shows that, although the hydration of ZrO_2 is energetically very favorable, soluble ionic species like ZrO^{+2}, Zr^{+4}, and $HZrOO_3^-$ occur only below pH 2 and above pH 17. Hence, zirconia is a very desirable addition for alkaline durability over the whole range from neutral (pH 7) to strongly alkaline (pH 12 to 14).

16.5 Tests for Corrosion Resistance

A number of tests are used in the industry to quantify the durability of a glass.[E30] Usually they involve exposing the sample to a controlled temperature, time, and pH. Depending upon the use envisioned, the attacking medium might be an acid, an alkali, or water. For example, home laundry enamels are evaluated in alkaline phosphates at pH 10. Hot water tanks are evaluated in superheated water. Dinnerware are evaluated in mild acids (usually acetic)

Figure 16.9

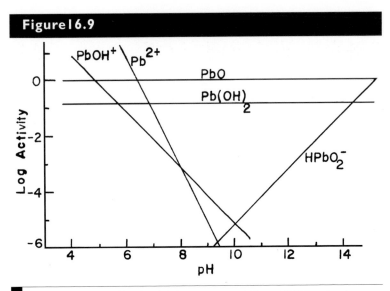

Stability diagram of lead oxide in aqueous solution at 25°C and various pH (ref. P4).

to simulate acidic foods, and in alkaline phosphates to simulate dish washing.

The details of the various tests appear in volumes 2.05 (tests for porcelain enamels) and 15.02 (tests for ceramic glazes) of the ASTM standards. Table 16-1 lists the principal methods used as of 1997 for the testing of ceramic coatings. They are divided into three categories: tests of acid resistance, tests of alkali resistance, and other tests. The ASTM books of standards are reissued annually, as all the methods are under the active management of a committee of experts on the technology relevant to the method.

16.6 Lead and Cadmium Release from Ceramic Coatings

Lead and cadmium release from ceramic coatings is an example of the use of one of these testing methods, as well as an important subject in itself. Particular emphasis will be placed on those surfaces used for the consumption of food and drink.

Lead oxide has been widely used in the formulation of vitreous coatings.[E14] There were a number of reasons for this. The strong fluxing action of lead oxide permits greater flexibility in glaze formulation. PbO reduces viscosity and allows for satisfactory processing over a wider firing range and under the varying conditions that may occur in a production-scale piece of equipment. PbO imparts low

Table 16-1. Corrosion Resistance Tests

Tests for Acid Resistance

C282	Acid Resistance of Porcelain Enamels (Citric Acid Spot Test)[n1]
C283	Resistance of Porcelain Enamel Utensils to Boiling Acid[n1]
C1034	Lead and Cadmium Extracted from Glazed Ceramic Cookware[n2]
C738	Lead and Cadmium Extracted from Glazed Ceramic Surfaces[n2]
C895	Lead and Cadmium Extracted from Glazed Ceramic Tile[n2]
C872	Lead and Cadmium Release from Porcelain Enamel Surfaces[n1]

Tests for Alkaline Resistance

C614	Alkali Resistance of Porcelain Enamels[n1]
C556	Detergents, Resistance of Overglaze Decorations to Attack by[n2]

Other Corrosion Tests

C650	Chemical Substances, Resistance of Ceramic Tile to[n2]

surface tension, a high index of refraction, and resistance to devitrification. This combination of properties is difficult to reproduce on a production scale in leadless systems. It is for these reasons that PbO was used for many years.

Cadmium was much less widely used than lead, but it is considerably more toxic.[E32] Its use is confined to the CdS-Se pigments that are used to impart red color to glass coatings. These pigments contain large amounts of cadmium and are fairly soluble in acidic media. Moreover, when CdS-Se is used in a glass coating, it is usually necessary to add 3 to 5% CdO to the coating formula to improve the color stability.

Over the years, occasional episodes of lead toxication have resulted from the use of improperly formulated and fired lead-containing coatings on ceramic ware.[E30] Usually, these episodes of lead toxication have resulted from the use of improperly made vessels for acid beverages consumed regularly in large quantities for a prolonged period of time. The pieces of ware implicated in these cases have come from a variety of sources, but in most cases have been manufactured by hobbyists or some artware manufacturers ignorant of the proper ways to assure the production of safe coatings.[E12]

16.6.1 The kinetics of the lead release process has received particular attention.[E13, E47, Y2] Three stages have been identified. The initial logarithmic mechanism is observable only in the most durable glazes, because it occurs almost instantaneously in less

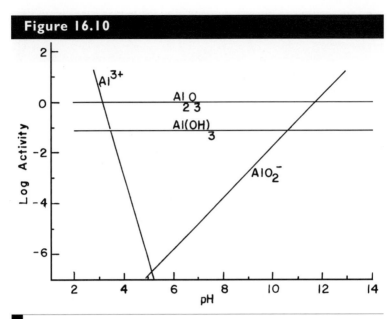

Figure 16.10

Stability diagram of alumina in aqueous solution at 25°C and various pH
(ref. P4).

durable coatings. It is associated with the release of loosely held lead
ions near the surface of the glaze. The intermediate mechanism is
superficially linear in time, but recent studies have identified the
mechanism as a combination of chemical reaction between lead in
the glass and a "proton" from the solution, with the diffusion of the
Pb^{+2} ions to the reaction site. The long time logarithmic mechanism
has been identified as a diffusion of Pb^{+2} ions through a barrier layer.

16.6.2 Procedures have been developed for controlling
lead and cadmium release under production conditions. A standard
test has been developed for determining the lead and cadmium
release from glass surfaces (C738—See Table 16-1), so various
surfaces can be examined and rated.[n2] This test is specific for Pb and
Cd, accurate to low release levels in the ppm range, and readily
reproducible in different laboratories and under field conditions.

In this test, a sample is first washed with detergent, and rinsed in
distilled water. It is then exposed to a 4% acetic acid solution for 24
hours at room temperature while covered with a watch glass or other
suitable cover. The leachate solution is then placed in an atomic
absorption spectrometer and the ppm of Pb and Cd are determined.

Current (1998) United States Food and Drug Administration
standards[n8] for lead release are 3 ppm average from six samples for

Figure 16.11

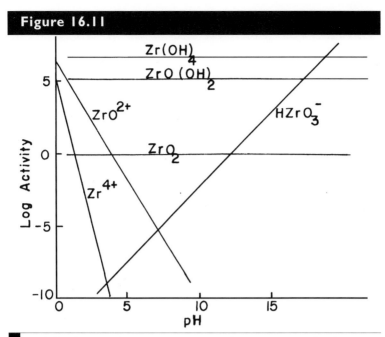

Stability diagram of zirconia in aqueous solution at 25°C and various pH (ref. P4).

flatware, 2 ppm from a maximum of six samples for small holloware, 1 ppm maximum from six samples for large holloware, and 0.5 ppm from a maximum of six samples for cups, mugs, and pitchers. For cadmium, the standards[n7] are 0.3 ppm average from six samples for flatware, 0.2 ppm average from a maximum of six samples for small holloware, and 0.1 ppm average from a maximum of six samples for large holloware, cups, mugs, and pitchers. Revisions to these levels are periodically under consideration. Moreover, because of statistical fluctuations during production, operating standards must be less than half these values.[M18]

16.6.3 The typical results obtained in the testing of tableware for lead release are dramatic.[E14] Commercial tableware glazes almost always give values of less than 0.2 ppm. Properly designed commercial artware will be somewhat higher, so they cannot always be used in contact with food and drink. By contrast, the materials involved in health cases have all given tests in excess of 50 ppm.

The results with cadmium are more specialized.[E23] Most glazes have no added cadmium and will not give a measurable reading. Those that do contain cadmium will show 0.1 to 0.2 ppm even when

Figure 16.12

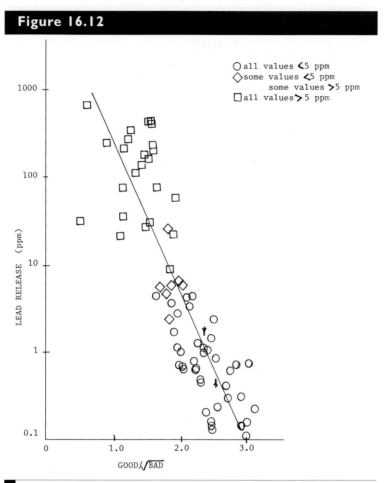

Comparison of lead release data with the figure of merit (revised from ref. E12).

properly formulated. Thus, it is best if CdS–Se red colors are not used for surfaces that will come in contact with food or drink.

16.6.4 Formulating a coating for low lead release involves a number of factors that must be considered in order to achieve low lead and cadmium release.[E12] These include total glaze composition, including opacifiers and colorants when used, the thermal history of the glaze during processing, the effectiveness and uniformity of glaze application, glaze-body solution at the coating-substrate interface, and atmospheric conditions that exist during the firing process—in particular, the flow of air over the ware during high-temperature processing. It is for this reason, as well as all the environmental regulations applicable to the use of lead and cadmium oxide, that the use of these oxides in coatings is no longer recommended.[E38]

16.6.5 The lead release of a ceramic coating can be predicted from experimental knowledge about the acid resistance of various glasses.[E12] It has been shown that silica, alumina, zirconia, and similar oxides such as titania and tin oxide are effective in lowering the lead release of a glaze.

Referring to the equations in section 16.4.1, the concentrations are expressed in molar ratios, and they reflect the ionic nature of the ion exchange process. These equations also show that alkalis, alkaline earths, B_2O_3, fluoride, phosphate, ZnO, CdO, and PbO are all more or less detrimental to the lead release in a glaze. These detrimental oxides consist of the soluble glass former B_2O_3, those ions such as F that disrupt the silicate network, and all of those ions that do not enter the basic glass structure.

These factors have been related to a database of 77 glazes (see Figure 16.12) and examined by a regression technique. As a result the figure of merit mentioned earlier was developed.

When the figure of merit exceeds 2.48, the lead release is below the FDA standard of 3 ppm. When it is less than 2.30, some measurements are always greater than 3.0 ppm. The figure of merit is not able to predict acceptability in the small interval 2.30 to 2.48. The different values from those published previously[E12] reflect changes in the Compliance Policy Guides[n7,n8] since they were published.

Thus, in most cases, the figure of merit provides a simple, straightforward calculation to predict the acceptability of the lead release of a glaze. In terms of industrial practice, the figure of merit almost always gives a definite prediction of the lead release, since glazes of marginal lead release have been emphasized in this study but occur infrequently in the real world. Note that this calculation assumes proper glazing and firing procedures.[E12] Also, while the figure of merit is useful for predicting the acceptability of a lead-containing glaze, the lead release should always be verified by testing, using the standard test (ASTM C-738).

A few qualifications have been noted. This calculation does not apply to multiphase systems, because the formulation of the least durable component is the durability to be used. Second is the effect of cupric oxide. CuO in the glaze has the unique effect of turning an otherwise safe glaze into an unsafe one.[12] Thus, glazes containing CuO should never be used in contact with food or drink.

16.7 Summary

Chemical resistance in service is a major consideration in the selection of a vitreous material as a coating material.[E30] Ceramic coatings can be designed to be highly resistant to practically all liquid media except hydrofluoric acid and related fluorides.

There are two processes at work in the aqueous corrosion of a vitreous surface. In acidic media, an ion exchange process dominates. In alkaline media, the process is one of bulk dissolution of the glass surface.

The ion exchange process is a function of the total composition of the coating, and not merely those constituents that are extracted. A figure of merit has been developed to predict the acid resistance of various formulations.

There is only one element that significantly improves the alkaline resistance of a silicate-based glass coating. That additive is zirconia.

The role of glaze composition has been worked out to the extent of a first-order correlation. Beyond that, our understanding of compositional effects is fragmentary, largely limited to the effects of alkali adjustment.

Over 90% of the aqeuous corrosion of ceramic coatings can be accounted for by a consideration of only three parameters: the time and temperature of corrosion and the pH of the attacking medium.

While the basic phenomena involved in the corrosion of ceramic coatings are well understood, many of the details of the processes are not. The properties of the corrosion layers that form in response to ion exchange have been examined only superficially. The exact nature of the species in the attacking solution sometimes make a difference in the corrosion rate.

Chapter 17
Gloss

Gloss is a very important visual property of glazed whitewares[E40] For example, high gloss is especially valued in high-quality ware such as fine china.[D8] Unfortunately, gloss is one of the most difficult properties of a glaze to measure, to specify accurately, and to relate to the composition and processing of the glaze.[E36]

One reason for these difficulties is that gloss is not easy to define quantitatively.[D6] It consists of an impression formed in the mind of the observer of the reflected light distribution from the surface of the sample. It has been found to be most closely related to the sharpness and perfection of the reflected image, and thus to the intensity of the specular reflection.

Figure 17.1 shows a light beam incident onto a solid surface.[K5] Some of the light is reflected off the surface at the same angle to the surface as the incident beam. This is the specular reflection. Other light is reflected at other angles. This is called the diffuse reflection.

Figure 17.2 shows the difference in the reflective response of various surfaces. At the left in this diagram, a high-gloss surface exhibits a high percentage of specular reflection compared to diffuse reflection. In the center, a satin finish has only a little specular reflection, and more diffuse reflection. At the right, a matte surface shows no specular gloss; essentially all the reflectance is diffuse.

Thus, the attempts to quantify gloss actually measure specular reflectance. Glossmeters measure the reflectance at the same angle as the instrument's incident light. Another technique is to measure the color with an abridged spectrophotometer (see section 8.3) both with and without specular reflectance, and determine the difference between the two measurements.

The factors that affect the intensity of the specular reflectance include the surface smoothness, the presence in the glaze of internal

Figure 17.1

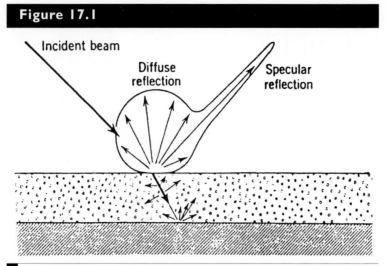

Diffuse and specular reflectance from a coating surface.

surfaces caused by crystals or phase separation, and the refractive index of the glaze.[D8]

The effect of surface roughness[D6] is illustrated by Figure 17.3. When a surface is less than smooth, some of the light reflected specularly from the surface is reflected at angles other than the incident angle, because the surface was not flat at the point of interaction. Hence, the apparent specular reflectance is reduced, and with it, the gloss.

Thus, a textured glaze can never be a high-gloss glaze! Said another way, attaining a high gloss requires developing a smooth surface. On the other hand, an isolated defect, however large, that does not disturb the human response to the rest of the surface will not lower the gloss in the way that texture will.

Figure 17.2

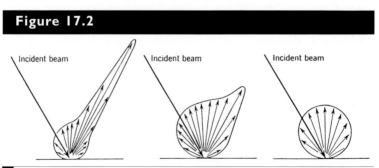

Light reflection from (left to right) a high gloss, a satin, and a matte coating.

Figure 17.3

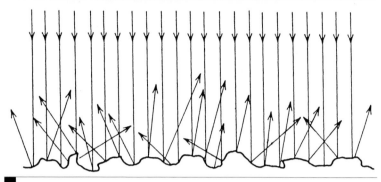

Light reflection from a rough surface.

This concludes what will be said about texture. The rest of this discussion will assume that the surface is smooth.

When a glaze has crystals dispersed within it, or when the glaze phase separates, there are internal interfaces within the glaze that can themselves cause reflection. Reflection from these internal surfaces produces the phenomenon called scattering.[E5] Scattering is the basis for opacification, or the production of an opaque white color. The effect of internal scattering on gloss depends on the difference between the refractive index of the glaze and that of the dispersed crystal. When the refractive index difference is large, the gloss may be enhanced by additional specular reflectance from crystals near the surface. On the other hand, when the refractive index difference is small, but not zero, scattering from the crystals causes the diffuse reflectance to become overwhelming, leading to a matte glaze. The scattering effect is discussed more fully in section 17.2.

17.1 Gloss Coatings

Let us consider the development of gloss coatings, where we try to optimize the gloss in order to provide a brilliant surface. The specular reflection from the surface of a glaze is governed by Fresnel's Law:

$$\frac{R}{I_o} = \frac{(m-1)^2}{(m+1)^2}$$

where

R = intensity of specular reflection
I_o = intensity of the incident light
m = relative refractive index of material on
either side of an interface

For the external surface of a ceramic coating, the refractive index of air is 1, so the relative refractive index equals the refractive index of the glaze:

$$\frac{R}{I_o} = \frac{(n-1)^2}{(n+1)^2}$$

where

n = refractive index of the glaze.

This overriding effect of refractive index in producing a high gloss makes it difficult to attain a high gloss in a leadless glaze. The reason for this difficulty is explained by the Gladstone and Dale formula[M21] for the specific refractivity, or reflectance per unit of composition, which is:

$$Sp.R = \frac{(n-1)M}{\rho}$$

where

M = molecular weight

ρ = density

As one goes from a light oxide such as MgO to a heavy oxide such as PbO, the molecular weight increases about twice as much as the density. Hence, we see that specular reflectance increases when the mean atomic number of the constituents of a glaze increases.

Table 17.1 gives the atomic number of the cations in the oxides commonly found in glazes. The right column shows that there are not many alternatives to lead oxide for adding high index-of-refraction oxides to a glaze. Bismuth oxide is a very low melting, relatively volatile, high-cost material, suitable only for very low-firing applications such as glass colors. WO_3 and MoO_3 are high-cost specialties.

Table 17-1. Atomic Number of Cations in Oxides Commonly Used in Glazes

Li_2O	3	V_2O_5	23	ZrO_2	40
B_2O_3	5	Cr_2O_3	24	MoO_3	43
Na_2O	11	MnO_2	25	CdO	48
MgO	12	Fe_2O_3	26	SnO_2	50
Al_2O_3	13	CoO	27	Sb_2O_3	51
SiO_2	14	NiO	28	BaO	56
K_2O	19	CuO	29	WO_3	74
CaO	20	ZnO	30	PbO	82
TiO_2	22	SrO	38	Bi_2O_3	83

Sb_2O_3, SnO_2, and ZrO_2 are opacifiers. Cadmium oxide is more toxic than lead oxide. That leaves one with very few possibilities.

One of the few possibilities for raising the mean atomic number of the cations in a leadless glaze is to substitute strontium oxide for calcium oxide or the alkalis. When this was done for two glazes that differ essentially by the substitution of SrO for CaO, the gloss was modestly improved.[E40]

Another choice with the potential for a modest increase in gloss is to substitute zinc oxide for calcium oxide. When this was done for two glazes that differ only by the substitution of ZnO for CaO, the gloss was again modestly increased.[E40]

17.2 Satin and Matte Coatings

Now let us examine the reverse case, the production of a matte or satin coating. Here, the purpose is to reduce or eliminate the gloss, and hence the specular reflectance. This is normally accomplished by adding crystals that have a refractive index close to, but not equal to, the refractive index of the glaze. In such a case, there will be little if any increase in specular reflectance caused by the many reflections from the glaze-crystal interfaces. On the other hand, these same reflections will greatly increase the diffuse reflectance by the phenomenon of scattering.

The phenomenon of scattering from crystals dispersed in a glass matrix has been studied in detail.[E7] The diffuse reflectance caused by scattering from particles in a glaze is calculated by the Mie theory[M17] for diffraction from spherical particles dispersed in a fluid matrix. Provided the crystals do not vary greatly from spherical shape, the scattered reflectance is given by the equation:[Z3]

$$\frac{R}{I_o} = 1 - \exp[-N(d^2 LK/4)]$$

where

    R = intensity of the scattered light
    I_o = intensity of the incident light
    N = number of independent scatterers/
        unit volume
    d = diameter of a particle
    L = effective coating thickness
    K = scattering cross section

The number of scatterers per unit volume is proportional to the number of crystals per unit volume.[K5] Hence, a good way to control the tendency to produce a satin or a matte is to alter the ability of the glaze to crystallize. The higher the crystal content, the lower the gloss.

Conventional leadless glazes are composed of alkalis, alkaline earths plus MgO and ZnO, boron oxide, alumina, and silica.[D8] X-ray diffraction analysis shows that the crystals that form are alkaline earth aluminosilicates having silica concentrations lower than that of the glaze. Compositional changes that make the glaze composition closer to that of the crystals will serve to increase the concentration of crystals, and hence, to lower the gloss.

One such compositional change is to alter the silica content in the molecular formula. The lower the silica content, the lower should be the gloss. In a study of four glazes that differed primarily in their silica content, the expected lowering of the gloss was found as the silica was reduced.[E40]

Another compositional change is to alter the alkali-to-alkaline earth ratio. As the alkali-to-alkaline earth ratio decreases, so does the gloss. This was observed in a study of four glazes that differed only in their alkali to alkaline earth ratios.[E40]

A third way to change the gloss is by changing the concentration of crystals. In many formulations, alumina is the limiting material that determines how many crystals are possible. By increasing the alumina content sufficiently to exceed the solubility of the aluminosilicate crystals, it is possible to lower the gloss (see section 3.3.4). In a study of two glazes where the only compositional difference was alumina content, the glaze with higher alumina had a lower gloss.[E40]

Chapter 18
Color of Vitreous Coatings

W hile essentially all color hues or types of color can be obtained in ceramic coatings, there is considerable variation in the purity of color that can be obtained.[E34] Some colors can be obtained with excellent purity. Others are only available in muted tones. In addition, some pigments are unaffected by the coating constituents, while others are.

In Chapter 8, the methods for measuring color were discussed, along with the pigments available. There are only a limited number of pigments suitable for use in ceramic glazes.[B11] The main reason for this is that only a few materials can withstand the high temperatures and corrosive environment of a molten glaze.

18.1 Purity of Color

Figure 18.1 is a plot in a/b coordinates (see Chapter 8) that indicates the colors obtainable from the various pigment families.[E28] On this plot, the origin is the locus of white, gray, and black. As we move away from the origin, the purity or saturation of color increases.

The scale on this plot is a measure of the ability of the human eye to distinguish colors.[B3] It is not a measure of relative saturation. Hence, a red of poor saturation may have as large a + a as a blue of excellent saturation may have a − b. For a given hue, however, the larger the distance from the origin, the purer the color.

Typical values for the color coordinates of the various pigment families are indicated on this plot.[E34] This data was taken on tile samples having leadless glazes with 5% pigment and 4% opacifier added.

Figure 18.1

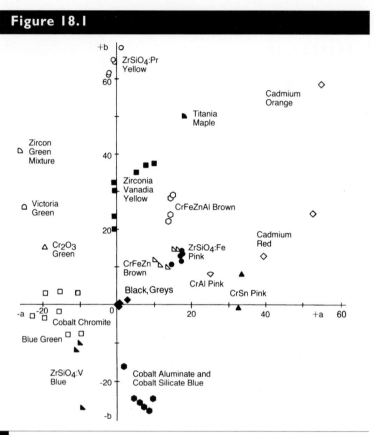

CIELAB chroma diagram showing colors obtained from the major ceramic pigments.

18.1.1 For blue there are three possibilities.[E34] Two of
them are cobalt-containing pigments: the cobalt-aluminate spinel and the cobalt-silicate olivine. These are the strongest of the ceramic pigments, producing a very pure, navy blue color. The other important blue pigment is the vanadium-zircon blue. That pigment is less intense than the cobalt pigments and is a turquoise. Thus, blue is a color that is obtainable with good purity in ceramic coatings.

18.1.2 A green color can be obtained in several ways.[E34]
Chromium oxide yields a dark green of moderate purity. The cobalt-chromite blue-green spinels yield a range of dark blue and green shades, but they can only be used in masstone. The Victoria green garnet yields a bright transparent green of good purity, but it is not satisfactory for opaque glazes or pastel shades. Bright green glazes with good purity can be made by combining a zircon-vana-

278

dium blue pigment with about twice as much of a praseodymium-zircon yellow pigment. Finally, copper compounds yield green with many subtle shade variations, but they are very difficult to control. The purity of the copper greens varies from moderate to good. Thus, the purity of green colors also varies from moderate to good. It is easier to obtain purity of color in dark masstones than in letdowns with opacifier.

18.1.3 Yellow is probably the most important color.[E34]

Consumption of yellow exceeds that of all other colored pigments. Three important yellow pigment families are suitable for ceramic glazes. Zirconia-vanadia yellows are economical pigments of poor to modest purity. Tin-vanadia yellows are very pure, opaque pigments. However, they are sensitive to reducing conditions, incompatible with chrome-containing pigments, and are very costly. Praseodymium-zircon pigments have excellent tinting strength and purity. To obtain the best purity, products introduced after 1990 must be used.

For lower-firing coatings such as porcelain enamels, the lead-antimony yellow and the chrome-titania maple can be used. They have excellent purity, provided their thermal stability is not exceeded. In summary, yellow is another color that can be obtained with excellent purity in ceramic coatings

18.1.4 Browns.

The zinc-iron chromite brown spinels produce a wide palette of brown and tan shades in good purity, although the shade and purity are affected by the presence or absence of zinc oxide (see section 18.2). Additions of nickel to the zinc-iron chromite pigment yield a much darker chocolate brown. The addition of alumina to a zinc-iron chromite brown yields a warm, orange-brown pigment. It is of modest purity, but it is the strongest orange available aside from the cadmium sulfoselenides. It requires a glaze high in zinc and alumina and low in calcium oxide. The manganese brown yields a deep brown color of low purity and stability. It tends to produce a poor coating surface. Essentially all of the many shades of brown are obtainable in ceramic coatings.

18.1.5 Pinks and purples are strongest

when made with the chrome-tin pink.[E34] Shades vary from orchid to light pink to reddish pink to maroon to purple to green. The reddish shades are the closest approach to red possible in ceramic glazes, unless nonoxide pigments (the cadmium sulfoselenides) are used. The purity is moderate.

The most stable pink pigment is the iron-zircon pink. Shades of this pigment extend from coral to pink and are of moderate purity. Variations on the iron-zircon pinks are the inclusion pigments. These products are modestly stronger and redder than the iron-zircon pinks, but they do not reach a pure red color.

A third pink is the chrome-alumina pink, which yields a baby pink, providing the coating to which it is added is free of calcium oxide, low in boron oxide, and high in zinc oxide and alumina. The manganese-alumina pink corundum is similar in color, but with improved purity. A zinc-free glaze, high in alumina, is required.

It is in this area of pink, purple, orange, and red that the limitations of ceramic pigments become evident. The possibilities mentioned do a good job for pink colors, and a fair approach to maroon and purple shades. However, among oxide pigments there are no alternatives for bright orange or red.

18.1.6 The possibilities for a red color are indeed limited and unsatisfactory. The iron-zircon pinks approximate a brick color, as do the inclusion pigments. For some applications, the cadmium sulfoselenide pigments can be used. They give very pure red and orange colors. However, these pigments require a glaze specially designed for this purpose. It is a low-alkaline borosilicate. It contains a few percent of cadmium oxide in the glaze, to retard attack on the pigment. For many whiteware bodies, such a glaze leads to crazing.

Moreover, these pigments are temperature sensitive. They can only be used in glazes fired below cone 1. They are highly toxic, and are very sensitive to acid attack. Hence, for many applications, there is no way to achieve a red color.

18.1.7 Black ceramic pigments are formed by the calcination of several oxides to yield an intense, uniform absorption over the entire visible spectrum. As the color of the glaze itself has some effect on the color, no one black will work in all cases. Most of these pigments are variations on cobalt iron chromite.

In addition, the nickel-iron-chromite spinel, and the iron chrome hematite are both cobalt-free systems of moderate to good purity in some coatings. By examining several products to select the product that gives the best results, a black color of high tinting strength can be obtained.

18.1.8 Gray can be made by mixing a black with a white opacifier. Unless this is done with great care, it leads to mottling. More uniform results are obtained with the cobalt-nickel periclase pigment, or by mixing a pink, a yellow, and a blue. Between these methods a wide variety of gray colors are obtainable in good purity.

Thus, while all hues are available in ceramic pigments, the purity of color varies significantly.[E34] Blues, yellows, browns, pinks, blacks, and grays are available in high purity. Greens and purples are available in fairly good purity. However, the purity of red and orange is very poor, unless cadmium sulfoselenide pigments are used. The latter are highly toxic and are difficult to stabilize in a ceramic glaze.

18.2 Effect of Coating Constituents

To be successfully used, a ceramic pigment must function as a component in an integral glaze or porcelain enamel coating.[E28] Hence, it must be compatible with the coating itself, the opacifier(s), and the coating additives.

Pigment-opacifier compatibility consists of matching elemental types in order to reduce pigment solubility. Zircon opacifiers should be used with all zirconia and zircon pigments. Titania opacifier should be used with titanium-containing pigments. Pigments containing tin oxide, such as chrome-tin pinks and tin-vanadium yellows, should be matched with at least a small amount of tin oxide opacifier.

There is a large variability in coating-pigment interaction during firing.[E28] Some pigments, such as the zircon pigments, are relatively inert in conventional coatings. Other pigments are much more reactive. Moreover, some coating constituents are more interactive than others.

Probably the most important coating consideration is the presence or absence of zinc oxide in the coating. The manganese-alumina pink corundum, chromium green-black hematite, Victoria green garnet, chrome-tin orchid cassiterite, and chrome-tin pink sphene pigments are not very stable in the presence of zinc oxide. On the other hand, the iron brown hematite, chrome-alumina pink spinel, iron chromite brown spinel, zinc-ferrite brown spinel, and zinc-iron chromite brown spinel require high zinc oxide for best results.

Calcium oxide concentration is important for a number of pigment systems. High concentrations of calcium oxide are required for the stability of Victoria green garnet and chrome-tin pink sphene. By contrast, calcium oxide should be avoided when using chrome alumina pink spinel, zinc-ferrite brown spinel, and zinc-iron chromite brown spinel.

High alumina concentrations are needed for the stability of chrome-alumina pink corundum, manganese-alumina pink corundum, chrome-alumina pink spinel, and zinc-iron chromite brown. Reactive ingredients such as lead oxide or boron oxide should be minimized when using zirconium-vanadium yellow baddeleyite, chrome-alumina pink spinel, and the cadmium sulfoselenide pigments. The latter require the addition of several percent cadmium oxide to the coating for adequate stability.

Another important color change is that which occurs when one converts from a lead-containing coating to one that is free of lead oxide.[E31,E33] The cobalt aluminate blue, cobalt silicate blue, chrome oxide green, tin-vanadium yellow, zircon-praseodymium yellow, and the zinc-iron-nickel chromite pigments work equally well in both high-lead and lead-free coatings. The Victoria green and cobalt black pigments work better in the lead-containing coating, primarily because of the improved glaze clarity obtainable there. Cupric oxide and ferric iron oxide solution colors are also in this category.

The strength of the tin-vanadium yellow, the zirconia-vanadia yellow, and the zirconia gray pigments are inversely proportional to the lead content of the coating. The mixed zircon green and the zinc-iron chromite brown work better in the low-lead or lead-free glazes, where the pigment solubility in the glaze is reduced. In clear coatings, the zircon-vanadium blue, the zircon-iron pink, and the chrome-tin pink pigments are only suitable for lead-free systems, where they have adequately low solubility. In opacified coatings, a little lead oxide can be tolerated.

There is only one important incompatibility between pigments.[E28] Pigments containing chromium III oxide are incompatible with pigments containing tin oxide. This incompatibility extends even to the sequential passage of ware through a kiln, as trapped volatiles from one can affect the other.

Part V
Concluding Remarks

Chapter 19
Conclusion

The concepts developed in this book are only worthwhile if they can be combined to formulate useful glazes for specific applications. Therefore, the following examples will illustrate the application of these ideas.

19.1 A Cone 8 Sanitary Ware Glaze

A conventional opacified gloss glaze for sanitary ware, firing at cone 8, has the following molecular formula:

OXIDE	AMOUNT
Na_2O	0.01589
K_2O	0.02396
CaO	0.12091
ZnO	0.00825
Al_2O_3	0.07221
SiO_2	0.72430
ZrO_2	0.03448

The alkali content in this formula is near the top of the limits given in Chapter 3, as the thermal expansion of sanitary ware bodies is higher than other high-fire bodies. The alumina content is slightly lower than the optimum for clarity, which can be tolerated in a highly opacified glaze. The zirconia content is in the range where opacification occurs. The silica level is adjusted to the desired firing cone. The other constituents are within the limits given in Chapter 3.

As described in Chapter 6, the process of obtaining a batch recipe involves converting to weight percent and then selecting suitable raw materials, as discussed in Chapter 5.

Converting to weight percent, one obtains:

OXIDE	AMOUNT
Na_2O	1.496
K_2O	3.438
CaO	10.301
ZnO	1.019
Al_2O_3	11.185
SiO_2	66.117
ZrO_2	6.453

There is no B_2O_3 in the formula, and the intended firing is cone 8. Hence, no frit is needed in the formula. The potash is higher than the soda, so a potash feldspar (G-200) is selected. For the CaO source, wollastonite is selected. The residual alumina is sufficient to select a kaolin clay as the suspending agent. Zircon is selected as opacifier and zirconia source. Finally, zinc oxide is specified for the ZnO, and 325 mesh silica for the residual SiO_2. The firing conditions are high enough that using silica in the glaze batch is acceptable.

As discussed in Chapter 7, in addition to the raw materials to yield the oxide formula, additives are needed to facilitate the preparation and application processes. One quarter of one percent of CMC is selected as a binder, and one quarter of one percent tetrasodium pyrophosphate is selected as a deflocculant.

Following the calculation procedure in Chapter 6, the batch recipe is calculated:

G-200 feldspar	34.50 wt%
wollastonite	20.50
EPK kaolin	11.00
zircon	10.00
zinc oxide	1.00
silica	23.00
CMC	0.25
tetrasodium pyrophosphate	0.25

As a check, the molecular formula is recalculated. The result is:

OXIDE	AMOUNT
Na_2O	0.01586
K_2O	0.02391
CaO	0.12068
MgO	0.00050
ZnO	0.00823
Fe_2O_3	0.00105
Al_2O_3	0.07207
SiO_2	0.72291
ZrO_2	0.03441
TiO_2	0.00039

In this formula, the MgO, Fe_2O_3, and TiO_2 concentrations are due to impurities in the raw materials.

The glaze is prepared by weighing out and blending the dry ingredients. The blended ingredients are then placed in a ball mill and milled, as described in Chapter 9. After sitting for at least 24 hours, to assure that the blended additives are fully effective, the milled slip is ready for application. Because of the complex shapes of sanitary ware, the application is by spraying, as described in Chapter 10. The sprayed ware is then dried and fired to cone 8 in a tunnel kiln (see Chapter 12).

The result is a smooth, white opaque, high-gloss glaze. The coefficient of thermal expansion (Chapter 15) is $6.8 \times 10^{-6}/°C$. The color data (Chapters 8 and 18) are $L = 92.7$, $a = -1.1$, $b = +2.3$.

19.2 A Cone 1 Opaque White Gloss Glaze for Fast-Fire Tile

An opaque white gloss glaze for fast-fire tile application has the following molecular formula:

OXIDE	AMOUNT
Na_2O	0.03746
K_2O	0.01175
CaO	0.11041
SrO	0.01746
ZnO	0.03052
B_2O_3	0.03354
Al_2O_3	0.06654
SiO_2	0.64834
ZrO_2	0.04398

This formula contains zinc oxide because it is a low-grade opacifier, helping the zircon opacifier to produce the desired white color, as discussed in Chapter 5. As discussed in Chapter 3, this zinc oxide in the formula requires lower boron oxide and lower alkali than a cone 1 formula without zinc oxide. The zirconia level is raised to that appropriate to a white color. The other constituents are within the limits given in Chapter 3.

As described in Chapter 6, the process of obtaining a batch recipe involves converting to weight percent, and then selecting suitable raw materials, as discussed in Chapter 5. Converting to weight percent, one obtains:

OXIDE	AMOUNT
Na_2O	3.434
K_2O	1.652
CaO	9.183
SrO	2.682
ZnO	3.683
B_2O_3	3.464
Al_2O_3	10.084
SiO_2	57.781
ZrO_2	8.037

As this formula contains both boron oxide and strontium oxide, a frit or frits are required. Other considerations are that rapid melting is needed for fast-fire, and a high seal-over temperature is also needed. This led to the selection of two frits from Table 6-2. Frit F300 is selected as the strontium source, and as a frit with high seal-over temperature. Frit FZ376A is selected as a rapid-melting frit and as a source of the rest of the boron oxide.

At cone 1, and in fast-fire, melting rate is very important, so a soda feldspar is selected instead of a potash feldspar. In addition, raw materials are selected so that the SiO_2 requirement can be met without using flint. At cone 1 fast-fire, the melting rate of flint is not adequate, as discussed in Chapter 5. Bentonite is used as the suspending agent, to limit the total clay content.

As discussed in Chapter 7, in addition to the raw materials to yield the oxide formula, additives are needed to facilitate the preparation and application processes. One quarter of one percent of CMC is selected as a binder, and one quarter of one percent tetrasodium pyrophosphate is selected as a deflocculant.

Following the calculation procedure in Chapter 6, the batch recipe is calculated:

Frit FZ376A	15.27 wt%
Frit F300	30.18
NC-4 feldspar	22.30
wollastonite	10.51
milled zircon	10.72
zinc oxide	3.43
bentonite	1.05
calcined kaolin	1.04
pyrophyllite	5.20
silica	23.00
CMC	0.25
tetrasodium pyrophosphate	0.25

As a check, the molecular formula is recalculated. The result is:

OXIDE	AMOUNT
Na_2O	0.03741
K_2O	0.01173
CaO	0.11024
MgO	0.00067
SrO	0.01743
ZnO	0.03047
Fe_2O_3	0.00065
B_2O_3	0.03349
Al_2O_3	0.06644
SiO_2	0.64736
ZrO_2	0.04391
TiO_2	0.00022

In this formula, the MgO, Fe_2O_3, and TiO_2 concentrations are due to impurities in the raw materials.

The glaze is prepared by weighing out and blending the dry ingredients. The blended ingredients are then placed in a ball mill and milled, as described in Chapter 9. After sitting for at least 24 hours, to assure that the blended additives are fully effective, the milled slip is ready for application. The application is by a waterfall technique, as described in Chapter 10. The coated ware is then dried and fired to cone 1 in an electric-fired fast-fire kiln (see Chapter 12).

The result is a smooth, white, high-gloss glaze. The coefficient of thermal expansion (Chapter 15) is $6.1 \times 10^{-6}/°C$. The color data (Chapters 8 and 18) are $L = 88.9$, $a = -1.2$, $b = +5.9$.

19.3 A Cone 1 Opaque Colored Glaze for Fast-Fire Tile

To make a light-colored glaze, the same base glaze as recommended in section 19.2 can be used. Appropriate pigments are added to the base glaze to produce the color (see Chapter 8). In addition, the amount of opacifier is reduced so that effective use is made of the pigments. This is important, because the pigments are, by far, the most expensive components of the glaze.

Thus, the opaque colored gloss glaze for fast-fire tile application has the following molecular formula:

OXIDE	AMOUNT
Na_2O	0.03874
K_2O	0.01215
CaO	0.11416
SrO	0.01805
ZnO	0.03155
B_2O_3	0.03468
Al_2O_3	0.06880
SiO_2	0.65338
ZrO_2	0.02849

This is the same formula as that in section 19.2, except for the lower zirconia and silica caused by reducing the zircon opacifier. Converting this formula to weight percent, one obtains:

OXIDE	AMOUNT
Na_2O	3.589
K_2O	1.729
CaO	9.613
SrO	2.807
ZnO	3.856
B_2O_3	3.625
Al_2O_3	10.555
SiO_2	58.983
ZrO_2	5.271

This formula is the same as that of section 19.2, except for the zircon level. The raw materials selected are the same. The additives needed, in addition to those just described, are appropriate pigments to produce the desired color. For a light pink color, we add one half of one percent of an iron-zircon coral pigment.

The calculation procedure then yields the batch recipe:

Frit FZ376A	16.03 wt%
Frit F300	31.67
NC-4 feldspar	23.41
wollastonite	11.03
milled zircon	6.30
zinc oxide	3.66
bentonite	1.10
calcined kaolin	1.09
pyrophyllite	5.46
CMC	0.25
tetrasodium pyrophosphate	0.25
iron-zircon coral pigment	0.50

As a check, the molecular formula is recalculated. The result is:

OXIDE	AMOUNT
Na_2O	0.03868
K_2O	0.01213
CaO	0.11398
MgO	0.00069
SrO	0.01802
ZnO	0.03150
Fe_2O_3	0.00067
B_2O_3	0.03463
Al_2O_3	0.06869
SiO_2	0.65235
ZrO_2	0.02844
TiO_2	0.00023

Again, the MgO, Fe_2O_3, and TiO_2 concentrations are due to impurities in the raw materials.

The glaze is prepared by weighing out and blending the dry ingredients. The blended ingredients are then placed in a ball mill and milled, as described in Chapter 9. After sitting for at least 24 hours, to assure that the blended additives are fully effective, the milled slip is ready for application. The application is by a waterfall technique, as described in Chapter 10. The coated ware is then dried and fired to cone 1 in an electric-fired fast-fire kiln (see Chapter 12).

The result is a smooth, pink, high-gloss glaze (see the opacified tile in Figure 8.37). The coefficient of thermal expansion (Chapter 15) is $6.7 \times 10^{-6}/°C$. The color data (Chapters 8 and 18) are $L = 71.7$, $a = +11.7$, $b = +9.0$.

Many producers, prefer to use the same glaze for white and for light colors, adding only pigment to the colors. This can still be done, using the base glaze in this section, and treating the extra zircon used in section 19.2 as a pigment when making the white glaze.

19.4 A Cone 1 Clear Glaze for Tile

To make a glaze with a dark color, or a transparent glaze, a clear glaze is required. Such a glaze, for tile application at cone 1, has the following molecular formula:

OXIDE	AMOUNT
Na_2O	0.04143
K_2O	0.01355
CaO	0.13009
SrO	0.01467
ZnO	0.02837
B_2O_3	0.03117
Al_2O_3	0.07292
SiO_2	0.66113
ZrO_2	0.00667

This formula is similar to those in sections 19.2 and 19.3, but not the same. The zirconia is reduced to below the solubility. The zinc oxide and boron oxide are modestly reduced, to insure that they do not contribute opacity. Converting to weight percent, one obtains:

OXIDE	AMOUNT
Na_2O	3.943
K_2O	1.961
CaO	11.203
SrO	2.335
ZnO	3.545
B_2O_3	3.333
Al_2O_3	11.417
SiO_2	61.001
ZrO_2	1.263

While this formula is slightly different than those of sections 19.2 and 19.3, the raw materials selected are the same. To produce a dark color, appropriate pigments must be added. For a deep blue-green color, we add 2% of a cobalt-chrome blue-green spinel pigment.

The calculation procedure then yields the batch recipe:

Frit FZ376A	15.91 wt%
Frit F300	26.46
NC-4 feldspar	30.72
wollastonite	15.36
zinc oxide	3.36
bentonite	1.17
calcined kaolin	1.16
pyrophyllite	5.83
CMC	0.25
tetrasodium pyrophosphate	0.25
cobalt-chrome blue-green spinel pigment	2.00

As a check, the molecular formula is recalculated. The result is:

OXIDE	AMOUNT
Na_2O	0.04125
K_2O	0.01353
CaO	0.12984
MgO	0.00079
SrO	0.01464
ZnO	0.02832
Fe_2O_3	0.00084
B_2O_3	0.03111
Al_2O_3	0.06869
SiO_2	0.65987
ZrO_2	0.00666
TiO_2	0.00028

Again, the MgO, Fe_2O_3, and TiO_2 concentrations are due to impurities in the raw materials.

The glaze is prepared by weighing out and blending the dry ingredients. The blended ingredients are then placed in a ball mill and milled, as described in Chapter 9. After sitting for at least 24 hours, to assure that the blended additives are fully effective, the milled slip is ready for application. The application is by a waterfall technique, as described in Chapter 10. The coated ware is then dried and fired to cone 1 in an electric-fired fast-fire kiln (see Chapter 12).

The result is a smooth, deep blue, high-gloss glaze (see the masstone glaze in Figure 8.22). The coefficient of thermal expansion (Chapter 15) is $6.5 \times 10^{-6}/°C$. The color data (Chapters 8 and 18) are $L = 28.2$, $a = -6.7$, $b = -23.3$.

19.5 A Matte Glaze For Tile

As discussed in section 3.6, for a matte glaze the formulation must be adjusted to promote the crystallization of a matting crystal. Such a formulation for tile application at cone 1 has the following molecular formula:

OXIDE	AMOUNT
Na_2O	0.04913
K_2O	0.01405
CaO	0.22971
ZnO	0.01612
B_2O_3	0.00941
Al_2O_3	0.09150
SiO_2	0.59008

This formula is much lower in silica and higher in alkaline earth than the gloss glazes described previously. The zinc oxide and boron oxide are also lower. Converting to weight percent, one obtains:

OXIDE	AMOUNT
Na_2O	4.758
K_2O	2.067
CaO	20.128
ZnO	2.050
B_2O_3	1.024
Al_2O_3	14.578
SiO_2	55.395

As stated, this formula will produce a translucent glaze, because the matting crystals yield a low level of opacity. Hence, it is best to use it as a base for whatever color (including white) that is desired. For a blue-green color, we add 2% of a cobalt-chrome blue-green spinel pigment.

The calculation procedure then yields the batch recipe:

Frit F495	6.99 wt%
A-200 nepheline syenite	39.60
wollastonite	40.00
zinc oxide	2.03
bentonite	1.75
calcined kaolin	9.41
CMC	0.25
tetrasodium pyrophosphate	0.25
cobalt-chrome blue-green spinel pigment	2.00

As a check, the molecular formula is recalculated. The result is:

OXIDE	AMOUNT
Na_2O	0.04900
K_2O	0.01401
CaO	0.22912
MgO	0.00148
ZnO	0.01608
Fe_2O_3	0.00044
B_2O_3	0.00939
Al_2O_3	0.09127
SiO_2	0.58909
TiO_2	0.00012

Again, the MgO, Fe_2O_3, and TiO_2 concentrations are due to impurities in the raw materials.

The glaze is prepared by weighing out and blending the dry ingredients. The blended ingredients are then placed in a ball mill and milled, as described in Chapter 9. After sitting for at least 24 hours, to assure that the blended additives are fully effective, the milled slip is ready for application. The application is by a waterfall technique, as described in Chapter 10. The coated ware is then dried and fired to cone 1 in an electric-fired fast-fire kiln (see Chapter 12).

The result is a smooth, blue, matte glaze. The coefficient of thermal expansion (Chapter 15) is $7.4 \times 10^{-6}/°C$. The color data (Chapters 8 and 18) are $L = 36.9$, $a = -6.9$, $b = -17.8$.

References

A1. Andrew I. Andrews, *Porcelain Enamels*, (Champaign, IL: Garrard Press, 1961), p. 14.

B1. George H. Beall, "Glass Ceramics," pp. 157–73 in *Commercial Glasses*, David C. Boyd and John F. MacDowell, eds. (Columbus, OH: American Ceramic Society, 1986).

B2. L. G. Berry and Brian Mason, *Mineralogy: Concepts, Descriptions, Determinations, .*, (San Francisco, CA: W. H. Freeman & Co., 1959), pp. 560–61.

B3. F. W. Billmeyer, Jr., and M. Saltzman, *Principles of Color Technology* (New York: Wiley, 1981).

B4. Z. Boksay, G. Bouquet, and S. Dubos, "The Kinetics of the Formation of Leached Layers on Glass Surfaces," *Phys. Chem. Glasses* 9[2]:69–71 (1968).

B5. Wallace P. Bolen, "Silica," *Am. Ceram. Soc. Bull.* 76[6]:130–35 (1997).

B6. F. T. Booth and G. N. Peel, "The Principles of Glaze Opacification with Zirconium Silicate," *Trans. J. Br. Ceram. Soc.* 58[9]:532–64 (1959).

B7. F. T. Booth and G. N. Peel, "Preparation and Properties of Some Zircon Stains," *Trans. J. Br. Ceram. Soc.* 61[7]:359–400 (1962).

B8. Marcus P. Borum and Joseph A. Pask, "Role of Adherence Oxides in the Development of Chemical Bonding at Glass-Metal Interfaces," *J. Am. Ceram. Soc.* 49[1]:1–6 (1966).

B9 Marcus P. Borum, James A. Longwell, and Joseph A. Pask, "Reactions between Metallic Iron and Cobalt Bearing Sodium Disilicate Glass," *J. Am. Ceram. Soc.* 50[2]:61–66 (1967).

B10. D. W. Budworth, M. S. Smith, and M. E. Rose, "Firing of Bone China Glazes," *Trans. Brit. Ceram. Soc.* 73[2]:57–59 (1974).

B11. Aladar Burgyan and Richard A. Eppler, "Classification of Mixed-Metal-Oxide Inorganic Pigments," *Am. Ceram. Soc. Bull.* 62[9]:1001–3 (1983).

B12. Bruno Burzacchini, "Technical Developments in Ceramic Tile Glazes and Related Applications," *Ceram. Eng. Sci. Proc.* 12[1–2]:261–74 (1991).

C1. David G. Carl, "Hot and Cold Inks," *Proc. Ann. Semin. Glass Ceram. Decorators* 1991, p. 42.

C2. Robert J. Castilone and William M. Carty, "The Metal Marking Behavior of Matte, Gloss, and Zircon-Opacified Glazes," *Ceram. Eng. Sci. Proc.* 18[2]:81–95 (1997).

C3. CIE (International Commission on Illumination), *Proceedings of the Eighth Session, Cambridge, England,* Bureau Central de la CIE, Paris, 1931.

C4. CIE (International Commission on Illumination), "Colorimetry, Official Recommendations of the International Commission on Illumination," *Publication CIE #15* (E-1.3.1), 1971, Bureau Central de la CIE, Paris, 1971.

C5. CIE (International Commission on Illumination), "Recommendations on Uniform Color Spaces, Color-Difference Equations, Psychometric Color Terms," *Supplement #2 to CIE Publication #15*, (E1.3.1) 1971/(TC-1.3) 1978, Bureau Central de la CIE, Paris, 1978.

C6. David E. Clark and Edwin C. Ethridge, "Corrosion of Glass Enamels," *Am. Ceram. Soc. Bull.* 60[6]:646–49 (1981).

C7. Emmanuel Cooper, *The Potter's Book of Glaze Recipes,* (London: B. T. Batsford, Ltd., 1980).

C8. Emmanuel Cooper and Derek Royle, *Glazes for the Potter,* (New York: Charles Scribner's Sons, 1978).

C9. A. N. Copp, "Magnesia/Magnesite," *Am. Ceram. Soc. Bull.* 76[6]: 112–15 (1997).

C10. Ian Currie, *Stoneware Glazes, A Systematic Approach,* (Maryvale, Australia: Bootstrap Press, 1986).

D1. C. R. Das and R. W. Douglas, "Studies on the Reaction between Water and Glass, Part 3," *Phys. Chem. Glasses* 8[5]:178–84 (1967).

D2. *DCMA Classification and Chemical Description of the Mixed Metal Oxide Inorganic Colored Pigments,* 2nd ed., Metal Oxides and Ceramic Colors Subcommittee, Dry Color Manufacturers Assn., Arlington, VA, 1982.

D3. H. D. deAhna, "Inclusion Pigments: New Types of Ceramic Stains and Their Applications," *Ceram. Eng. Sci. Proc.* 1[9–10]:860–62 (1980).

D4. Temel Demiray, D. K. Nath, and Floyd a. Hummel, Zircon-Vanadium Blue Pigments," *J. Am. Ceram. Soc.* 53[1]:1–4 (1970).

D5. Morris F. Dilmore, David E. Clark, and Larry L. Hench, "Chemical Durability of $Na_2O-K_2O-CaO-SiO_2$ Glasses," *J. Am. Ceram. Soc.* 61[9–10]:439–43 (1978).

D6. Allen Dinsdale and F. Malkin, "The Measurement of Gloss with Special Reference to Ceramic Materials," *Trans. Brit. Ceram. Soc.* 54[7]:94–112 (1955).

D7. Allen Dinsdale, "Crystalline Silica in Whiteware Bodies," *Trans. Brit. Ceram. Soc.* 62[4]:321–88 (1963).

D8. Allen Dinsdale, *Pottery Science—Materials, Processes, and Products* (New York: Wiley, 1985).

D9. John W. Donahey, and Ralston Russell, Jr., "Color Fading of Underglaze Decalcomania," *J. Am. Ceram. Soc.* 33[9]:283–90 (1950).

D10. P. J. Doyle, *Glass-Making Today* (London: Portcullis Press, Ltd., 1979), p. 169.

E1. K. A. Ellis, "Mechanized Decorating Within the Ceramic Industry," *Interceram* 22[4]:305–08 (1973).

E2. Richard A. Eppler and William A. McLeran, Jr., "Kinetics of Opacification of a TiO_2-Opacified Cover-Coat Enamel," *J. Am. Ceram. Soc.* 50[3]:152–56 (1967).

E3. Richard A. Eppler, "Crystallization and Phase Transformation in TiO_2-Opacified Porcelain Enamels," *J. Am. Ceram. Soc.* 52[2]:89–99 (1969).

E4. Richard A. Eppler and George H. Spencer-Strong, "Role of P_2O_5 in TiO_2-Opacified Porcelain Enamels," *J. Am. Ceram. Soc.* 52[5]:263–66 (1969).

E5. Richard A. Eppler, "Reflectance of Titania-Opacified Porcelain Enamels," *Am. Ceram. Soc. Bull.* 48[5]:549–54 (1969).

E6. Richard A. Eppler, "Mechanism of Formation of Zircon Stains," *J. Am. Ceram. Soc.* 53[8]:457–62 (1970).

E7. Richard A. Eppler, "Use of Scattering Theory to Interpret Optical Data for Enamels," *J. Am. Ceram. Soc.* 54[2]:116–20 (1971).

E8. Richard A. Eppler, "Formation of Praseodymium-Doped Zircon Colors in the Presence of Halides," *Ind. Eng. Chem. Prod. Res. Dev.* 10[9]:352–55 (1971).

E9. Richard A. Eppler, "The Crystallization of Some Ceramic Coatings," Ch. 24 in *Advances in Nucleation and Crystallization in Glasses*, L. L. Hench and S. W. Freiman, eds. (Columbus, OH: Am. Ceram. Soc., 1971).

E10. Richard A. Eppler, "Solid State Reactions in the Preparation of Zircon Stains," pp. 1021–45 in *Physics of Electronic Materials*, Part B, L. L. Hench and D. B. Dove, eds. (New York: Marcel Dekker, 1972).

E11. Richard A. Eppler, "Niobium and Tungsten Oxides in Titania-Opacified Porcelain Enamels," *Am. Ceram. Soc. Bull.* 52[12]:879–81 (1973).

E12. Richard A. Eppler, "Formulation of Glazes for Low Lead Release," *Am. Ceram. Soc. Bull.* 54[5]:496–99 (1975).

E13. Richard A. Eppler and William F. Schweikert, "Interaction of Dilute Acetic Acid with Lead-Containing Vitreous Surfaces," *Am. Ceram. Soc. Bull.* 55[3]:277–80 (1976).

E14. Richard A. Eppler "Formulation and Processing of Ceramic Glazes for Low Lead Release," Chapter 10, pp. 74–96 in *Proceedings International Conference Ceramic Foodware Safety,* Jerome F. Smith and Malcolm H. Mc Laren, eds. (New York: Lead Industries Assn. 1976).

E15. Richard A. Eppler, "Lattice Parameters of Tin Sphene," *J. Am. Ceram. Soc.* 59[9–10]:455 (1976).

E16. Richard A. Eppler, "Zirconia-Based Colors for Ceramic Glazes," *Am. Ceram. Soc. Bull.* 56[2]:213–15,18,24 (1977).

E17. Richard A. Eppler, Robert L. Hyde, and Howard F. Smalley, "Resistance of Porcelain Enamels to Attack by Aqueous Media: I> Tests for Enamel Resistance and Experimental Results Obtained," *Am. Ceram. Soc. Bull.* 56[12]:1064–67 (1977).

E18. Richard A. Eppler, "Resistance of Porcelain Enamels to Attack by Aqueous Media: II. Equations to Predict Enamel Durability," *Am. Ceram. Soc. Bull.* 56[12]:1068–70 (1977).

E19. Richard A. Eppler, "Kinetics of Formation of an Iron-Zircon Pink Color," J. Am. Ceram. Soc. 62[1–2]: 47–49 (1979).

E20. Richard A. Eppler, "Cobalt-Free Black Pigments," *Am. Ceram. Soc. Bull.* 60[5]:562–65 (1981). See also *Ceram. Eng. Sci. Bull.* 1[9–10]:863–70 (1980).

E21. Richard A. Eppler, "Resistance of Porcelain Enamels to Attack by Aqueous Media: III. Mechanism of the Corrosion of Water Tank Enamels," *Am. Ceram. Soc. Bull.* 60[6]:618–22 (1981).

E22. Richard A. Eppler, "Resistance of Porcelain Enamels to Attack by Aqueous Media: IV. Effect of Anions at pH 5.5," *Am. Ceram. Soc. Bull.* 61[9]:989–95 (1982).

E23. Richard A. Eppler and Dodd S. Carr, "Cadmium in Glazes and Glasses," *Proc. 3rd Int. Cadmium Conf.,* (New York: International Lead Zinc Research Organization, 1982).

E24. Richard A. Eppler, "Glazes and Enamels," Ch. 4, pp. 301–337 in *Glass Science & Technology,* Vol. 1, D. R. Uhlmann and N. J. Kreidl, eds. (New York: Academic Press, 1983).

E25. Richard A. Eppler, "Inverse Spinel Pigments," *J. Am. Ceram. Soc.* 66[11]: 794–801 (1983).

E26. Richard A. Eppler, "Glazes and Enamels," Ch. 6 in *Commercial Glasses,* David C. Boyd, and John F. MacDowell, eds. (Columbus, OH: American Ceramics Society, 1986).

E27. Richard A. Eppler, "Ceramic Colorants," *Ullmann's Encyclopedia of Industrial Chemistry,* Vol. A5. (5th Ed., VCH Verlagsgesellschaft mbH, Wertheim, Germany, 1986), pp. 545–56.

E28. Richard A. Eppler, "Selecting Ceramic Pigments," *Am. Ceram. Soc. Bull.* 66[11]:1600–04 (1987). See also *Ceram. Eng. Sci. Proc.* 8[1–2]:1137–49 (1987).

E29. Richard A. Eppler, "Colorants for Ceramics," *Kirk-Othmer Encyclopedia of Chemical Technology,* 4th ed., Vol. 6, pp. 877–92, 1992.

E30. Richard A. Eppler, "Corrosion of Glazes and Enamels," Ch. 12 in *Corrosion of Glass, Ceramics, and Ceramic Superconductors*, David E. Clark and Bruce K. Zoitos, eds. (Park Ridge, NJ: Noyes Pubs., 1992.

E31. Richard A. Eppler and Douglas R. Eppler, "Color in Lead and Lead-Free Glazes," *Ceram. Eng. Sci. Proc.*, 13[1–2]:338–57 (1992).

E32. Richard A. Eppler, "Bubble Defects in Leadless Glazes," *Am. Ceram. Soc. Bull.* 72[9]:62–65,[10]8 (1993).

E33. Douglas R. Eppler and Richard A. Eppler, "Color in Lead and Lead-Free Glazes II," *Ceram. Eng. Sci. Proc.* 14[1-2]:137–54 (1993).

E34. Richard A. Eppler and Douglas R. Eppler, "Which Colors Can and Cannot Be Produced in Ceramic Glazes," *Ceram. Eng. Sci. Proc.* 15[1]:281–88 (1994).

E35. Richard A. Eppler, "Crazing on Whitewares Having Both an Engobe and a Glaze," *Ceram. Eng. Sci. Proc.* 15[1]:138–45 (1994).

E36. Richard A. Eppler, "The Fundamentals of Leadless Glaze Development," *Ceram. Eng. Sci. Proc.* 15[1]:118–25 (1994).

E37. Richard A. Eppler, "Ceramic Pigments," Ch. 23 in *Paint and Coating Testing Manual*, 14th ed. of the Gardner-Sward Handbook, Joseph V. Koleske, ed. (Philadelphia: ASTM, 1995).

E38. Richard A. Eppler, "Leadfree Glazing Trends for Whiteware," *Ceram. Ind.* 145[6]:33–37 (1995).

E39. Richard A. Eppler, "Glazing Defects and Their Control," *Ceram. Eng. Sci. Proc.* 16[3]:43–50 (1995).

E40. Richard A. Eppler, "Controlling the Gloss of Leadless Glazes," *Ceram. Eng. Sci. Proc.* 16[1]:40–45 (1995).

E41. Richard A. Eppler and Douglas R. Eppler, "Formulating Lead-free Glazes," *Am. Ceram. Soc. Bull.* 75[9]:62–65 (1996); see also *Ceram. Eng. Sci. Proc.* 18[2]:150–58 (1997).

E42. Douglas R. Eppler and Richard A. Eppler, "Analyzing the Color of Reddish Glazes," *Ceram. Eng. Sci. Proc.* 17[1]:77–87 (1996).

E43. Douglas R. Eppler and Richard A. Eppler, "On the Relative Stability of Ceramic Pigments," *Ceram. Eng. Sci. Proc.* 18[2]:139–49 (1997).

E44. Douglas R. Eppler and Richard A. Eppler, "Calculating Glaze Color from Pigment and Opacifier Standards," *Ceram. Eng. Sci. Proc.* 19[2]:17–37 (1998); see also *Ceram. Ind.* 148[10]:40–46 (1998).

E45. Frederick M. Ernsberger, "The Role of Molecular Water in the Diffusive Transport of Protons in Glasses," *Phys. Chem. Glasses* 21[4]:146–49 (1980).

E46. A. Escardino, J. de la Torre, and A. Blasco, "Lead Release from a Bisilicate Glaze in Acid Media: II. Kinetic Model for All the Reaction Period," *J. Brit. Ceram. Soc.* 86:118–23 (1987).

E47 Richard A. Eppler, "Selecting Raw Materials for Glazes," *Am. Ceram. Soc. Bull.* 77[3]:71–74 (1998); see also *Ceram. Eng. Sci. Proc.* 19[2]:9–15 (1998).

F1. J. Francel, "Sealing Glasses," In *Commercial Glasses,* David C. Boyd and John F. MacDowell, eds. (Columbus, OH: Amercian Ceramic Society, 1986.

F2. H. Fraser, *Glazes for the Craft Potter,* (New York: Watson-Guptill Publications, 1974.

F3. Warren D. Fuller, "Milling Practices and Parameters," *Ceram. Eng. Sci. Proc.* 12[5–6]:749-54 (1991).

G1. Laurence D. Gill and Richard A. Eppler, "Lead Frits," ch. 7, pp 99–105 in *Lead in the World of Ceramics,* John S. Nordyke, ed. (Columbus, OH: American Ceramic Society, 1984).

G2. Albert Granger, *Die Industrielle Keramik,* (Trans. Raymond Keller, p. 401, (Berlin: Julius Springer, 1908).

G3. Thomas J. Gray, "Strontium Glazes and Pigments," *Am. Ceram. Soc. Bull.* 58[8]:768–70 1979.

G4. David Green, *A Handbook of Pottery Glazes,* (London: Watson-Guptill Publications, 1979).

G5. R. M. Gruver, "Differential Thermal Analysis Studies of Ceramic Materials: I. Characteristic Heat Effects of Some Carbonates," *J. Am. Ceram. Soc.* 33[3]:96–101 (1950).

G6. Benjamin Gutmann and Alan Chalup, "Barium Carbonate," *Am. Ceram. Soc. Bull.* 76[6]:74–77 (1997).

H1. Cullen L. Hackler, "Formation and Control of Textured Tear Glazes," *Am. Ceram. Soc. Bull.* 56[6]:647–48 (1980).

H2. P. W. Harben, ed., *Processing of Minerals and Chemicals in Glass and Ceramics—the Next Decade,* (London: Ind. Min., 1981).

H3. Ralph L. Hawks, "Chrome-Alumina Pink at Various Temperatures," *Am. Ceram. Soc. Bull.* 40[1]:7–8 (1961).

H4. James B. Hedrick, "Mica," *Am. Ceram. Soc. Bull.* 76[6]:115–17 (1997).

H5. Paul Henry, "Ceramic Green Colors for Whiteware Glazes," *Am. Ceram. Soc. Bull.* 40[1]:9–10 (1961).

H6. Jonathan W. Hinton, "Lead-free Glaze for Alumina Bodies," U. S. Patent 4,084,976, April 18, 1978.

H7. David A. Hopkins, "Dolomite," *Am. Ceram. Soc. Bull.* 76[6]:95–96 (1997).

H8. Richard S. Hunter, "Photoelectric Tristimulus Colorimetry with Three Filters," NBS Circular 429, U.S. Government Printing Office, Washington, DC, 1942: see also *J. Opt. Soc. Am.* 32,509–38(1942).

H9. Richard S. Hunter, *The Measurement of Appearance,* (New York: Wiley 1975).

I1. Herbert Insley, George W. Morey, Frederick D. Rossini, and Alexander Silverman, "Data on Chemicals for Ceramic Use," *Bull. Nat'l. Res. Coun.* No. 118, June 1949.

I2. International Lead Zinc Research Organization, "Lead Glazes for Dinnerware," (New York: ILZRO Manual Ceramics #1, ILZRO, 1970).

J1. Charles W. F. Jacobs, "Opacifying Crystalline Phases Present in Zircon-Type Glazes," *J. Am. Ceram. Soc.* 37[5]:216–20 (1954).

J2. Barbara Ann Jacoby, "Practical Solutions for Fast-Fire Tile Faults," *Ceram. Eng. Sci. Proc.* 11[3–4]:314–19 (1990).

J3. Randall L. Johnson, "Talc," *Am. Ceram. Soc. Bull.* 76[6]:136–37 (1997).

J4. Deane B. Judd and Gunter Wysocki, *Color in Business, Science, and Industry,* 3rd ed., (New York: Wiley, New York, 1975).

K1. B. Kerl, *Handbuch der Gesammten Thonwaarenindustrie,* Braunschweig: p. 1149, Viereg and Son, 1907.

K2. Burnham W. King and Andrew I. Andrews, "Reactions Taking Place During Smelting of Superopaque Antimony Enamel," *J. Am. Ceram. Soc.* 23, 225–28 (1940).

K3. Burnham W. King and Andrew I. Andrews, "Reactions Taking Place During Smelting of Superopaque Antimony Enamel II," *J. Am. Ceram. Soc.* 23, 228–35 (1940).

K4. Burnham W. King, H. P. Tripp, and Winston H. Duckworth, "Nature of Adherence of Porcelain Enamels to Metals," *J. Am. Ceram. Soc.* 42[11]:504–25 (1959).

K5. W. David Kingery, H. Kent Bowen, and David R. Uhlmann, *Introduction to Ceramics,* 2nd ed. (New York: Wiley, 1976).

K6. Randy O. Knapp, "Lead-Free Glaze for Alumina Bodies," U. S. Patent 4,256,497, Mar. 17, 1981.

K7. Joseph V. Koleske, "Oil Absorption of Pigments," Ch. 28, pp. 252–58 in *Paint and Coating Testing Manual,* Joseph V. Koleske, ed. (West Conshohocken, PA: ASTM, 1995).

K8. P. Kubelka and F. N. Munk, "A Contribution to the Optics of Pigments," *Z. Tech. Phys.* 12:593–601 (1931).

L1. Chi-Hang Li, Douglas R. Eppler, and Richard A. Eppler, "Iron Zircon Pigments," *Ceram. Eng. Sci. Proc.* 13[1–2]:109–18 (1992).

L2. Hans-Peter Lisson, "Precision Screen Printing Fabrics," *Proc. Ann. Semin. Glass Ceram. Decorators* 1992, pp. 50–54.

L3. Loris Lorici and Augusto Brusa, "Porous and Vitrified Single-Fired Tiles," *Ceram. Eng. Sci. Proc.* 12[1-2]:183–221 (1991).

L4. Carolyn B. Luttrell, "Glazes for Zircon Porcelains," *J. Am. Ceram. Soc.* 32[10]:327–32 (1949).

M1. Masaki Madono, Raymond P. Racher, and Marilyn K. Kunka, "Alumina," *Am. Ceram. Soc. Bull.* 76[6]:65–69 (1997).

M2. Rick Malmgren, "Glaze Calculation Software," *Ceram. Monthly* 40[1]:29–33 (1992).

M3. Rick Malmgren, "More Glaze Calculation Software," *Ceram. Monthly* 42[3]:52–53,86–90 (1994).

M4. Rick Malmgren, "A Look at Glaze Calculation Software, with Using Glaze Programs," *Ceram. Monthly* 46[6]:38–45 (1998).

M5. John E. Marquis and Robert E. Carpenter, "Plant Control Problems with Whiteware Glazes Containing Brown and Tan Stains," *Am. Ceram. Soc. Bull.* 40[1]:19–24 (1961).

M6. John E. Marquis, "Lead in Glazes—Benefits and Safety Precautions," *Am. Ceram. Soc. Bull.* 50[11]:921–23 (1971).

M7. John E. Marquis and Richard A. Eppler, "Leadless Glazes for Dinnerware," *Am. Ceram. Soc. Bull.* 53[5]:443–45,449 (1974).

M8. K. A. Maskall and D. White, *Vitreous Enamelling*, (Oxford: Pergamon Press, 1986).

M9. Ronald K. Mason, "Use of Cobalt Colors in Glazes," *Am. Ceram. Soc. Bull.* 40[1]:5–6 (1961).

M10. Derek J. McCracken, and Mike Haigh, "Lithium Minerals," *Am. Ceram. Soc. Bull.* 76[6]:110–12 (1997).

M11. E. S. McCutchen, "Strontia and Its Properties in Glazes," *J. Am. Ceram. Soc.* 27[8]:233–38 (1944).

M12. K. McLaren, *The Color Science of Dyes and Pigments*, Bristol, UK: Adam Hilger, 1986).

M13. George W. McLellan and Errol B. Shand, *Glass Engineering Handbook*, 3rd ed., (New York: McGraw-Hill, 1984).

M14. Jason T. McCuistion, "Ball Clay," *Am. Ceram. Soc. Bull.* 76[6]:73–74 (1997).

M15. Peter W. McMillan, *Glass Ceramics*, 2nd ed. (New York: Academic Press, 1979).

M16. J. W. Mellor, "The Durability of Pottery Frits, Glazes, Glass, and Enamels," *Trans. Brit. Ceram. Soc.* 34:113–90 (1935).

M17. Gustav Mie, "Optically Active Media, Specifically Colloidal Metal Solutions," *Ann. Phys.* (Leipzig) 25[3]:377–450 (1908).

M18. F. Moore, "Some Statistical Aspects of Metal Release Regulations," *Trans. J. Brit. Ceram. Soc.* 76[3]:52–57 (1977).

M19. H. Moore, "The Structure of Glazes," *Trans. J. Brit. Ceram. Soc.* 55:589–600 (1956).

M20. Neil V. Moresca, "Safe Use of Lead Compounds," Ch. 12, pp. 159–62 in *Lead in the World of Ceramics*, John S. Nordyke, ed., (Columbus, OH: American Ceramic Society, 1984).

M21. George W. Morey, *The Properties of Glass*, New York: Reinhold Publishing Company, 1938), pp. 389–91.

M22. A. N. Munsell, *Munsell Book of Color*, (Baltimore: Munsell Color Company, 1929 to date).

M23. Stephen H. Murdock and Richard A. Eppler, "Zinc Iron Chromite Pigments," *J. Am. Ceram. Soc.* 71[4]:C212–14 (1988). See also *Ceram. Eng. Sci. Proc.* 8[11–12]:1162–67 (1987).

M24. Stephen H. Murdock, Terry D. Wise, and Richard A. Eppler, "Predicting the Color of a Ceramic Glaze," *Am. Ceram. Soc. Bull.* 69[2]:228–30 (1990).

M25. Stephen H. Murdock, Terry D. Wise, and Richard A. Eppler, "Blending of Pigments in Ceramic Glazes," *Ceram. Eng. Sci. Proc.* 11[3–4]:278–87 (1990).

M26. Stephen H. Murdock, Terry D. Wise, and Richard A. Eppler, "Measurement and Interpretation of Color in Glazes," *Ceram. Eng. Sci. Proc.* 11[3–4]270–77 (1990).

M27. O. Muller, and R. Roy, *The Major Ternary Structural Families*, (New York: Springer-Verlag, 1974), p. 41.

N1. John S. Nordyke, "Lead Compounds and Their Properties," Ch. 1 in *Lead in the World of Ceramics*, John S. Nordyke, ed., Columbus, OH: American Ceramic Society, 1984).

O1. Joyce A. Ober, "Strontium," *Am. Ceram. Soc. Bull.* 76[5]:154–57 (1996).

O2. Mimi Obstler, *Out of the Earth, into the Fire* (Westerville, OH: American Ceramic Society 1996).

O3. Eugene F. O'Conor and Richard A. Eppler, "Semicrystalline Glazes for Low Expansion Whiteware Bodies," *Am. Ceram. Soc. Bull.* 52[2]:180–84 1973).

O4. H. J. Orlowski and John E. Marquis, "Lead Replacements in Dinnerware Glazes," *J. Am. Ceram. Soc.* 28[12]:343–57 (1945).

O5. H. J. Orlowski and John E. Marquis, "Lead Replacements in Dinnerware Glazes," *Ohio State Univ. Eng. Expt. Sta. Bull.* #125, 58 pp. (1946).

O6. William H. Orth, "Effect of Firing Rate on Physical Properties of Wall Tile," *Am. Ceram. Soc. Bull.* 46[9]:841–44 (1967).

P1. Cullen W. Parmalee and Cameron G. Harmon, *Ceramic Glazes*, (Boston: Cahner's Books, 1973).

P2. Joseph A. Pask, "Chemical Reactions and Adherence of Glass-Metal Interfaces," *Proc. PEI Tech. Forum* 33:1–16 (1971).

P3. Robert F. Patrick, "Some Factors Affecting Opacity, Color, and Color Stability of Titania-Opacified Enamels," *J. Am. Ceram. Soc.* 34[3]:96–102 (1951).

P4. A. Paul, *Chemistry of Glasses*, (London: Chapman and Hall, Ltd., 1982), pp. 108–47.

P5. Linus Pauling, *The Nature of the Chemical Bond*, 3rd ed. (Ithaca, NY: Cornell University Press, 1960).

P6. Allen S. Perl, "Zinc Oxide, " *Am. Ceram. Soc. Bull.* 76[6]:140–43 (1997).

P7. Michael J. Potter, "Feldspar," *Am. Ceram. Soc. Bull.* 76[6]:96–99 (1997).

P8. W. Pukall, "Bunzlauer Feinsteinzeng," *Sprechs.* 48:1–3,18–19, 33–35,47–49 (1910).

R1. Paul Rado, *An Introduction to the Technology of Pottery,* 2nd ed., (Oxford: Pergamon Press, 1988).

R2. Mushtaq A. Rana, and R. W. Douglas, "The Reaction of Glass and Water, Part 1, Experimental Methods and Observations," *Phys. Chem. Glasses* 2[6]:179–95 (1961).

R3. H. Rawson, *Properties and Applications of Glass,* (Amsterdam: Elsevier, 1980), p. 189.

R4. E. H. Ray, T. D. Carnahan, and R. M. Sullivan, "Tin-Vanadium Yellows and Praseodymium Yellows," *Am. Ceram. Soc. Bull.* 40[1]:13–16 (1961).

R5. James S. Reed, *Introduction to the Principles of Ceramic Processing,* (New York: Wiley, 1988), Ch. 13.

R6. Konrad C. Reiger, "Wollastonite," *Am. Ceram. Soc. Bull.* 76[6]:139–40 (1997).

R7. J. A. Reising, "Zinc Oxide and Crawling of Glazes," *Am. Ceram. Soc. Bull.* 41[8]:497–99 (1962).

R8. Daniel Rhodes, *Clay and Glazes for the Potter,* Rev. Ed. (Radnor, PA: Chilton Publ., 1973).

R9. Prudence Rice, *Pottery Analysis, a Sourcebook,* (Chicago: University of Chicago Press, 1987).

R10. Rustum Roy, "Rational Molecular Engineering of Ceramic Materials," *J. Am. Ceram. Soc.* 60[7–8]:350–63 (1977).

S1. George Sanderson, "Transfer Printing for Ceramics from the 1700s to the Present Day," *Br. Ceram. Reviews* #80, 1989, pp. 24–25.

S2. J. L. Saunderson, "Calculation of the Color of Pigmented Plastics," *J. Opt. Soc. Am.* 32[12]:727–36 (1942).

S3. N. Irving Sax and Richard J. Lewis, Sr., "Hazardous Chemicals Desk Reference," (New York: Van Nostrand Reinhold Company, 1987).

S4. Charles A. Seabright and H. C. Draker, "Ceramic Stains from Zirconium and Vanadium Oxides," *Am. Ceram. Soc. Bull.* 40[1]:1–4 (1961).

S5. Zeke C. Seedorff, Richard C. Patterson, Heinz J. Pangels, and Richard A. Eppler, "Testing for Metal Marking Resistance," *Ceram. Eng. Sci. Proc.* 13[1–2]:196–209 (1992).

S6. Hermann Seger, *Collected Writings,* Vol. 2 (New York: Chemical Publishing Company, 1902).

S7. Daniel J. Shanefield and Richard E. Mistler, "The Manufacture of Fine-Grained Alumina Substrates for Thin Films," *Western Electric. Eng.* 15[2]:26–31 (1971).

S8. Robert D. Shannon and Arthur L. Friedberg, "Titania Opacified Porcelain Enamels," *Univ. Illinois Eng. Expt. Sta. Bull.* #456, 1960.

S9. Kenneth Shaw, *Ceramic Colours & Pottery Decoration*, (London: MacLaren & Sons, Ltd., 1962).

S10. Julia G. Shteinberg and M. I. Nevorotina, "New Compositions of Strontium Colored Glazes for Majolica," *Glass Ceram.* 25[1–2]:46–47 (1968).

S11. Julia G. Shteinberg, *Strontium Glazes*, (trans. T. J. Gray), Kaiser Strontium, Div. of Kaiser Aluminum & Chemical of Canada, Halifax, NS, 1974.

S12. Felix Singer and W. L. German, *Ceramic Glazes*, (London: Borax Consolidated, Ltd., 1964).

S13. Felix Singer and Sonja S. Singer, *Industrial Ceramics*, (London: Chapman and Hall, 1963).

S14. Stefan Stefanov and Svetlan Batschwarov, *Ceramic Glazes*, (Weisbaden: Bauverlag GmbH, 1988).

S15. W. Steger, "Neue Untersuchungen uber Warneaysdehnung ubd Entspannungstemperatur von Glasuren (mit besonderer Berucksichigung der Anpassung der Glasur au den Scharben)," *Ber. Deut. Keram. Ges.* 8[01]:24–43(1927).

T1. J. R. Taylor and A. C. Bull, *Ceramics Glaze Technology* (Oxford: Pergamon Press, 1986).

T2. Robert Tichane, *Those Celadon Blues*, (Painted Post NY: New York State Institute for Glaze Research, 1983).

T3. Shoji Tsuchihashi, "Dissolution Phenomenon of Some Optical Glass in an Acid," *Bull. Chem. Soc.* Japan 24:161–64 (1951).

V1. Pamela B. Vandiver and W. David Kingery, "The Technology of Celedon Glazes," *Ceram. Monthly* 35[7]:55–58(1987).

V2. Pamela B. Vandiver, "Ancient Glazes," *Sci. Am.* 262[4]:106–13 (1990).

V3. Werner F. Votava, "Gray and Black Stains in Whiteware Glazes," *Am. Ceram. Soc. Bull.* 40[1]:17–18 (1961).

W1. Arthur S. Watts, "The Practical Application of Bristol Glazes Compounded on the Eutectic Basis," *Trans. Am. Ceram. Soc.* 18:631–41 (1916).

W2. Anthony Weiss, "Zircon," *Am. Ceram. Soc. Bull.* 75[6]:165–69 (1996).

W3. Hugh H. Wilson and Henry G. Lefort, "Quantitative Studies of Enamels for Continuous Cleaning Ovens," *Am. Ceram. Soc. Bull.* 52[8]:610–11 (1973).

W4. Shawn Wingfield, "Color Manufacturing and Control Standards," *Ann. Semin. Glass Ceram. Decorators*, 1991, pp. 23–26.

W5. Gunter Wysecki and W. S. Stiles, *Color Science—Concepts and Methods, Quantitative Data and Formulas* (New York: Wiley, 1967).

Y1. Michael J. Yarborough, "Kaolin," *Am. Ceram. Soc. Bull.* 76[6]:105–9 (1997).

Y2. Soo-Choon Toon, Gerda B. Krefft, and Malcolm G. McLaren, "Lead Release from Glazes and Glasses in Contact with Acid Solutions," *Am. Ceram. Soc. Bull.* 55[5]:508–10, 12 (1976).

Y3. Mike Young, "The Art of Successful Screen Printing," *Glass* 70[7]:271–72 (1993).

Z1. W. H. Zachariasen, "The Atomic Arrangement in Glass," *J. Am. Chem. Soc.* 54[10]:3841–51 (1932).

Z2. Jeff Zamek, "Gerstley Borate and Colemanite," *Ceram. Monthly* 46[6]:118–20 (1998).

Z3. Gene A. Zerlaut and Brian H. Kaye, "Summary of Investigations of Light Scattering in Highly Reflecting Pigmented Coatings," *Technical Report NASA* CR-844, July 1967.

n1. *ASTM Annual Book of Standards,* Part 2.05 (West Conshohocken, PA: American Society for Testing and Materials).

n2. *ASTM Annual Book of Standards,* Part 15.02 (West Conshohocken, PA: American Society for Testing and Materials).

n3. "C-242 Standard Terminology of Ceramic Whitewares and Related Products," *ASTM Annual Book of Standards,* Part 15.02, (West Conshohocken, PA: American Society for Testing and Materials).

n4. *Pemco Technical Notebook on Ceramic Glazes and Stains,* (Baltimore, MD: Pemco Corp.).

n5. "Pemco Porcelain Enamel Technical Manual," (Baltimore, MD: Pemco Corp.), 1970.

n6. *Pottery Gazette* 83(973):866–67 (1958).

n7. Section 546.400 Pottery (Ceramics); Imported and Domestic— Cadmium Contamination, *U.S. Food and Drug Administration Compliance Policy Guide* 7117.06.

n8. Section 546.400 Pottery (Ceramics); Imported and Domestic—Lead Contamination, *U.S. Food and Drug Administration Compliance Policy Guide* 7117.07.

Appendix I
My Solution to the Batch Calculation Problem

NOTE: Depending on what raw materials you select, your solution may differ from mine. As long as you add the oxides desired, and don't add others, your solution is as good as mine.

Molecular Formula

Na_2O	0.0303
K_2O	0.0081
CaO	0.1515
MgO	0.0101
B_2O_3	0.0253
Al_2O_3	0.0657
SiO_2	0.7070

1. Calculate the weight percent.

Oxide	Seger x Molecular Weight	Weight Ratio	Wt%
Na_2O	0.0303 x 62	1.879	3.103
K_2O	0.0081 x 94	0.761	1.366
CaO	0.1515 x 56	8.484	13.560
MgO	0.0101 x 40	0.404	0.646
B_2O_3	0.0253 x 70	1.771	2.825
Al_2O_3	0.0657 x 102	6.701	10.702
SiO_2	0.7070 x 60	42.420	67.798

2. To supply the B_2O_3, I selected Frit F19.

Amount of frit = 2.825/14.41 = 19.604%

Na_2O	19.604 x 0.0652	=	1.278
K_2O	19.604 x 0.0072	=	0.141
CaO	19.604 x 0.1409	=	2.762
B_2O_3	19.604 x 0.1441	=	2.825
Al_2O_3	19.604 x 0.1000	=	1.960
SiO_2	19.604 x 0.5429	=	10.643

After which, the amounts remaining are:

Na_2O	3.103 – 1.278	= 1.825
K_2O	1.366 – 0.141	= 1.225
CaO	13.560 – 2.762	= 10.798
MgO	0.646 – 0	= 0.646
B_2O_3	2.825 – 2.825	= 0
Al_2O_3	10.702 – 1.960	= 8.742
SiO_2	67.798 – 10.643	= 57.155

3. More than half the remaining alkali is soda. Therefore, I select soda feldspar as the next raw material.

Amount of soda feldspar = 1.825/ 0.067 = 27.239%

Na_2O	27.239 x 0.067	=	1.825
K_2O	27.239 x 0.045	=	1.225
CaO	27.239 x 0.016	=	0.436
Al_2O_3	27.239 x 0.189	=	5.148
SiO_2	27.239 x 0.682	=	18.577

After which, the amounts remaining are:

Na_2O	1.825 – 1.825	= 0
K_2O	1.225 – 1.225	= 0
CaO	10.798 – 0.436	= 10.362
MgO	0.646 – 0	= 0.646
Al_2O_3	8.742 – 5.148	= 3.594
SiO_2	57.155 – 18.577	= 38.578

4. With over 3% alumina remaining, I selected kaolin for my suspending agent.

Amount of kaolin = 3.594/0.396 = 9.076%

Al_2O_3	9.076 x 0.396	=	3.594
SiO_2	9.076 x 0.470	=	4.266

After which, the amounts remaining are:

CaO	10.362 – 0	=	10.362
MgO	0.646 – 0	=	0.646
Al_2O_3	3.594 – 3.594	=	0
SiO_2	38.578 – 4.266	=	34.312

5. For the magnesia, I selected talc.

Amount of talc = 0.646/0.306 = 2.111%

CaO	2.111 x 0.078	=	0.165
MgO	2.111 x 0.306	=	0.646
SiO_2	2.111 x 0.547	=	1.155

After which, the amounts remaining are:

CaO	10.362 – 0.165	=	10.197
MgO	0.646 – 0.646	=	–
SiO_2	34.312 – 11553	=	33.157

6. For the remaining calcia, I selected wollastonite:

Amount of wollastonite = 10.197/0.421 = 24.221%

CaO	24.221 x 0.421	=	10.197
SiO_2	24.221 x 0.519	=	12.571

After which, the amounts remaining are:

CaO	10.197 – 10.197	=	0
SiO_2	33.157 – 12.571	=	20.586

7. The remaining silica can be added as flint. Therefore, the final recipe is:

Material	Weight Ratio	Wt%
Frit F19	19.604	19.06
Soda feldspar	27.239	26.49
Kaolin	9.076	8.83
Talc	2.111	2.05
Wollastonite	24.221	23.55
Silica	20.586	20.02
	102.837	100.00

Appendix II
Some Manufacturers/ Suppliers of Color Measuring Equipment

Color Instruments, Inc., 319 Mola Avenue, Fort Lauderdale, FL 33301, 954-525-6044.

Colortec, 28 Center Street, Clinton, NJ 08809, 908-735-2248.

Hunter Associates Lab., Inc., 11491 Sunset Hills Road, Reston, VA 22090, 703-471-6870.

MacBeth, division of Kollmorgen Instruments Corporation, 405 Little Britain Road, New Windsor, NY 12553, 914-565-7660.

Milton Roy Company, Analytical Products Division, 820 Linden Avenue, Rochester, NY 14625, 716-248-4000.

Minolta Corporation, Instrument Systems Division, 101 Williams Drive, Ramsey, NJ 07446, 888-473-2656.

Pacific Scientific Company, 11801 Tech Road, Silver Spring, MD 20904, 301-680-7000.

X-Rite, Inc., 358-T Nye Avenue, Grandville, MI 49418-2567, 800-545-0694.

Appendix III

Temperature Equivalents for Orton Pyrometric Cones

TEMPERATURE EQUIVALENTS °C FOR ORTON PYROMETRIC CONES

These tables provide a quide for the selection of cones. The actual bending temperature depends on firing conditions. Once the appropriate bending cones are selected, excellent, reproducible results can be expected.

	Self Supporting Cones						Large Cones				Small
	Cone Type and Composition										
	Regular			Iron Free			Regular		Iron Free		Regular
	Heating Rate °C/hour (last 90-120 minutes of firing)										
Cone	15	60	150	15	60	150	60	150	60	150	300
022		586	590				N/A	N/A			630
021		600	617				N/A	N/A			643
020		626	638				N/A	N/A			666
019	656	678	695				676	693			723
018	686	715	734				712	732			752
017	705	738	763				736	761			784
016	742	772	796				769	794			825
015	750	791	818				788	816			843
014	757	807	838				807	836			870
013	807	837	861				837	859			880
012	843	861	882				858	880			900
011	857	875	894				873	892			915
010	891	903	915	871	886	893	898	913	884	891	919
09	907	920	930	899	919	928	917	928	917	926	955
08	922	942	956	924	946	957	942	954	945	955	983
07	962	976	987	953	971	982	973	985	970	980	1008
06	981	998	1013	969	991	998	995	1011	991	996	1023
05 1/2	1004	1015	1025	990	1012	1021	1012	1023	1011	1020	1043
05	1021	1031	1044	1013	1037	1046	1030	1046	1032	1044	1062
04	1046	1063	1077	1043	1061	1069	1060	1070	1060	1067	1098
03	1071	1086	1104	1066	1088	1093	1086	1101	1087	1091	1131
02	1078	1102	1122	1084	1105	1115	1101	1120	1102	1113	1148
01	1093	1119	1138	1101	1123	1134	1117	1137	1122	1132	1178
1	1109	1137	1154	1119	1139	1148	1136	1154	1137	1146	1184
2	1112	1142	1164				1142	1162			1190
3	1115	1152	1170	1130	1154	1162	1152	1168	1151	1160	1196
4	1141	1162	1183				1160	1181			1209
5	1159	1186	1207				1184	1205			1221
5 1/2	1167	1203	1225				1201	1223			N/A
6	1185	1222	1243				1220	1241			1255
7	1201	1239	1257				1237	1255			1264
8	1211	1249	1271				1247	1269			1300
9	1224	1260	1280				1257	1278			1317
10	1251	1285	1305				1282	1303			1330
11	1272	1294	1315				1293	1312			1336
12	1285	1306	1326				1304	1324			1355

TEMPERATURE EQUIVALENTS °F
FOR ORTON PYROMETRIC CONES

These tables provide a quide for the selection of cones. The actual bending temperature depends on firing conditions. Once the appropriate bending cones are selected, excellent, reproducible results can be expected.

Self Supporting Cones						Large Cones				Small	
Cone Type and Composition											
Regular			Iron Free			Regular		Iron Free		Regular	
Heating Rate °F/hour (last 90-120 minutes of firing)											
27	108	270	27	108	270	108	270	108	270	540	Cone
	1087	1094				N/A	N/A			1166	022
	1112	1143				N/A	N/A			1189	021
	1159	1180				N/A	N/A			1231	020
1213	1252	1283				1249	1279			1333	019
1267	1319	1353				1314	1350			1386	018
1301	1360	1405				1357	1402			1443	017
1368	1422	1465				1416	1461			1517	016
1382	1456	1504				1450	1501			1549	015
1395	1485	1540				1485	1537			1598	014
1485	1539	1582				1539	1578			1616	013
1549	1582	1620				1576	1616			1652	012
1575	1607	1641				1603	1638			1679	011
1636	1657	1679	1600	1627	1639	1648	1675	1623	1636	1686	010
1665	1688	1706	1650	1686	1702	1683	1702	1683	1699	1751	09
1692	1728	1753	1695	1735	1755	1728	1749	1733	1751	1801	08
1764	1789	1809	1747	1780	1800	1783	1805	1778	1796	1846	07
1798	1828	1855	1776	1816	1828	1823	1852	1816	1825	1873	06
1839	1859	1877	1814	1854	1870	1854	1873	1852	1868	1909	05 1/2
1870	1888	1911	1855	1899	1915	1886	1915	1890	1911	1944	05
1915	1945	1971	1909	1942	1956	1940	1958	1940	1953	2008	04
1960	1987	2019	1951	1990	1999	1987	2014	1989	1996	2068	03
1972	2016	2052	1983	2021	2039	2014	2048	2016	2035	2098	02
1999	2046	2080	2014	2053	2073	2043	2079	2052	2070	2152	01
2028	2079	2109	2046	2082	2098	2077	2109	2079	2095	2163	1
2034	2088	2127				2088	2124			2174	2
2039	2106	2138	2066	2109	2124	2106	2134	2104	2120	2185	3
2086	2124	2161				2120	2158			2208	4
2118	2167	2205				2163	2201			2230	5
2133	2197	2237				2194	2233			N/A	5 1/2
2165	2232	2269				2228	2266			2291	6
2194	2262	2295				2259	2291			2307	7
2212	2280	2320				2277	2316			2372	8
2235	2300	2336				2295	2332			2403	9
2284	2345	2381				2340	2377			2426	10
2322	2361	2399				2359	2394			2437	11
2345	2383	2419				2379	2415			2471	12

© 1996 The Edward Orton Jr. Ceramic Foundation

Temperatures shown are for specific mounted height above base. For Self-Supporting — 1 3/4". For Large — 2". For Small Cones, — 15/16".
For Large Cones mounted at 1 3/4" height, use Self-Supporting temperatures.

Raw Materials and Oxides

Name of Material	Formula	Mol. Wt.	Oxides Provided	Conversion Factor
Albite	$Na_2OAl_2O_36SiO_2$	524	Na_2O Al_2O_3 SiO_2	0.118 0.195 0.687
Alumina	Al_2O_3	102	Al_2O_3	1.000
Alumina hydrate	$Al(OH)_3$	78	Al_2O_3	0.654
Antimony oxide	Sb_2O_3	292	Sb_2O_3	1.000
Arsenic oxide	As_2O_3	198	As_2O_3	1.000
Barium carbonate	$BaCO_3$	197	BaO	0.777
Barium oxide	BaO	153	BaO	1.000
Baryta, barytes	$BaSO_4$	233	BaO	0.658
Bismuth oxide	Bi_2O_3	464	Bi_3O_3	1.000
Bone ash	$Ca_3(PO_4)_2$	310	CaO P_2O_5	0.542 0.458
Boric acid	H_2BO_3	62	B_2O_3	0.565
Borax, 10 mol	$Na_2O_2B_2O_310H_2O$	382	Na_2O B_2O_3	0.162 0.366
Borax, anhydrous	$Na_2O_2B_2O_3$	202	Na_2O B_2O_3	0.307 0.693
Boric oxide	B_2O_3	70	B_2O_3	1.000

Name of Material	Formula	Mol. Wt.	Oxides Provided	Conversion Factor
Cadmium oxide	CdO	128	CdO	1.000
Cadmium sulfide	CdS	144		
Calcium borate	$2CaO3B_2O_35H_2O$	412	CaO	0.272
			B_2O_3	0.510
Calcium carbonate	$CaCO_3$	100	CaO	0.560
Calcium chloride	$CaCl_2$	111		
Calcium fluoride	CaF_2	78	CaO	0.718
			F	0.487
Calcium oxide	CaO	56	CaO	1.000
Calcium phosphate	$Ca_3(PO_4)_2$	310	CaO	0.542
			P_2O_5	0.458
Celestite	$SrSO_4$	183	SrO	0.570
Cerium oxide	CeO_2	176	CeO_2	1.000
China clay	$Al_2O_32SiO_2 2H_2O$	258	Al_2O_3	0.395
			SiO_2	0.465
Chromium III oxide	Cr_2O_3	152	Cr_2O_3	1.000
Cobalt oxide, black	Co_3O_4	241	CoO	0.934
Cobaltous oxide	CoO	75	CoO	1.000
Copper carbonate	$CuCO_3$	124	CuO	0.645
Copper oxide, black	CuO	80	CuO	1.000
Copper oxide, red	Cu_2O	144	CuO	1.111
Cornish stone*	$(Na_2,K_2,Ca)O2.5Al_2O_320SiO_2$	1550	Al_2O_3	0.164
			SiO_2	0.775
Cryolite	$3NaFAlF_3$	210	Na_2O	0.443
			Al_2O_3	0.243
			F	0.543

*Ratio of Na_2O, K_2O, and CaO depends upon the particular source used. Consult supplier.

Name of Material	Formula	Mol. Wt.	Oxides Provided	Conversion Factor
Dolomite	$CaCO_3MgCO_3$	184	CaO	0.304
			MgO	0.218
Feldspar, potash	$(K,Na)_2OAl_2O_36SiO_2$	548	Na_2O	0.035
			K_2O	0.095
			CaO	0.013
			Al_2O_3	0.195
			SiO_2	0.659
Feldspar, soda	$(Na,K)_2OAl_2O_36SiO_2$	548	Na_2O	0.067
			K_2O	0.045
			CaO	0.016
			Al_2O_3	0.189
			SiO_2	0.682
Ferric oxide	Fe_2O_3	160	Fe_2O_3	1.000
Ferrous oxide	FeO	72	Fe_2O_3	1.130
Flint	SiO_2	60	SiO_2	1.000
Fluorspar	CaF_2	78	CaO	0.718
			F	0.487
Gold chloride	$AuCl_3$	303.5		
Gypsum	$CaSO_42H_2O$	172	CaO	0.326
Iron oxide, black	Fe_3O_4	232	Fe_2O_3	1.035
Iron oxide, red	Fe_2O_3	160	Fe_2O_3	1.000
Iron oxide, yellow	FeOOH	89	Fe_2O_3	0.870
Kaolin	$Al_2O_32SiO_22H_2O$	258	Al_2O_3	0.396
			SiO_2	0.470
Lead, White	$2PbCO_3Pb(OH)_2$	775	PbO	0.863
Lead, Red (Minium)	PbO	685	PbO	0.975
Lead Oxide	PbO	223	PbO	1.000
Lime	CaO	56	CaO	1.000
Litharge	PbO	223	PbO	1.000

Name of Material	Formula	Mol. Wt.	Oxides Provided	Conversion Factor
Lithium carbonate	Li_2CO_3	74	Li_2O	0.405
Lithium oxide	Li_2O	30	Li_2O	1.000
Magnesium carbonate	$MgCO_3$	84	MgO	0.476
Magnesium oxide, heavy	MgO	40	MgO	1.000
Manganese carbonate	$MnCO_3$	115	MnO	0.610
Manganese dioxide	MnO_2	87	MnO	0.817
Manganous oxide, green	MnO	71	MnO	1.000
Nickel carbonate	$NiCO_3$	119	NiO	0.630
Nickel oxide, black	Ni_2O_3	166	NiO	0.903
Nickel oxide, green	NiO	75	NiO	1.000
Pearl ash	K_2CO_3	138	K_2O	0.680
Plaster of paris	$CaSO_4 1/2H_2O$	145	CaO	0.387
			K_2O	0.472
Potassium carbonate	K_2CO_3	138	K_2O	0.680
Potsssium nitrate	KNO_3	101	K_2O	0.465
Potassium oxide	K_2O	94	K_2O	1.000
Potassium silicofluoride	K_2SiF_6	220	SiO_2	0.273
			F	0.518
Pyrolusite	MnO_2	87	MnO	0.817
Selenium	Se	79		
Silica	SiO_2	60	SiO_2	1.000
Soda Ash	Na_2CO_3	106	Na_2O	0.585
Sodium antimonate	$Na_2OSb_2O_3$	386	Na_2O	0.160
			Sb_2O3	0.757

Name of Material	Formula	Mol. Wt.	Oxides Provided	Conversion Factor
Sodium carbonate	Na_2CO_3	106	Na_2O	0.585
Sodium chloride	NaCl	58	Na_2O	0.535
Sodium fluoride	NaF	42	Na_2O F	0.738 0.452
Sodium nitrate	$NaNO_3$	85	Na_2O	0.365
Sodium oxide	Na_2O	62	Na_2O	1.000
Sodium silicofluoride	Na_2SiF_6	188	Na_2O SiO_2 F	0.330 0.320 0.452
Stannous oxide	SnO	135	SnO_2	1.120
Stannic oxide	SnO_2	151	SnO_2	1.000
Strontium carbonate	$SrCO_3$	148	SrO	0.703
Strontium oxide	SrO	104	SrO	1.000
Talc	$3(Mg,Ca)O4SiO_2H_2O$	378	CaO MgO SiO_2	0.078 0.306 0.547
Titanium oxide (anatase, rutile)	TiO_2	80	TiO_2	1.000
Uranium oxide	U_2O_3	525	U_3O_8	1.070
Wollastonite	$CaOSiO_2$	116	CaO SiO_2	0.421 0.519
Zinc oxide	ZnO	81	ZnO	1.000
Zircon	$ZrSiO_4$	183	ZrO_2 SiO_2	0.672 0.316
Zirconium oxide	ZrO_2	123	ZrO_2	1.000

Index

Note: Page entries in *italics* refer to figures; entries followed by *t* refer to tables.

A

abridged spectrophotometry, 125–26, 271
acidic oxides, 16
acid resistance, 52, 260–61, 265*t*
additives
  binders, 103–4, 110, 226
  deflocculants, 104–5, 220
  effect on gas release, 220
  flocculants, 105–6
  functions of, 101, 102*t*
  suspending agents, 106–7
adherence oxides, 4, 49–50, 231–37.
  See also porcelain enamels
agglomeration, 75
alkali-boron frits, 86*t*
alkali content
  ion exchange and, 260–61
  limits on, 29, 220
alkaline durability, 261–63
alkaline earths
  in Bristol and wall tile glazes, 23*t*
  corrosion resistance and, 260
  effect on gloss, 276
  as fluxes, 19
  in high-temperature leadless glazes, 21*t*
  limits on, 31
  in tableware glazes, 24, 26–27*t*
alkali resistance, 52, 265*t*
alkali-to-alkaline earth ratios, 276
alum, 102*t*
alumina
  in Bristol and wall tile glazes, 23*t*
  in brown pigments, 279
  in commercial frits, 86–87*t*
  durability and, 260–61, 262–63
  effect on gloss, 276

  in enamels, 20, 51*t*, 54*t*, 56*t*
  in high-temperature leadless glazes, 21*t*
  in lead glazes, 35*t*
  limits on, 30–31
  in low-expansion glazes, 28*t*
  melting properties of, 76, 219*t*
  in opaque glazes, 39*t*
  pigment interactions with, 281–82
  in pink pigments, 161
  in satin and matte glazes, 39*t*
  sources of, 59*t*, 67
  in special-effects glazes, 41*t*, 47*t*
  in tableware glazes, 26–27*t*
  thermal expansion factor of, 251*t*
alumina hydrate, 59*t*, 67, 76, 219*t*
aluminum, 238
ammonium chloride, 102*t*
ammonium hydroxide, 102*t*, 105
amphoteric oxides, 16
anatase, 59*t*, 68–69
antifoam agents, 107–8
antimony oxide
  in black pigments, 144–45, 146
  in enamels, 51*t*, 56*t*
  thermal expansion factor of, 251*t*
application techniques, 187–95
ash glazes, 45–46, 47*t*
atomic numbers, 274
automation
  of coating techniques, 189, 191, 194
  of decorating techniques, 201–2, 204, 207–8
aventurine glazes, 40, 41*t*

B

back stamping, 207–8
baddeleyite pigments, 139*t*

323

lithia
  in commercial frits, 86t, 87t
  in enamels, *51t*, 54t, 56t
  fluxing properties of, 18
  in low-expansion glazes, 28t
  sources of, 59t, 60
  in tableware glazes, 26–27t
  thermal expansion factor of, *251t*
lithopones, 166
low-expansion glazes, 25–29
Lung Chuan celadon, 46–48
luster glazes, 43, *44*

M

macrocrystalline glazes, 38–40
magenta glaze, *116*
magnesia
  in Bristol and wall tile glazes, 23t
  in commercial frits, 86t, 87t
  in enamels, *51t*, 54t
  fluxing properties of, 19
  in high-temperature leadless glazes, *21t*
  limits on, 31–32
  in low-expansion glazes, 28t
  melting properties of, 79, 219t, 220
  sources of, 59t, 62–63, 64
  in special-effects glazes, *41t*, 47t
  in tableware glazes, 26–27t
  thermal expansion factor of, *251t*
magnesium carbonate
  melting properties of, 79
  oxides in, 59t, 63
  sources of, 63
magnesium sulfate, *102t*
majolica glazes, *26t*
manganese alumina pink, 161, *164*, 280
manganese brown, 159, *162*, 279
manganese oxide
  in ground coat enamels, *51t*
  in pigments, 161, *164*
  thermal expansion factor of, *251t*
maroon pigments, 164, 169, *172*
matte glazes
  formulation of, 37–38, 39t, 294–95
  reflectance of, 275–76
matting agents, 38
melters, 77–78
melting temperatures, 17–18, 219t
metakaolin, 219t
metal marking, 226–27
metamerism, 119
methyl cellulose, 104

Mie theory, 275
mill additives. *See* additives
milling methods, 179–85, 199
modifiers, 11t
molecular formulas, 15, 16t, 17
mole ratios, 84, 89
molybdenum oxide, *56t*, *251t*
monopressatura, 194
montmorillonite clays, 76
mordant pigments, 128
multicolor direct application, 200
multiple crazing, 244
Munsell system, 119–20
muscovite mica
  melting properties of, 77
  oxides in, *59t*, 61
  sources of, 61

N

Naples yellow, 155–56, *157*
neodymium oxide, 251t
nepheline syenite
  melting properties of, 77, 219t
  oxides in, *59t*, 61
  sources of, 61
network formers, 9, 11t
network modifiers, 9
nickel flash, 237
nickel-iron-chromite spinel, 280
nickel oxide
  in brown pigments, 279
  in enamels, 50, *51t*, 234–35
  thermal expansion factor of, *251t*
niobium pentoxide, 54t, 55
nonoxide pigments, 127–28, 129, 165–72
nonplastic raw materials, 76–77

O

oil absorption, 111
olivine pigments, 139t
opacifiers
  interaction with coatings, 281–82
  metal marking and, 227
  pigments for, 138–42
  solubility of, 174–76
  sources of, 68–69
opaque enamels, 53, *54t*
opaque frits, 86t
opaque glazes, 34–36, 39t. *See also* opacifiers
opponent-color system, 123–25
orange peel, 217
Orlowski and Marquis's glazes, *26t*